ANNA OF DENMARK, QUEEN OF ENGLAND

ANNA OF DENMARK, QUEEN OF ENGLAND

A Cultural Biography

LEEDS BARROLL

UNIVERSITY OF PENNSYLVANIA PRESS

Philadelphia

10 9 8 7 6 5 4 3 2 1

Published by
University of Pennsylvania Press
Philadelphia, Pennsylvania 19104-4011

Library of Congress Cataloging-in-Publication Data

Barroll, J. Leeds (John Leeds), 1928–
   Anna of Denmark, Queen of England : a cultural biography /
by Leeds Barroll.
     p. cm.
   Includes bibliographical references and index.
   ISBN 0-8122-3574-6 (cloth : alk. paper)
   1. Anne, Queen, consort of James I, King of England, 1574–1619.
2. Anne, Queen, consort of James I, King of England, 1574–1619—
Art patronage.   3. James I, King of England, 1566–1625—Marriage.
4. Art patronage—Great Britain—History—17th century.   5. Great
Britain—History—James I, 1603–1625.   6. Arts, Modern—17th
century—Great Britain.   7. Queens—Great Britain—Biography.
8. Arts, British.   I. Title.
DA391.1.A6 B37 2001
941.06′1′092—dc21
[B]   00-062861

For Joseph D. Robinson, M.D.

Humanist, humanitarian, dedicated to the
life both of the body and of the mind

CONTENTS

1. QUEEN ANNA AS CONSORT ESTABLISHING A LOCAL HABITATION AND A NAME

The cultural efflorescence often associated with the onset of the Stuart period has usually been attributed to the presence of King James as a new high cultural force. This viewpoint is not necessarily wrongheaded, as two considerations seem to render it highly tenable. James's many and diverse writings—including poetry—are eloquent argument for a general literary ambience surrounding England's new monarch, a specific event that followed his accession even urging that he gave a special impetus to the stage. Scarcely a month after James assumed the throne in 1603, William Shakespeare and his fellows were patented as "the King's Servants." Less than a year later, the first of a long series of brilliant masques made its appearance at court. Additionally, in testimony to the specifically intellectualist tenor of the new king's reign, there appeared a new translation of the Scriptures, the King James Version arranged for by the monarch himself. In these times, William Shakespeare also completed the balance of his plays, Ben Jonson most of his comedies and masques, and John Donne most of his poetry, and there appeared translations of the essays of Montaigne and of Seneca, and of the Homeric versions of the *Iliad* and the *Odyssey*. The stimulus provided by James I of England, so goes literary tradition, must have made important contributions.

I shall propose that this new king's influence on the high culture of the Stuart period, although considerable in certain discrete areas, has been misunderstood in terms of innovations at the court itself, and that during the first decade of his reign, these innovations were fundamentally shaped by James's much neglected queen consort, Anna of Denmark.[1] Her role as a cultural force at the Jacobean court has, however, been long eclipsed, owing, I believe, to two major critical predispositions. The first of these is the assumption in many cultural histories of the early modern period, at least until the late 1990s, that James himself, as monarch, was synonymous with a kind of monolithic, hegemonic power in early modern England—a power that dictated the shape of court politics as well as the court arts connected to these politics. The second critical predisposition, which inevitably follows from privileging the notion that James dominated all sectors of Stuart court activity, is the assumption that Anna, being a negligible influence on court culture, was therefore not an appropriate subject for serious scholarly investigation. This critical neglect of James's queen consort has, it would seem, been reinforced by the tendency in most biographies of James to focus on events subsequent to 1614, rendering the first decade of the new reign important only insofar as it helps elucidate the crises of later years.[2]

This tendency derives, in turn, from certain theoretical assumptions about Jacobean statecraft that have served to foreground James as catalytic center of Stuart culture, assumptions that require some brief comment as my way of clarifying my own approach to redressing the imbalance that I claim. One such assumption, often found in literary studies, has generally structured the early modern English state as a binary, with the Crown (synonymous with the "state") in ideological opposition to those whom the Crown rules. Such a polarizing of "ruler" and "ruled," supposing that the king and those around him contend with those whom they subjugate —the "people"—has generated a concept of "hegemonic" force in opposition to subversive counterforce. In turn, this oppositional paradigm, persisting in literary criticism of the 1990s, has established a view of the arts as important to both sides of the social equation: to the oppressor as social propaganda, and to the oppressed as a mode of expressing resistance. Thus the "arts" become crucial for the "state" or the Crown to appropriate: they are the spoils of the patron as ideological victor.

In the dynamics of such a dualist political structuring, however, early Stuart society actually disappears as a "state" to become the kind of political entity that S. N. Eisenstadt has defined as an "empire." That is, the early modern state vanishes within a supposed political enterprise wherein a sole ruler possesses all organized power so as to contain the resistance inevitably generated by a subjugated populace—a populace which, in turn, exists in a constant, subversive, and uniform resistance.[3] Such an imperial model of early modern English polity, as a consequence, will not only locate the Stuart Crown as the unquestioned center of political power but will inevitably associate the Stuart monarch (as "emperor") with the appropriation, for hegemonic purposes, of all the arts. In effect, all high cultural activity to be associated with the royal court of early modern England will naturally seem to emanate, specifically, from the figure of the monarch, James I.

In contrast, the view of the early modern English state advanced in this study, as defined by Fernand Braudel, François Chabaud, and John Guy, is of a polymorphic body politic, comprising not one but a number of constituencies. Not a political entity wherein the Crown (James and his advisers) subjugated a populace, this Stuart state was, like other early modern European states, an aggregate. Each of the constituencies in this aggregate operated as a social force within the polity, with political significance and leverage (virtually) equal to that of the Crown. The peerage, for example, and also the body of the gentry, many of them quite wealthy and influential in the areas where they resided, were two such constituencies, as were the merchants of the more important cities. Their collective power was expressed in the age-old institution of the guilds, as well as by means of the annual election through which one of their number was chosen to serve as Mayor or Lord Mayor. In London, for instance, this office was so important that when James's son Henry was installed as Prince of Wales in 1610, the ceremony began, according to Dudley Carleton, when Henry came from Richmond by water "and was met by the way by the Lord Mayor and all the Companies much after the fashion of bringing the Lord Mayor to Westminster."[4]

Despite the Stuart rhetoric of absolute kingship, it was these constituencies — *including* the Crown — that made up the early modern state by relating to one another within a general formation characterized by the constant mobility of power centering.[5] As a multiplex organism composed of competing social groupings of which the Crown was only one, the early Stuart polity was thus an entity composed of constituencies that tended to centrifuge. The peerage, for example, was not a monolith, as witnessed by the 1601 Essex uprising: four earls rode at the head of this rebellion against the monarch who was, however, supported by a conclusive majority of the peerage. Nor, as witnessed by the many antitheatrical orders from London's Lord Mayor and aldermen (elected by the guilds), was the constituency of merchants and traders a monolith: these antitheatrical orders attempted to repress a new London theater which was itself a business. Indeed Shakespeare, though from the distance of a Roman setting, seems to show Coriolanus as a figure incapable of envisaging these complexities of competing constituencies.

It is, then, in the context of the Jacobean state as polymorphic that I urge the resituation of Anna of Denmark in the high court culture of the first years of the Stuart reign. This said, however, I must render at the outset the caveat that this study is by no means intended as a historical biography, a systematic recording and documenting of all evidence available about Stuart England's first queen consort. Rather, I am here concerned, first, with advancing the *idea* of Anna's relevance to the artistic production of the very early Stuart court—a notion not readily embraced by literary scholars—and then with suggesting how our sense of the interaction between the arts and the early Stuart court may require some reconfiguration.[6] Yet because Anna's distinctive role in these matters must be viewed in terms of her earlier experiences at the Danish court of her childhood and the Scottish court of James VI, some biographical commentary concerning events hitherto absent from traditional literary history is relevant to my project.

Reference to this background can serve several purposes: it helps elucidate the configuration of Anna's court patronage of the arts during the early Stuart years, and it clarifies her relationship to those brilliant masques that, though featuring her person, are usually ascribed to the imaginings of Ben Jonson and Inigo Jones, as if working in a vacuum. The chief concern of this book, then, is to establish Anna's dynamic relevance to the Stuart court, particularly to its cultural accomplishments from 1603 to 1614. Deferring a start on the specifics of this matter to Chapter 2, I must conclude my introduction with several general observations that will, I hope, establish a broader framework for this discussion that seeks to companion the influence of James I on the high culture of the Stuart court with that of his queen.

First, we must consider the importance of recognizing how the long reign of the unmarried Queen Elizabeth I may distort our sense of the usual English royal situation wherein the Crown was not necessarily, or even customarily, wholly centered in one person. Now, it was, at least in some respects, ambiguously bifurcated. Unlike the unwed Elizabeth, who was in this sense a sovereign totality, James was married. Thus he brought with him to England a royal duality—theoretically two regal figures, and two courts. And although, clearly, James's queen consort could not in any way challenge the ultimate political power of the monarch in early modern England, it is reasonable to suppose that the constituency and institution of the Crown, by admitting a consort, introduced a certain degree of conceptual confusion to the antecedent model.

As an idea, that is, the consort was an entity that was *of* the Crown but not the Crown: the admission of a "royal" spouse for the monarch, paradoxically, extended the monarchical constituency of the state that was the "Crown" to some royal "other" who, as royalty, nevertheless ambiguously commanded ambiguous obedience. To obey the queen was not necessarily to disobey the king—or to obey him; to disobey the queen was not necessarily to obey the king—or to disobey him. At the same time, Anna of Denmark functioned as "wife" in the patriarchally configured institution of matrimony, owing submission within the royal household to her husband; and she also functioned as subject in the state, owing homage to James as her king, to whom disobedience could indeed be high treason.[7] Further, there were many arenas in which a queen consort in England could hardly act as "queen": for example, she could not command the local political allegiances that, say, the earl and countess of Derby held on the Isle of Man, or the earl and countess of Southampton held on the Isle of Wight. On the other hand, it is equally misleading to think of Anna of Denmark—in contrast with Elizabeth I—merely as some Cinderella swept up from her ashes into the arms of a magnanimous prince-monarch.

Beyond her functions as wife and subject, rather, Anna of Denmark was herself wrapped in the mystique of monarchy. Paradoxically deriving her influence through the very institution of patriarchy that was in place to subjugate her, she was not merely a commoner or even merely a peer: she was royalty in several degrees. Because (as was true of many queen consorts) her own father had been a king, Anna of Denmark had "royal blood" in her veins before she married James VI of Scotland. Her wedding to him only reaffirmed in this sense her own "intrinsic" royalty while giving her a title that magnified it. As James's Scottish queen consort, crowned 17 May 1590, she was owed by all the people of the Scottish state the same kind, if not the same degree, of homage as they gave their king. Further, as the official copulation-partner of the king—his royal "bedfellow" as so many official documents put it—she was also the mother of the royal heir; her *own* royal blood ran in this future monarch's royal veins.

Thus a queen consort, in theory, effectively and potentially incorporated several personae. It could, in fact, be argued that a woman such as Anna of Denmark was in the best of all possible positions at court to transcend constituency boundaries. From the viewpoint of the peerage, she could theoretically deploy transcendence over them. Officially she was, in effect, a kind of super peer with excellent access to the monarch, holding the unofficial position analogous to that of a favorite, and in this sense—

in the matter of privileged access—she was a favorite's natural enemy. But from the viewpoint of the city, of the guilds, and of other constituencies in the general population, she was, if nothing else, an unquestionably royal figure, perceived as *part* of the Crown. Finally, if, in the king's view, Anna was supposed to represent the wifely "body" of which he was the patriarchal "head," still, if pushed too far, she could find a formidable ally in a foreign potentate of almost equal power with her husband (her brother, king of Denmark), just as, later, Henrietta-Maria, consort to the next Stuart king, remained to some extent within the protective ambience of her father, the king of France.[8]

Indeed, such a potential royal dualism in the European monarchic institution (a dualism not extant, by comparison, in Ottoman monarchic practice), while in abeyance for the forty-five years of Queen Elizabeth's reign, was nonetheless common enough on the Continent. There, royal mothers, royal wives, and even royal sisters often played significant political roles, made possible by the very state of their royalty. By no means viewed as irrelevant, we find the significance of such women exemplified in the activity of Philip II of Spain who, in 1583, asked his sister Maria, wife of the emperor Maximilian II, to take up the post of governor of Portugal when he had to absent himself from Lisbon. He also corresponded with his daughter, Catalina, duchess of Savoy, about the Armada in 1588, and he nominated another daughter, Isabella, for the Catholic throne of France during the 1590 effort to prevent the then-Protestant Henri IV from acquiring that crown.[9] His son, Philip III, we learn from a recent study, had to contend with court factions generated by his consort, Margaret of Austria, interacting with his grandmother, Empress Maria, and her daughter, Margaret of the Cross.[10] And, of course, after Henri IV was assassinated in 1610, during the consequent minority of Louis XIII, French affairs came into the hands of his mother, Marie de Medici.[11]

In Anna's case her father, Frederick II, was king of Denmark; he was succeeded by her brother, Christian IV, in 1596. This Danish kingship was, politically, no mean position in Europe. Denmark's king was sovereign over not only Denmark itself—this consisting of the Jutland Peninsula, the islands of Fyn and Sjaelland and their island groups—but also a large collection of other Scandinavian and German territories. Danish rule extended to the north over all of Norway; to the east over the provinces of the Scandinavian peninsula in present-day Sweden, and the Baltic islands of Bornholm and Gotland; to the northwest, over Iceland, Greenland, the Faeroe Islands, and the Orkneys; and to the south over the German duchies of Schleswig and Holstein. Since the latter was within the recognized boundaries of the Holy Roman Empire, Anna's brother was thus also an Imperial prince, a "vassal" of the emperor of Vienna, with a real stake in German affairs. Further, because of its geographical position, Denmark in the late sixteenth century could effectively block all three entrances from the Atlantic to the Baltic with its powerful navy and a dense ring of coastal fortifications to maintain that crucial seaway as *Danish* territorial waters.[12] Thus, this Danish (Oldenberg) state, as one of the largest political entities on the early modern European continent, wielded, as Lockhart has put it, "tremendous international influence," possessing formidable prestige. By the end of the sixteenth century, owing to the moneys exacted from foreign ships as toll for passing through the Denmark Sound into the Baltic, and from duties exacted for the export of timber from Norway, the Danish monarchy was among the wealthiest in all of Europe and could boast the largest and most efficient naval force in northern Europe.[13]

Therefore, if the early Stuart era became a site of cultural production that we now view as transhistorically significant, the potential contribution of Anna of Denmark is hardly, on the face of it, an absurd proposition. Yet the fact that such a statement must still be made is also owing to the persistence of a well-entrenched critical view of Anna herself. One finds it, for instance, in the work of so distinguished a historian of art as Roy Strong. The primary purpose of Strong's 1986 book on Stuart culture — akin to the thrust of this study — is to locate the patronage of the arts in the early Stuart period outside the purview of King James, but Strong deems Anna of Denmark to be so irrelevant to court politics that he turns his attention to another royal male: Henry, Prince of Wales. The bent of Strong's argument is that Henry's early death served to abort a special English Renaissance that was taking its shape from this cultured young prince's own precocity. And in this context, Anna of Denmark simply did not register as a serious factor: "On the whole, Anne lived for pleasure, passing her time moving from one of the palaces assigned to her to the next," Strong asserted. She "deliberately avoided politics," merely "devoting herself instead to dancing, court entertainments, and the design and decoration of her houses and gardens." Indeed, Prince Henry (we gather from Strong) was familiar enough with her character, for "even at sixteen he was keenly aware of his mother's pettiness."[14]

Yet, although Prince Henry's arrival in England may have preceded such a "new Renaissance," it did not necessarily precipitate it. Henry was only nine years old in 1603 when his father's English reign began, and if, at the time of his death at eighteen in 1612, the young prince and his court had all the promise of becoming a center of high culture, it was hardly likely that Henry was himself the sole agent of this phenomenon. Since Henry could hardly have invented himself *in vacuo*, we must consider the constellation of events during his youth, beginning with the introduction to the English court of a boy who before June 1603 had never left the Scottish castle of Stirling. Finally, if the prince and his own circle (which was not in place formally until 1610) are to be identified as the inspiration for new royal accomplishments, then we at least need to locate the royal impetus for the flourishing of court culture during Henry's childhood—say, from 1603 to 1607.

Strong, however, is certainly not alone in passing over Anna. So notable and able a historian as Maurice Lee has recently observed that "Queen Anne's influence on the court is hard to detect," and David Mathew also elaborated on this theme, opining only that the queen was a great patron of the masque "and liked to take part in these fine and very costly shows." [15] Indeed, we are to gather that the closest Anna came to wielding influence at court was when Ben Jonson conveniently provided her with masques on which she was presumably allowed to spend money and in which she was presumably allowed to dance. In sum, then, the wide-ranging, dismissive judgments of Anna in literary and historical scholarship before 1990, when Linda Levy Peck described her household as "a political web from which patronage radiated," have hardly encouraged any sense of her importance as the potential center of an intellectual circle in the early Stuart court. [16]

Of course, the court of the Stuart king was obviously the center of administrative rule, and it should not be denied that James himself was an "intellectual" monarch. That said, however, James's own sophistication can hardly rule out the possibility that Anna may have exerted, especially in spheres important to historians of high culture, a presence and an intellect appropriate to her role as consort. Indeed, one must ask why the cultural influence of James I and that of Anna of Denmark must be regarded in terms of an either/or proposition: why one necessarily precludes the other. Nonetheless, substantiating a claim that Anna of Denmark was something other than a royal idler, and, more challengingly, that she was the important precipitant of that "atmosphere" of high cultural patronage which we associate with the early Stuart court, requires that the weight of that long-held tradition to the contrary be balanced by an equivalent *gravitas* of response. If Anna of Denmark was sufficiently motivated or sufficiently energetic to be active—not passive—as an influence on the arts, we must ask why the vibrations occasioned by her agency have not resounded more in historical accounts than they have.

An acceptable counternarrative should thus establish the queen's interaction with persons and events already associated with the arts of the Stuart court, and it is just this issue of plausibility that Chapter 2 will begin to address. It does so by presenting a generally neglected but sharply etched counter-record of Anna's activities, dating from when she was sixteen, that may alter long-held notions of what might plausibly constitute her behavior. Before James's English accession, we recall, she had been his queen in Scotland for almost thirteen years, from 1590 to 1603, and this sojourn in Scotland generated far more detailed records than those available for her years in England. These Scottish records, which had not been calendared until relatively recently, portray Anna—surprisingly to many—engaged in startlingly vigorous political activity. In fact, such materials portray a woman so different from that of her familiar image as to reconfigure Anna's construction in the cultural history of the Jacobean period. As Scottish consort, Anna was able to exert significant influence on what might be called matters of politics and government: she played the factions that divided James's court for her own purposes. Understanding this earlier avatar of Anna is important for our purposes here—but not in terms of the political history of Scotland. The issue is what Anna's behavior there suggests about her personal resources, intelligence, and drive for self-assertion. The queen consort who greeted England in 1603 had already demonstrated a propensity for behaving in ways sufficiently iron-willed and imaginative to render her traditional reputation for triviality almost ludicrous. The fact that the English court offered Anna virtually none of the same political opportunities as did Scotland was, from this perspective, a challenge to Anna to redefine herself, to construct another kind of visibility in accordance with new constraints. The queen consort's investment in high court culture, I shall suggest, represents this newfound sphere of influence. Thus Anna's contribution to the arts can be fully understood only in terms of the considerable energy and ambition that she characteristically displayed—in any court—to establish a royal presence that would demand attention.

Having argued for Queen Anna as a potentially formidable presence in England, I turn in Chapter 3 to the extremely important issue of the construction of her own English court. To describe it, however, is to delineate the many circles of artistic patronage that it comprehended. These included not only Anna's own direct artistic patronage but also that of the noblewomen, hitherto little discussed, whom Anna appointed to her inner circle, and that of the men to whom these women were allied by friendship, kinship, or marriage. In fact, some of the most active artistic patrons of the time could be numbered among Anna's circle, such as the countess of Bedford, Penelope Rich (the sister of the earl of Essex), Robert Sidney (brother of Sir Philip and father of Lady Mary Wroth), and two daughters of the earl of Oxford, to name only a few. Indeed, embracing as it did such powerful social networks, Anna's court can be associated with artists as diverse as Samuel Daniel, William Shakespeare, Ben Jonson, Thomas Middleton, John Donne, John Florio, Lady Mary Wroth, John Dowland, and Inigo Jones, among others. In effect, to study the social structuring of Anna's court is to delineate what was probably the most prestigious and promising "atmosphere" available to successful or aspiring poets, musicians, and painters and even to writers of public plays.

But Anna is, of course, specifically and traditionally associated with the masque—that brilliant and spectacular court production which best defines her English identity (even though, ironically, her masquing activities may in the long run actually have occupied her *least*). My emphasis on these productions in Chapter 4 will deliberately avoid formalist concerns as to their iconology, as well as intentionalist theories concerning Ben Jonson's scripts, to stress the social and political court relations that these spectacles displayed and enhanced. I shall argue that, rather than functioning as Ben Jonson's symbolic messages to monarch or peers regarding the manner in which England was to be governed, Anna's extant corpus of six masques—only four of which had scripts written by Ben Jonson—is best viewed as a series of self-conscious presentations by the queen of herself, of chosen members of her female court, and of noblemen whom she particularly favored.[17]

Inaugurated in the first Christmas season of the Stuart reign, Anna's masques need to be envisaged as court spectacles that for the first time in over forty years showcased a queen consort. Including not only selected noblewomen but also noblemen sympathetic to the queen's interests, these dazzling events thus emphasized the circles of influence operant in Anna's Privy Chamber and Bed Chambers. Accordingly, in Chapter 4, I focus on formal dance structure as a sociopolitical phenomenon in order to deliberately shift our critical emphasis from the written scripts of the masques to an analysis of their cultural politics. I shall view two masques in some detail from this sociopolitical viewpoint and conclude that Anna's masques, danced exclusively by her and by her ladies-in-waiting, represent more than simply her contribution to the development of Jacobean court art. They reached out socially and politically—not to poets and other artists but to the peerage.

Indeed, that such spectacles may have served a purpose other than the propagation of innovations in music, drama, and painting is attested to by the little-noted fact that, after having established masques as her own annual signature events, Anna then unilaterally relinquished them: after Christmas 1611 she never presented another masque. Although the reason for this change of behavior can never be confidently adduced, the death of Henry, Prince of Wales, in November 1612 reportedly prostrated Anna for several months, canceling plans for the Christmas masque of that year. But is it likely that events in 1612 marked the end of her interest altogether in matters of art? Cultural historians could claim that the brilliant sequence of Ben Jonson's masques certainly did not end with the termination of Anna's own interest here. Jonson wrote masques for others well beyond 1611. So where are we to locate the queen consort in matters of literary significance subsequent to Prince Henry's death? Certainly, when she abruptly ceased masquing, there were left at least five years before her "dropsy" began to affect her physical activity. Must we then conclude that during this period Anna withdrew from the court, an assumption which might seem retroactively to negate the supposed strength of her early influence? Or, to put it another way, between 1612 and her death in 1619, was Anna of Denmark still a figure whom scholars need to take into account in any narrative that concerns the cultural history of these years?

In a final chapter, I shall be arguing that Anna's last years complement rather than contradict my representation of the queen consort as a significant presence at court. It seems to be the case that while in the years before 1612 Anna's influence was exercised primarily in the cultural activities of her own court, her last years took a somewhat different turn. Certainly, she continued to be involved in the masques of others, but in ways that emphasize the specifically political encounters taking shape between her (with her allies) and other members of the Jacobean court. In effect, Anna's latter years saw the reemergence of a woman akin to the Scottish queen of Chapter 2, suggesting that perhaps her influence on the arts, her Twelfth Night spectacles, and the entire structure of her court had always been manifestations of a larger energy. That is to say, up to 1612, Anna's scope of activities had been effectively held in check by the structure of James's English ruling circle, which for eight years had been impervious to any Scottish-like maneuvers on her part. But the multiple deaths that occurred between 1612 and 1614 provided Anna with an opportunity to reposition herself. Within three years King James lost his eldest son as well as several skilled advisers. Robert Cecil, earl of Salisbury and first secretary, a bulwark of the state, succumbed to his long illness in the summer before Henry's November death. In June 1614, James also lost George Home, earl of Dunbar, and Henry Howard, earl of Northampton, both mature and seasoned politicians crucial to James's attainment of the English Crown and integral to his inner circle of rule. It was in the power vacuum that resulted from these losses that such favorites as Somerset, and then Buckingham, had freer political play than might otherwise have been possible.

But so, it seems, did Anna of Denmark. In Chapter 5 I approach this issue of repositioning through several masques best contextualized by Anna's relationship with Henry — and with Somerset. Beginning with her moves at the time of James's accession to bind the nine-year-old prince closely to herself and her circle, this last chapter will briefly note how, as Henry matured, he and his mother jointly opposed the growing influence of Robert Carr who, as James's favorite, was viewed as a natural antagonist to the aspirations of such a forceful Prince of Wales as Henry. In fact, Jonson's *Oberon*, Daniel's *Hymen's Triumph*, and Jonson's *Golden Age Restored* are court spectacles best contextualized in terms of Anna's activities with regard to Prince Henry and Carr. *The Golden Age Restored*, in particular, is important in light of the fact that, after Henry's death and Carr's rise to almost transcendent supremacy under James, it was Anna who appears to have been the center of an extended anti-Howard circle. Her involvement in the introduction of Buckingham to supplant Carr and with a new political alignment that positioned the earl of Pembroke as James's Lord Chamberlain, an involvement that ultimately sped Buckingham in James's favor and to his earldom — as, in effect the new Robert Cecil — strongly suggests that Anna's legacy for Stuart cultural history represents something more than masquing.

But these last are controversial topics subject to disputation. I include them in this study because I believe that such matters, considered in terms of the trajectory of Anna's entire life, do put to rest the last — and culminating — myth of the queen, in which she ekes out her last years as a pale ghost, playing with her dogs.[18] Even so I have not envisaged this book as a revisionist history of Anna's later political machinations nor as a comprehensive biography of the full range of her royal accomplishments. Rather, this study is always concerned with demonstrating Anna's substantiality — as opposed to her triviality — as a royal figure with considerable influence at the Stuart court, particularly during its first decade, and preeminently in matters concerning the arts. Thus my brief review of Anna's post-masquing political life is designed to suggest that a woman of such formidable energy would not be likely to disengage from court activities while still healthy and empowered.

In the end, then, understanding what Anna actually accomplished through her enlarged sphere of influence seems less important than understanding that her full-spirited commitment to the development of high court culture proceeded from the restless and ambitious temperament of an intelligent and capable woman. Her reputation as a empty-headed gadfly — subservient to James and beholden to Ben Jonson — needs to be understood as a fiction, one perhaps as great as any produced by the Jacobean arts that she enhanced.

2. ANNA
IN SCOTLAND
STYLE AND
SUBSTANCE

Feminist studies have rewritten the history of letters and the fine arts in the early modern period, an era that has hitherto commanded attention primarily because William Shakespeare and other male dramatists and poets were part of it. By focusing on women who produced poetry, prose, painting, and music, this new body of criticism, especially in the past two decades, has led to an importantly reconfigured approach to the early modern cultural milieu. But because the emphasis in much of this scholarship has rightfully been on the emergence of voices in nonaristocratic settings, innovations in the arts produced by aristocratic women at court have been largely unexplored, or have been bracketed off as an essentially separate phenomenon. This notion of social division is, however, misleading. Many nonaristocratic women artists were themselves inevitably connected to, and influenced — positively or negatively — by aristocracy-based systems of aid and influence.

Because the tendency of many critical studies has been to isolate artistic production from the social conditions that made it possible, perhaps a predictable result of this critical misperception has been to discover the significant social roles of early modern women only in the expressions of their literature, music, or painting. Nonetheless, few scholars would directly claim that women of the period discovered or revealed their personal potentials only through the practices of art. When offered advantages in other areas of endeavor, advantages that rivaled those available to men, women of talent — in any social sphere — exploited these as well. Indeed, the inevitable intersection of social opportunity and talent seems especially evident in the provenances that are the concern of the present study: the complex, politically based networks of court patronage which was an essential component of the early modern cultural scene.

This activity of women — not regnal as was that of Elizabeth I, nor artistic, as was that of an Aemilia Lanyer — has, however, been obfuscated by lingering distortions of the copious indications of how many of these early Jacobean cultural networks actually fashioned themselves. Because these misperceptions, as I have already suggested, would view early modern English systems of patronage as primarily male-dominated, it is precisely this way of viewing the situation that may usefully be corrected by a sustained and revisionist account of Anna of Denmark's cultural impact. Not as the monarch, and not as an artist, the queen consort's centrality to Stuart high culture can yet become clear from a viewing of particular aspects of her queenly life. That these were complex and of long standing, may, in fact, become apparent not only from the grouping of nobles she personally assembled to constitute her English court in 1603, but even earlier. If in England Anna would make manifest her concept of her majesty by ruling a "world" created by the arts, her impulse to assert this majesty in one way or another — with or without the arts — was strongly foreshadowed from her earliest days and throughout her sojourn in Scotland, where she became queen before the age of eighteen.

What is striking about Anna of Denmark's thirteen years as queen consort of Scotland is the number of records her presence generated there, since this contrasts strongly with the scant materials available about the queen's English years. Indeed, the relative prolixity of this Scottish commentary offers us a sustained view of that elusive figure whose identity at the English court seems to evade us, leaving only traces that literary tradition has reconstructed into a woman notable chiefly for her frivolity. It is thus the Scottish scene that instructs us about some of Anna's qualities denied or occluded by the narrative of her English years. In Scotland, the queen emerges as a person of substance with a strong sense of her royal position and with so acute an urge to define and maintain it that her efforts constantly caused political problems for King James VI. In fact, as a political force, Anna often required James's full attention, and it is this Anna who can credibly be imagined as insisting on a royal presence in England as well, although there she shifted her sphere of influence to the arts.

The Scottish Anna should be introduced first in terms of the environment that shaped her, one that certainly did not presage an adulthood innocent of either sophistication or maturity. Briefly, her father was Frederick II, king of Denmark and Norway, whose support of learning is well known

to Danish historians. Illustrative in this respect is Frederick's generous patronage of the astronomer Tycho Brahe, who discovered the famous nova
in Cassiopeia in 1572 and whose other observational data, refined by Kepler,
actually laid the groundwork for Newton's law of gravitation. In addition to
sponsoring Brahe's research, Frederick funded the astronomer's renowned
castle-laboratory, Uraniborg, on the island of Hven. Designed with the help
of a number of specialists, this observatory was regarded as one of the most
architecturally and scientifically advanced buildings in Europe.[1]

Frederick's queen consort and Anna's mother, Sofie or Sophia, daughter of Ulric III, duke of Mecklenburg, was a highly gifted woman in her own
right. Also interested in the arts and the sciences, she too supported Brahe
(who was, in fact, the son of her mistress of the wardrobe), helping him gain
power of appointment over the succession to the control of Uraniborg.[2]

Queen Sophia, twenty-four years her husband's junior, had seven children, the second oldest of whom was Anna, born 12 December 1574.[3] Notwithstanding the Danish queen's royal position, she differed from her
English royal counterparts by taking a personal interest in her children's
education, being described in 1588 by an Englishman writing to Lord Burleigh as "a right virtuous and godly princess which with a motherly care
and great wisdom ruleth the children."[4] But Sophia was also interested in
power. When Frederick died in 1588, she laid claim as the dowager queen to
the right of governing Denmark and Norway during the minority of her son
Christian IV (the oldest of Anna's four brothers), then eleven. However, the
regency government, made up of well-established Danish aristocrats, refused her. Nevertheless, Sophia was able to secure very large sums of money
for the weddings of Elizabeth and Anna, although she overreached herself
when she attempted to provide lands for her children by carving up the
duchies of Schleswig and Holstein, then under the Danish Crown. After this
unsuccessful bid, Sophia was isolated politically on the island of Falster at
her own court in Nykjobing Castle. There, she continued her lifelong investment in learning, devoting part of her time to the study of astronomy,
chemistry, and other sciences. The Council did allow Sophia to receive ambassadors at her court, and it is likely that she also maintained a certain
degree of political leverage. She was independent and wealthy enough to
make two large loans to her son, the king of Denmark: the first in 1625,
during the Thirty Years' War, and then again in 1627, when she put 40,000
Rigsdaler (£10,000) at Christian's disposal.[5] Sophia died in 1631, outliving
her daughter Anna by twelve years. Thus Anna's parents represented strong
role models, both intellectual and political.

Seven months before her sixteenth birthday, in May 1589, and less than a year after the death of her father, Anna was married by proxy to James VI of Scotland. One year later, on 17 May 1590, she arrived in her adopted country and was crowned queen of Scotland.[6] At a rather early age, then, Anna was called upon to define a position as queen consort in an environment quite different from that of her Danish home. But the young queen[7] seems to have moved vigorously into court politics, an aspect of her new life not foregrounded by her few biographers. Despite the unfamiliarity of her surroundings and what might be viewed as the handicap of her youth, Anna nonetheless soon became a political presence at the Scottish court.

Because the general political ambience of the last decade of James's Scottish reign is obviously relevant to Anna's new situation, we need to recall that at this time the Crown was contending with three major problems: (1) the political challenges of those earls who resisted the broad entente generally prevailing between the Crown and the Scottish magnates who were indispensable to it, (2) the efforts by the Kirk to gain autonomy and then political power in Scotland through an elected internal hierarchy responsible in theory only to God, and (3) a political destabilization continually threatened by blood feuds among the nobility.[8]

Queen Anna, as early as 1590, seems to have made her weight felt in respect to several of these precarious balances.[9] In December, for instance, she developed what was to become an enduring friendship with the countess of Huntly, a woman close to her in age and a person of almost impeccable credentials from James's viewpoint.[10] She was Henrietta née Stuart, the daughter of James's second cousin and great favorite, Esmé Stuart.[11] This friendship may, in fact, have initiated the young queen into her first political activity. A year after her 1590 coronation, Anna joined a group of nobles at the Scottish court to petition the recall of the countess of Huntly's brother, Lodovick Stuart, second duke of Lennox, who had struck the Laird of Logie with his sword in the king's presence and had been forbidden the court. What subsequently transpired is not known, but the upshot involved Anna, since it was decided that "the Queen shall write him [Lennox] to come to her."[12]

The shape of Anna's political behavior in Scotland was largely configured, however, not by her friendships but by her enmities. Chief among her antagonists was the formidable chancellor, Sir John Maitland, who at some point in 1592 seems to have greatly offended Anna: presumably, as she later indicated, the cause of her anger was his "rash words to the King of Scots . . . narrowly touching her." Taking retaliatory action over an extended period, Anna actually managed, by August 1593, at age eighteen, to align with her against Scotland's chancellor (each for his own reasons, of course) such disparate figures as the duke of Lennox, the earl of Mar, the earl of Bothwell (James's almost murderous antimonarchist enemy), and Alexander Sixth Lord Home,[13] creating a near crisis whose seriousness is confirmed by a number of contemporary assessments. As early as January 1592, shortly after Maitland's initial offense, Lord Burleigh in England heard that Scotland "so now stands as there is but the King and Queen and the Chancellor, that the King must forsake and leave the Chancellor, or leave the Queen, for the Queen blames wholly the Chancellor."

Indeed, the pressure exerted by Anna on the man regarded by historians as one of Scotland's great chancellors continued so heavy that in November 1592, Maitland expressed the desire to go to England and live privately. But relentless in pursuit, "the Queen of Scots," so reports went, "has required the Queen of England to show the Chancellor no favor or reception in England."[14] A few months later, the situation between James and Anna had deteriorated to the point where James felt compelled to restrict Anna's movements, to her great unhappiness.[15]

Ultimately, the strain at court produced by Anna's continuing hostility toward Maitland was so persistent that James proposed to her "either as a party to declare his [Maitland's] fault, or else as a principal to hear his petition; whereupon it is advised that the Chancellor shall in humble wise submit and make suit to the Queen for her favour and good countenance, and when this has been got, the Duke [of Lennox] and other adversaries of the Chancellor shall be laid off by the King's means" (*CSPS*, 10:788).

In April 1593, however, Anna was still working against Maitland. "Sundry ministers have travailed lately and divers times with the Queen to pacify her wrath against the Chancellor that he might be restored to her good countenance and return to the Court to serve the King who greatly desires his service." But apparently Maitland "does not like and does not find any safety to come to court before he shall recover the Queen's favor, and thereon be reconciled with the Duke and the Master of Glamis" (*CSPS*, 11:78).

King James himself attested to the political difficulty Anna seems to have been capable of producing for him when he concluded that "only the Queen of England's letter to the Queen of Scots shall work the Chancellor's peace." James wrote Queen Elizabeth to this effect (*CSPS*, 11:80), while

Maitland pressed the English ambassador, Sir Robert Bowes, to do the same thing, and Bowes communicated with Burleigh seeking advice. Maitland himself undertook to write Anna "in very humble sort" (*CSPS*, 11:88). It did no good. Nor did the intervention of Queen Elizabeth, who by 20 May 1593 had also communicated with the Scottish queen. Not until Maitland began to offer substantial inducements did Anna relent, and then only insofar as to begin negotiations (*CSPS*, 11:88–100). Maitland had been litigating for some old interests that he claimed in the Abbey of Dunfermline, which was part of Anna's settlement as queen of Scotland (as were lands and strong-holds including Dunfermline, Leith, and Falkland), but he now abandoned the effort. The English ambassador, writing to Burleigh on 17 June 1593, re-marked that Anna and the ambassadors of Denmark, "by the King's advice, begin to like the Chancellor's offer of the lands in his hands, being parcel of Dunfermline, the Queen's dower." Indeed, it almost seems that Anna's openness to Maitland's overtures was the key to the resolution of a number of political tensions at court.

The Chancellor, hoping to be restored to the Queen's favor, trusts to return to the Court and to his office; whereupon it is looked that the reformation intended shall find the better progress, that the Chancellor and [the Earl of] Mar shall enter into good friendship, and that therein the Duke [of Lennox] and the Chancellor shall be reconciled, and other agreement made for the union of the councilors to serve the King with quietness. (*CSPS*, 11:100)

Even so, it was not until 30 November 1593 — almost two years after his origi-nal offense — that Maitland was formally reconciled with the queen. A week later, Bowes wrote Burleigh that "the Chancellor directs his course to please the Queen, and that by the means of the Queen and the Chancellor the court shall be reformed [reorganized]" (*CSPS*, 11:234, 237). Five days later, Anna turned nineteen. She was seven months pregnant.

    Anna's two-year confrontation with Maitland can be interpreted in several ways that are not necessarily mutually exclusive. On one level, Anna might appear as a highly offended young bride who also happened to be a queen and thus in a position to rage irresponsibly. But the interventions of both James and Queen Elizabeth suggest that they perceived here some-thing more than the self-indulgent behavior of a naive young woman. What these monarchs had to contend with was a person capable of asserting her-self forcefully with Maitland and other peers. Apparently feeling the chan-cellor held her queenship in light regard, Anna made him regret this attitude. In the end, Anna forced him to recognize that neither James nor Elizabeth could protect him or restore him to his former position without her personal acquiescence.

The real issues at stake in this crisis had little, of course, to do with Anna's personal grievance. James was in a power struggle, and Anna had adroitly used a Scottish court faction composed of formidable figures such as the duke of Lennox, the earl of Mar, the earl of Bothwell, and Lord Home to her own advantage—as they had used her as a means of legitimating their own resistance to centralized Crown control. The Maitland situation thus does not require us to imagine Anna as a political heavyweight in her own right. The point is that the youthful Anna was shrewd enough to identify a means of combining her own as yet undefined prerogatives with the resources of nobles who found it convenient to support her. Moreover, throughout her queenship in Scotland, Anna was able to repeat this kind of political maneuver even though the configuration of her supporting group of nobles continually shifted. Indeed, if there was a common denominator in the Scottish court factionalism surrounding Anna, it appears to have been Anna herself.

It may be useful to reiterate at this point that the present discussion is not intended as a political history of Scotland between 1593 and 1603. Rather, I am focusing on specific events that delineate Anna of Denmark as a catalyst for Scottish court intrigue in order to offer a counterargument to the literary tradition of her political irrelevance. And while Scottish accounts may not serve to dispel charges of Anna's frivolity (a subjective judgment, in any event), they do decisively demonstrate her strength of will and need for self-assertion—whatever the purposes for which these qualities may have been deployed.

This "drive," for want of a better term, seems significantly illustrated, in its important implications for Anna's future English reign, by events occurring just two months after her conflict with Maitland had ended. On 19 February 1594, she gave birth to Prince Henry, an event that was to precipitate serious and lasting conflict within the royal household. This was because, two days later, the Scottish Privy Council nominated one of the nobles who was James's closest supporter, John Erskine, second earl of Mar, to assume the formal guardianship of the Scottish heir apparent. Mar's nomination to the office was predictable, even routine, since his father and grandfather had served as royal guardians before him. The baby was thus to be taken from court to be kept at Mar's Castle of Stirling where Henry would be brought up by the earl, a widower, and his mother, Annabel Murray, dowager countess of Mar (*CSPS*, 11:280). The February 1594 ordinance for the nursing and keeping of Prince Henry was signed by twenty-three persons, including Mar and his mother. The order, in part, decreed

that his Grace's person no wise be removed or transported forth of the said castle [of Stirling] to any other place nor that none disobedient to our sovereign lord's authority or known not well affected to his Highness nor their wives, bairns, or servants, shall be received or suffered to have interest or residence within the said castle; and that no earl be received within the said castle with man nor servants, no lord with man nor servants, no baron with man nor servants, nor no gentleman but single and alone and all without armor or weapons and the number of the whole to be received at once to be within the ordinary number entertained in the said castle, and that the ordinary servants appointed presently by his Highness with advice of his Council to attend upon his dearest son, the Prince, shall not be removed from his Grace nor others placed in their charges and service without the special advice, warrant, and command of our said sovereign lord and his Privy Council.[16]

Anna's reaction to this decision, given her own background, is not surprising. Although her younger brother, the future king of Denmark, had, almost immediately after his baptism, been entrusted to the care of Duke Ulric and Duchess Elizabeth of Mecklenburg, with whom he remained for two years at Skandeborg Castle in Jutland, the important difference was that these were Christian's maternal grandparents. When Christian was eleven, however, Frederick II died and despite the efforts of his mother, Queen Sophia, to become his governor as well as regent, Anna's brother was entrusted to a regency government of Danish aristocrats who had all been loyal advisers of Christian's father.[17]

But Sophia, in the general context of *continental* royal activity, had not been attempting any unusual action. In Spain, for example, when Charles V, father of the infant Philip II, left the country for five years, he consigned the care of the heir apparent to his queen, Isabel, who was sister to the king of Portugal, thus making Isabel regent of the realm. Her letters to her husband at this time make clear her dominance over the regnal situation and certainly over her son. In fact, Isabel's largely Portuguese circle made such an impression on Philip that later in life, he appointed one of his former nurses in this circle, Leonor Mascarenhas, as an attendant on his own son. In France, too, there were (complicated) parallels for Anna of Denmark's determination to oversee the raising of her infant son and heir apparent. During a tournament celebrating the double marriage of Philip II of Spain to Elizabeth, daughter of the French king Henri II, and of the duke of Savoy to Henri II's sister, Marguerite, Henry was accidentally killed. At this time, Henri's son, Francis II (who would marry Mary Queen of Scots) was only fifteen, and the government of his part of France passed into the hands of his mother, Catherine de Medici. When Francis himself died soon thereafter, in 1560, Catherine became regent for the next in line, the ten-year-old Charles IX, who died in 1574. Catherine thus assumed a position at center stage that she continued to maintain until her own death in 1589, the same year in which her third son, Henri III, also died (and Anna married James VI). Indeed when all the male heirs of Henri II of France were deceased, Henry of Navarre, who had been raised a Protestant but later converted to Catholicism, became Henri IV of France. In 1572, he had married Catherine de Medici's daughter, Margaret of Valois; in 1600, he married Marie de Medici (niece of the duke of Tuscany), who bore him a son, Louis XIII, in 1601. Marie, as it happened, had been crowned queen regent on the day before Henri's assassination in 1610, the idea being that she would serve as regent during Henri's absence at his recently declared war against the Habsburgs. As both regent and now widow, Marie effectively ruled France during her son's minority, and she did not die until 1642.[18]

Evidently, the advisers to the Scottish Crown were unconcerned about how these continental precedents may have configured the Scottish queen's attitude toward their disposition of Henry. Of course, it is a reasonable assumption that Anna had been informed from the earliest months of her pregnancy what would happen if she gave birth to a son. Whatever the case, a little over a year after Henry's birth in March 1595, the twenty-one-year-old queen attempted to break Mar's guardianship by requesting that James assign to her the keeping both of the prince and of Mar's Castle of Stirling. The king, apparently quite dismayed, undertook to discover who had moved the queen to this action (assuming that she needed any instigation) (*CSPS*, 11:546, 553). Chancellor Maitland, an old enemy of Mar but now, significantly, allied with Anna, was greatly suspected in this connection: "There ariseth a variance at court. The Queen would have had the prince in keeping in the Castle of Edinburgh and Balcleuche [Buccleuch] to be captain. . . . It was thought the motion proceeded from the Chancellor who was now a great courtier with the Queen."[19]

But the king "finding that course to be so perilous to his own estate . . . could not let it proceed."[20] Maitland, who supported Anna's venture, withdrew from the situation (*CSPS*, 11:554) and also superficially reconciled with Mar (*CSPS*, 11:602). Anna, "degusted" with the chancellor, was forced for now to desist in her attempt. Yet despite her presumed understanding that in Scotland James's life may have depended upon keeping Prince Henry out of the hands of Bothwells or of Gowries, she persisted in her efforts to regain Henry, revealing a politically relentless streak. Thus, only a few months later, in May 1595, Roger Aston, the English agent in Scotland, reported to Robert Bowes that "the Queen speaks more plainly than before and will not cease till she has her son." We have "two mighty factions," he continued. "What will be the end God knows." "Some say," George Nicholson (Bowes's assistant) wrote to Bowes in June, that the queen would not go to James at Falkland so "that the King may come hither [to Edinburgh] where he may be more boldly dealt with in the motion for the young Prince, the Queen's faction being masters here and the King at Stirling." [21]

By July these new factions had defined themselves, the possession of the prince being the ostensible issue: Chancellor Maitland and seven nobles with the queen, in opposition to the king and the earl of Mar, his cousin, Thomas Erskine, and Sir James Elphinstone. [22] As Nicholson wrote to Bowes again on 15 July: "No good can come between the King and Queen till she be satisfied anent the Prince," there being "division of this land into two factions almost to the parting of the King and the Queen" (*CSPS*, 11:640). The situation seems to have been sufficiently tense to produce this letter, which James wrote the earl of Mar on 24 July: "Because in the surety of my son consists my surety and that I have concreditied unto you the charge of his keeping upon the trust I have of your honesty, this present therefore shall be a warrant unto you not to deliver him out of your hands except I command you with my own mouth, and being in such company as I myself shall best like of, otherwise not to deliver him for any charge or message that can come from me."

The scenario suggested here as subtext was that James might in the future become someone's prisoner. His awareness of his own physical vulnerability in the politically fraught situation in Scotland was also evident when he enjoined Mar that "in case God call me at any time, that neither for Queen nor Estates' pleasure ye deliver him [Henry] until he be eighteen years of age." [23]

The matter came to a climax in a reported episode that provides an interesting perspective on the historically obscured relationship between Anna and James. The king was at the Castle of Stirling while Queen Anna and her supporters were at her court in Edinburgh. Her supporters gave it out that the queen was ill and wanted to see James. But James's advisers thought it dangerous for him to go to Anna in these circumstances, kidnaping or even assassination having been the political mode in Scotland, as James himself knew from his own experience as a young man. [24] But as for the queen's party, "All their wits were laid together [to devise] how he [James] might be drawn to Edinburgh." No way could be better devised than to send "the doctores of fesike" to assure James of the queen's sickness. The king, being advised of this news and moved "to give a proof of his love to his wife" and to "set aside all occasion of suspicion, jealousy or [pleasures]," proceeded at once to Edinburgh, where he "found the Queen very merry and well disposed." Furthermore, it seems that, in the evening "the Queen insisted very earnestly in her suit and thought to have obtained her intent. The King, perceiving that she was purposed to follow out the matter, took it in a more higher sort than before and gave her this answer. 'My heart, I am sorry you should be persuaded to move me to that which will be the destruction of me and my blood.' Whereupon the Queen fell to tears and so left off that purpose" (*CSPS*, 11:662–63).

Whatever the accuracy of this account, the conflict between James and Anna appears to have been sufficiently well known to produce the story itself. The tense situation between the two continued for weeks. In England Cecil received an August report that Scotland was "now constantly divided into two factions, one for the King and another for the Queen." Colville wrote to Bowes on 20 August: "There is nothing but lurking hatred disguised with cunning dissimulation betwixt the King and the Queen, each intending by slight to overcome the other." All the parishes of Scotland, he wrote, were observing a fast "for the amendment of the present danger" (*CSPS*, 11:683).

Certainly the impression to be culled from the English and Scottish writers of these letters in the 1590s — however limited the sampling may be — is of a queen to be reckoned with, not a frivolous and vapid woman. Indeed, according to one letter of this period, outside intervention of the most telling kind seems to have been deemed necessary, and not, in this instance, from Queen Elizabeth. Rather, Anna received an explicit instruction from her mother, Queen Sophia, "to obey the King's will in all things, as she would have her blessing." Whether this maternal injunction or Anna's own intention defined her future course is unclear, but in the middle of August 1595, Anna superficially reconciled herself with the earl of Mar.[25] She was "something hard" with him at the beginning, for, as she told the king, "the cause of her earnest suit was that she thought she could not be crossed by any subject, but that she had as much credit as might countervail any" (*CSPS*, 11:681–83).

Even so, as late as October, Sir Robert Sidney in England (Anna's future English Lord Chamberlain) was hearing from his Scottish correspondent,

Thomas Lake, about the contention at court, here specifically, Chancellor Maitland's support of the queen's agenda.[26] And although the death (5 October 1595) of Maitland, adversary of the powerful earl of Mar, added to the general air of reconciliation in Scotland at this time, the English Crown was evidently disturbed by continuing reports of dissension. Given the incendiary situation precipitating the recent execution of Mary Queen of Scots, the English Crown may well have been concerned about instability in Scotland and, further, about possible Spanish influence among those nobles surrounding Anna who might thus be trying to overthrow James's Protestant rule.

Accordingly, six months after the reconciliation of Anna with Mar, Elizabeth's ambassador delivered a letter as well as a longish oral message to the Scottish queen on the classic *topos* of evil counselors. Such counselors, Elizabeth's oral message opined, were probably papists who were trying to seduce Anna from her Lutheran faith. Indeed, it would be good for the queen of England to know their names. Anna seems to have been unintimidated. She disingenuously replied that it was the dead Maitland who had put all those evil ideas about her infant son into her head. Others indeed had also tried to draw her from her religion, Anna observed, but they had not succeeded. So, Anna riposted, there was no point now in identifying anyone by name; nonetheless, if anyone tried to convert her in the future, Anna would immediately let Elizabeth know that person's identity (*CSPS*, 12:149–51). Elizabeth could not have been reassured by such responses, which merely attested to the fact that in Scotland, now, there was not only James VI to be dealt with but also Anna of Denmark.

Indeed, after bearing her second child in 1596, Anna again entered the political arena.[27] By December 1597, Robert Cecil was hearing that Anna "is presently and will be still [dealing] in matters of importance to the greatest causes." Again, in 1598: "Always the Queen knows all."[28] A month before the birth of her third child on Christmas Eve, for example, Anna informed King James of a plot being hatched against him by the Lords Erroll, Alexander Sixth Lord Home, Cessford, and others (*CSPS*, 13:333). But it was the Gowrie Plot of 4 August 1600, whatever its causes and whatever the true events constituting it, that again generated documents reporting a polarization of king and queen consort. For when James returned from that famous episode in which it was said that he was almost assassinated, he immediately caused the earl of Gowrie's two sisters, Barbara and Beatrix Ruthven, court ladies "in chiefest credit" with the queen, to be "thrust out of the house" over the queen's strong objections (*CSPS*, 13:679). Important officials urged that Anna herself had been connected with the Gowrie plot,[29] and on 21 October Sir John Carey, deputy governor of Berwick, England's military frontier with Scotland, wrote Cecil: "Our border news is that the Queen of Scots is very narrowly looked unto, and a strait watch kept about her; and it is further said that after she shall be brought to bed, she shall be kept as a prisoner ever after, and the King will no more come where she is. It is said that the Queen says plainly that she will be utter enemy to all that were at the murder of Gowry save the King himself."[30]

The Scottish noble, the Master of Grey, described to Robert Cecil the same suspicions about the queen, along with her testy response to her situation: "The King and the Queen are in very evil menage and now she makes to take upon her more dealing than hitherto she has done. At public table she said to him that he was advised to imprison her, but willed him to beware what he "mintit" at for she was not the Earl of Gowrie. He said he believed she was mad. She answered that he should find she was neither mad nor beside herself if he 'mintit' at that he intended."[31] Yet despite such a report, another account at this time described Anna as very loving with James as her latest pregnancy came to term. So reconciled were they, in fact, "that no man dare deal in that matter farther."[32]

Prince Charles was born 19 November 1600, on the evening of the day when the condemned corpses of the two Ruthvens, the brothers of Anna's former ladies-in-waiting, were hanged, drawn, and quartered in retroactive punishment for the Gowrie Plot.[33] Several months later, in January 1601, the queen was up and about and again working against the earl of Mar and his faction. By March she was apparently busy trying to "insinuate herself in the people's hearts" and also refusing to attend Patrick Galloway's sermons, which were framed to justify the king's procedure with the earl of Gowrie (*CSPS*, 13:789).[34] Even so, before James's accession to the throne of England, the royal domestic situation was said to have stabilized, "the Queen constant in her dislike of her conceived enemies, yet not able to hurt them. For now they rule more absolutely than ever."[35] Perhaps for this reason, in 1601, Anna offered forgiveness to her court enemies. Nevertheless Ralph Grey, writing to Robert Cecil, commented significantly on Anna's bent for political retaliation, observing that "if these gentlemen behave not themselves according to her Majesty's expectations, it had been better for them they had not as yet kissed her hands" (*CSPS*, 13:864). Further, the queen's forgiveness was conditioned on the premise that her former enemies would grant the following demands. They "should confess their fault and crave pardon for the same"; they should "obtain to her a yearly augmentation of twenty thousand pounds Scots, either of his Majesty's properties or the annuity of England" (sent by Elizabeth every year to help James balance the budget); and, significantly, they should persuade his Majesty "that herself should have the education of the Prince" (*CSPS*, 13:864).

As the Scottish sojourn drew to its end, Anna bore her fifth child, Robert, in January 1602—he died at four months, on 27 May[36]—but judging from the report of James Hudson, the new English agent, the queen's political activity continued. Writing Cecil in December 1602, on the eve of Queen Elizabeth's death, he described Anna as "that violent woman who will not leave til she either restore the last destroyed house [the Gowries?] or revenge the fall of it." But "the gentleman, her husband, is so 'syllid' in love that none dare deal in this matter as they would or should for fear of offense," he added. "Yet it has been plainly spoken in pulpits and so fervently that it has drawn out many tears from the auditors to hear so much of the peril of his person, and it has been plainly told herself that she must leave such matters and take a better course" (*CSPS*, 13:1092).

Two remarkable final episodes in Scotland offer grounds for Hudson's reactions and also reemphasize those traits in Anna of Denmark that strongly challenge her traditionally flaccid English court image. The first episode had to do with Gowrie's sisters, Beatrix and Barbara Ruthven. On an evening in January 1603, five months before Anna arrived in England, Beatrix Ruthven was smuggled into the palace as part of a group coming to visit the queen. Stowed "in a chamber prepared for her by the Queen's direction," Beatrix had "much time and conference" with Anna.[37] When James learned of this act, he was badly unsettled, especially, one might guess, by the security implications, for he immediately ordered workmen to seal up "all dangerous passages for coming near the King's chamber." All of Anna's servants were then called into the chapel and enjoined "on pain of death" to swear to have no dealings with the Ruthvens "without the King's and Queen's [*sic*] direction and privity."[38]

James's accession to the English throne less than two months later probably foreclosed any Scottish resolution of the Gowrie problem, but a conversation between Anna and the English agent in Scotland, Sir Roger Aston, one that he reported to James in February 1603, is nonetheless suggestive. "The two chief points I dealt with her in were [first] the countenance which she had given to the brethren and 'sesterne' of Gowrie; the second was the suspicion conceived of some late practice that should have been against his Majesty" (*CSPS*, 13:1110). Anna denied the second point, but she agreed to the validity of the first.

But it was the queen's last reported actions in Scotland that must finally disestablish that tradition of the English Anna as the pale and wavering queen of triviality. James was already in England when Anna, four months pregnant, was scheduled to begin her own progress on 14 May 1603. A week prior to her intended departure, on 4 May, Anna made a journey to the earl of Mar's Castle of Stirling actually to claim her son Henry and to bring him with her to England.[39] Joined at Stirling by a party that included a marquis, two earls, and other nobles, the queen demanded access to the castle.[40] But, according to the account in Calderwood, "Her purpose was perceived by the Lady Mar and her son [the earl of Mar's younger brother] and, when request prevailed not, the Lady Mar and her son and the Lord of Keir gave a flat denial and would not suffer the Prince to go out to the Torwood or whither the Queen would have had him." Nor were any of the nobles accompanying Anna allowed into the castle unless, as per Mar's original commission "they would enter, every principal man, with two [of Mar's men] and himself." Three days elapsed in this impasse. The incident increasingly alarmed supporters of the king because it coincided with James's accession to the English throne, showcasing a never-resolved area of acute conflict between king and queen. Thus Calderwood's sparse tale concerning the crisis must here be filled out with texts not hitherto invoked in connection with this event.

On 10 May the Lord Chancellor of Scotland, John, third earl of Montrose, conveyed to James in England his own concern about the situation:

Sir: Her Majesty's present estate and condition I refer to the bearer's report. Of Her Grace's departure to Stirling I was noways a mover thereof, neither scarce acquainted therewith. As this bearer coming in haste can sufficiently impart to Your Majesty Her Grace's present estate and company, so it were lost labor to me to write anything whereof I have no further warrant but of this bearer himself. Your Majesty shall be fully acquainted at all occasions how matters shall fall out here, but if her Highness' journey [to England] were once undertaken, Your Grace should see an amendment in bygane oversichts [previous negligences][41] that might be imputed to us in the government, and an honest and disposed resolution in myself at least to postpone [replace] all the fear of hazard, danger, or inconvenience to that which may redound in any ways to Your Majesty's honor.[42]

However, it was on this same day, according to Calderwood, that at Stirling, "the Queen went to bed in an anger and parted with child, the tenth of May, as was constantly [faithfully] reported." The event was enlarged upon by the Venetian ambassador in London, who did not write, as did Calderwood, for the reading public. Sending a confidential state communication to the doge on 18 May, the ambassador wrote that the queen "flew into a violent fury, and four months gone with child as she was, she beat her own belly, so that they say she is in manifest danger of miscarriage and death." Apparently for seventeen days Anna lay ill at Stirling among people she probably perceived as enemies.[43]

Very early in that illness, only two days after the miscarriage, the earl of Mar, in England with James, quickly returned to Scotland, "with full commission" to bring Anna back to England. Anna, however, "would not look upon him but desired to have the letters which were sent from the King. He [Mar] refused unless he got presence to discharge his secret commission. The Queen sent a letter with post to the King; the Earl of Mar did the like." [44]

On 13 May, Lord Chancellor Montrose, not having yet received a response from James to his letter, and alarmed by Anna's refusal to go with Mar, wrote again to the new English king:

I will noways renew the remembrance of that late accident so far to be sorrowed in the person of the Queen's Grace, albeit — praised be God — there is a full assurance of Her Majesty's preservation and full recovery of her wonted health. But . . . I could noways omit to impart the very true estate of matters as they stand here. . . . There is a controversy and jar entered betwixt some of the nobility anent this late question of the prince's delivery. These that accompanied the Queen's Majesty are accounted by the Earl of Mar to have been the movers and enticers of her Highness to that enterprise. They themselves by oaths protest that they had no intention at all but her Grace's convoy, being required by her missives thereto, which charge they could not goodly disobey. In either [each] of the contradictors there rests greater hatred and malice, nor as yet by action has budded forth, but if it be not prevented, no doubt it is able to make a greater stir in this country than any that has been there many years ago. . . . None here will press to meddle with the same, for by your Majesty's late warrant, it is ordained that the Earl of Mar shall have the prince's convoy in the Queen's company.[45]

But here, apparently, was the crux of the problem, for according to Montrose, Anna was not going to travel with Mar, nor was she going to go to England without her son.

The Queen's Majesty is not of mind to depart unless the prince go with her and will noways rest contented that the Earl of Mar should accompany her. . . . Only, I thought it not amiss to impart the same to your Majesty, most humbly beseeching your Highness to provide remedies how the Queen's Grace may rest satisfied and contented, the Earl of Mar exonerated of that great charge and bond that lies on him for keeping of the said Prince, and some order to be taken how this eilest [argument] [46] and controversy, likely to arise and increase amongst these of your nobility, may be settled and pacified.[47]

As the stand-off continued over the weekend, James decided to defuse the situation by removing Mar from the scene. Accordingly, on 14 May, James wrote to Mar from Greenwich that he should now defer in this matter "to our dearest cousin and counsellor," the duke of Lennox, whom James was about to dispatch from London to Stirling.[48] In the meantime, Anna continued to deny Mar access to her person; and, for his part, Mar still refused to deliver James's letters to her via anyone else. Indeed, James apparently felt it necessary actually to command Mar back to London. Enjoining him, "all excuses set aside," to "address yourself hither in all possible diligence," James's letter made it clear that, one way or the other, he wanted his message in Anna's hands:

> As for our letter sent [i.e., carried] by you to our dearest bedfellow, although you have done no thing in the not delivery thereof but according to our direction, yet since the contents thereof are not of so great consequence as they are particular and not fit to come into every man's hands, it is our will that for her better satisfaction you deliver the same to any of the [Privy] Council to be given to her and disposed upon as she pleaseth in case she continue in that wilfulness as she will not hear your credit nor receive the same from your own hands. In all other things concerning the transporting of our son you shall dispose yourself according as our cousin the Duke of Lennox will particularly acquaint you to that which is our pleasure and advise with him carefully upon our honor and his surety. To whose sufficiency remitting the rest and looking for you here in all haste we bid you farewell.[49]

In other words, Anna had contrived a situation that forced James to accede to her wishes. James's disparaging term, "wilfulness," summed up an intractable determination that James knew he could not deflect: only the personal acquiescence of Anna, one gathers, could resolve the present impasse.[50]

Accordingly, on 19 May, the duke of Lennox, one of the nobles whom Anna apparently trusted most, arrived from England to carry out the king's decision. Lennox set a mechanism in motion that would finally cancel the Scottish tradition of the Mars' guardianship, and at the same time protect the earl's honor.[51] Mar had insisted that before he would withdraw from Henry he must receive a formal revocation of his commission for protecting the king's heir. Clearly, the Scottish Privy Council took this demand seriously, for on 23 May are recorded two entries, "The Earl of Mar's discharge of his keeping of the Prince" and "Warrant for delivery of the Prince to the Duke of Lennox."[52] On the same day King James's formal discharge of the earl of Mar from his hereditary custodial office was registered in the "Books of Secret Council," declaring Mar and his descendants "to be freed and relieved thereof for now and ever" from any further responsibility for heirs apparent.[53]

These discharges having been executed so that the duke of Lennox was now Prince Henry's temporary (official) guardian, Anna was visited in Stirling by the Privy Council. Lord Fyvie (a member of the Privy Council so trusted that he had been made Prince Charles's guardian by James just before he left for England) described these proceedings in a letter to the new English king.[54]

I passed immediately, after the receipt of Your Highness' letter, to Stirling where first I dealt particularly with her Majesty as earnestly as I could, and with all the reason my wit might furnish me to that intent. Next, at the meeting of the Council I laid down such grounds and arguments as I thought meetest to be propounded and insisted on by us all commonly before Her Majesty to the same effect, which the Council thought so sufficient that, as they concluded best we should all go together to Her Majesty to propound and reason the same. So they burdened me to be the first propounder and reasoner thereof.[55]

Matters seem to have proceeded well enough, for Fyvie concluded, "I doubt not but her Majesty considers and understands sufficiently the best and the worst and all the right and the wrong in that matter. . . . At meeting with your Majesty, her Highness will think, esteem, and do in all that, and all belongs thereto, as shall please your grace to direct, signify, or dispose. This I understand to be her Majesty's mind and resolution."

Calderwood's account suggests the political upshot.

The Council convened in the Castle of Stirling. It was concluded that the four [*sic*] noblemen above mentioned who came to Stirling to the Queen repair not within ten miles to the Prince. It was thought good that the Earl of Mar should deliver the Prince to the Duke [of Lennox], and that the Duke again deliver him to the Council. The Council, to pleasure the Queen, delivered him to her and the Duke, to be transported and to be delivered by them to the King, and appointed so many noblemen to attend upon her, of which number the Earl of Mar was not one, to pleasure the Queen. All parties being contented, as it seemed, the Earl of Mar took journey toward England immediately after.[56]

Fyvie's letter casts additional light on Anna's forceful personality in that he defended himself to James for what he feared would be perceived as his ineffectiveness in not better controlling the queen. Since the crux of the problem was the fixedness of Anna's will, apparently the solution, in the opinion of all involved parties, was to accede to this will—because nothing else would work. "As to your Majesty's advocate's part [Sir Thomas Hamilton: later Lord Haddington] or mine in this, albeit we have had that honor and direction by your Majesties, to be as Her Highness' counsellors in the whole course of this business, I certify Your Majesty we have been more subject to obey commandments and directions, nor [rather than] well heard or taken with in our councils which we would never have given but to Your Majesty's contentment in the first place, and to the fulfilling of Your Highness' full will."

As for Hamilton, Fyvie suggested that he too apparently could do nothing with Anna:

> I was at Dunfermling when this stir fell forth and came not to Stirling till I was sent for by Her Majesty being in extremity of sickness and disease which state would not admit all that good reason might have furnished to any of us to be said to Her Majesty. Your Highness' advocate [Hamilton] chanced to be with Her Majesty present at the very worst. . . . At such a time, in such an accident, to such a person, what could he do or say? His due respect to Your Majesty and to your obedience behooved ever to have the first place in his mind, he was not ignorant of the great care and tender love your Majesty has to Her Highness's royal person. To dispute or contest what reason and wisdom would urge of her Highness' proceedings was but the way to incense Her Majesty farther against all and to augment her passion to greater peril which he was certain would have annoyed [disturbed] your Majesty above all and might have been justly imputed to lack of discretion on his part. All being weighed the best expedient was to comfort and encourage her Majesty, to give her good heart: in sum, physic and medicine requireth then greater place nor [than] economic or politic. Her Majesty's passions could not be so well moderated or mitigated as by seconding, following, and obeying all her directions which always was subject and depended wholly upon your sacred Majesty's answers and resolutions as oracles to give both health and full resolution of all doubts and difficulties.

In the end—and this is my general point here, as well as the point of this chapter—Fyvie's concluding words suggest the quality of the pressure Anna exerted, since the councillor, dwelling on the matter, reveals an anguish to the king about a situation "which I protest has grieved me so that to have all memories of the same extinguished and abolished I would be content almost to be buried therewith myself."[57]

On Friday, 27 May, Queen Anna left Stirling; she arrived in Edinburgh on Monday and attended church on Tuesday, "riding in a coach and accompanied with many English ladies in coaches, and some riding on fair horse." On 1 June, twenty-five days after the original incident, and nineteen days late for the scheduled beginning of her progress, "the Queen and Prince took journey about ten hours towards England."[58] On the eve of her departure, the Lord Chancellor penned a final letter and general warning to King James about the entire situation as he saw it. Her Majesty, wrote Montrose, remained as yet unreconciled with the earl of Mar "whose wrath, if it be not appeased" will necessarily produce one of several consequences. "For if her Highness will be satisfied, it is thought that the condition of that nobleman" shall not "answer to his expectation." On the other hand, if the queen consort's own sense of personal offense be not placated, "the uttering of her discontentments will breed small pleasure to Your Majesty. But lest Her Highness' wrath continuing, should hereafter produce unexpected tortures [troubles], I would most humbly entreat Your Majesty to prevent the same . . . and suffer not this canker or corruption to have any further progress."

Even though the Scottish stakes were now not so high, with James having assumed the added authority of the English Crown, England's new queen was riding south amid ominous warnings from James's Scottish Council (a fact not previously noted) that he had better exercise greater control over his wife. As for Anna's own motives in this episode, it seems impossible to separate her maternal and political instincts. For prior to Anna's effort to claim Henry from Stirling, Calderwood remarks, the queen had not been in the prince's vicinity "by the space of five years."[59] Nevertheless, the fact remains that it was Anna's desires, violently advanced, which in the end effected Henry's transfer to England.

The significance of this episode is underscored by the lack of evidence, otherwise, of any plans to raise Henry in England now instead of in Scotland. Did James originally intend for Henry to remain in the north to be further educated (as James had been) in a Scottish noble household until this heir apparent turned sixteen and was installed in England as a thoroughly Scottish prince of Wales? Certainly such a design seems implicit in the terms of the 1595 "Ordinance for the Nursing and Keeping of Prince Henry" in which James specified that Henry not be delivered from custody until he was eighteen "and that he command you [Mar] himself."[60] Further, Mar's own behavior—and Anna's unhappiness—suggest that James had not arranged to bring Henry to England at the time of his accession. Thus we may presume that Anna's actions precipitated a decision that resulted in an English rather than a Scottish upbringing for the prince, beginning at the age of nine. In light of this background, we must conclude—as against the views of Strong noted in Chapter 1 — any potential contribution Henry might have made to an artistic renaissance in England would not have been possible without his mother's aggressive interventions.[61]

But Anna abruptly ceased overt political activity in England — in a change so radical as to require a redefinition of her royal identity between 1603 and 1613 — and this, too, may have been the direct consequence of her Scottish history with James. In this connection, it seems highly significant that when James acceded to the English throne, he took advantage of his unique political opportunity to separate his Scottish nobles into two groups: quite simply, those whom he would take with him to England and those whom he would leave behind. Unsurprisingly, but portentously from Anna's perspective, James's new circle of intimates excluded nobles whom Queen Anna had been able to co-opt (or who had tried to co-opt her) in Scotland. Thus, although it has not generally been remarked, James selected only the Scottish nobles who had been of his own "faction," with the possible exception of the duke of Lennox, James's second cousin and close counselor, who had always been on friendly terms with Anna (as is obvious from the Stirling episode). But James's other Scottish advisers in England can be identified either as Anna's old enemies or as enemies of the factions successively associated with her. Thus, after this winnowing, James's Scottish group in England included the earl of Dunbar, Sir George Home, Sir James Elphinstone of Darnton (the future Lord Balmerino), Edward Bruce, Lord of Kinloss, Sir Thomas Erskine, Thomas Hamilton, and, of course, the earl of Mar.[62]

This isolation from her supporters in the Scottish peerage, coupled with the obviously different — and much more stable — political environment in England, forced Anna to reconfigure her role as queen consort. Her altered formulae for action, however, should not mislead students of the Stuart court as to her orientation and capabilities. Rather, we must reckon with the admittedly far-from-perfect recollections of that high French noble, close to Henri IV, who visited England as Henri's ambassador-extraordinary several months after James's accession. Writing his recollections of this time, he remarked of Anna:

> The character of this Princess was quite the reverse of her husband's; she was naturally bold and enterprising; she loved pomp and grandeur, tumult, and intrigue. She was deeply engaged in all the civil factions, not only in Scotland, in relation to the Catholics, whom she supported and had even first encourged, but also in England, where the discontented whose number were very considerable, were not sorry to be supported by a Princess destined to become their Queen. . . . She

was still in Scotland when I arrived at that city, and James wished she would not have departed from thence so soon, being persuaded that her presence would only be detrimental to affairs. He sent to acquaint her with his desire . . . but she was very little affected by it. Instead of obeying, the Queen prepared to quit Scotland after having, of her own accord, and against the King's expressed desire, appointed herself a great chamberlain of her household. She . . . brought with her the body of the male child of which she had been delivered in Scotland, because endeavors had been used to persuade the public that his death was only feigned.[63]

Temperamentally unsuited to a purely symbolic role, but now unable to maneuver in the more settled English political arena, which was further stabilized for King James by the controlling presences of Robert Cecil and the (future) earl of Northampton, Henry Lord Howard, the queen consort seems to have searched out new directions for her energies and considerable intelligence. Until such time as Robert Cecil's death in 1612 weakened the political structure of governance at court, Anna turned to social and intellectual concerns that not only reaffirmed a continuity with her Danish and Scottish past but also made her the center of high culture at the early Stuart court. For during the first decade of the Jacobean reign, Anna reconstituted her regnal identity in terms of this new arena, first, by bringing together circles of cultured nobles, then by creating the lavish spectacle of royal court masques that simultaneously gave sociopolitical weight to the showcasing of herself as spectacular queen. The next two chapters will discuss the importance of these activities to the creation of a particular English court milieu, a new ambience for high culture made possible largely by Anna's remarkable talent continually to reinvent herself.

3. QUEEN ANNA'S ENGLISH COURT CENTERING THE ARTS

In Scotland, Anna of Denmark had been an active and energetic organizer of peerage factions, which she used in pursuing her own goals. However, in May 1603, recovering from her self-induced miscarriage and ready to assume her role as England's queen consort, she faced quite a different court situation. Although something akin to the electric and often deadly factionalism of Scotland might have been found in England after the death of Henry VIII, such strife was, by 1603, effectively disempowered as a political mode. Decades of monarchic consolidation by Queen Elizabeth, first with Lord Burleigh and then with his son Robert Cecil as principal secretaries, had of course shaped the situation that prevailed at the end of the century.[1] The earl of Essex, the last earl openly to defy an English monarch, had been beheaded in 1601 with no unmanageable political consequences for the stability of Elizabeth's crown. Even more important, the almost unanimous choice of a foreigner, James VI, as Elizabeth's successor emphasized the existence of a consensus among the English nobility, rather than the kind of rampant divisiveness that Anna seems to have exploited so effectively in Scotland. Now Cecil, who, with a core of veteran English peers, had effected James's accession to the English crown, joined with James's own small group of seasoned Scottish advisers to form a strong political circle around the new king. Further, James had allowed no Scottish noble not wholly loyal to him to join the transition to England.

Concurrently, Anna's own most obvious incentive for court intrigue seems to have been removed. If indeed the earl of Mar's custody of Henry had been the galvanizing focus of her political career in Scotland, Anna had now broken Mar's claim to her son. Henry was no longer at Stirling, and

Mar was no longer his guardian. Instead, the prince in England was finally accessible to Anna whenever she desired. Nevertheless, given the intensity of Anna's former engagement in court affairs, it is difficult to imagine her as wholly passive — or indolent, as literary history would have her — in her new circumstances. Assuming then that this energetic queen, when confronted with the foreclosure of her former role, would be likely to evolve a new formula for royal activity, it seems plausible that she would redefine herself in terms of the possibilities of her own court.

I shall be focusing here solely on the composition and style of Anna of Denmark's new court because the purpose of this study is not to discuss all aspects of Anna's sojourn in England. Rather, it is to demonstrate how her court — without any intervention by James I — became a crucial center for early Stuart high culture. I shall be arguing that patronage of the arts during the first decade of James's reign flourished first around Anna and then, by extension, within both royal courts. To say this, however, is not necessarily to claim that in systematically organizing a court for which there had been no model since the time of Henry VIII, Anna herself had any specifically "humanistic" agenda. Indeed, the efflorescence of patronage that Anna inspired — whatever her original purposes — was doubtless a by-product of the high quality of the appointments, female and male, that she made to a group in which, at the same time, there was a remarkable and suggestive homogeneity of cultural tastes.

It is important at this point, however, to clarify the term *court* as I shall be using it, because very often the physical sense of the term is confused or conflated with the abstraction. Thus one could do worse than adduce an appropriate paragraph from William Harrison's (1587) *Description of England* in which, after he has named a number of buildings, he observes: "The court of England, which necessarily is holden always where the prince lieth, is in these days one of the most renowned and magnificent courts that are to be found in Europe. For whether you regard the rich and infinite furniture of household, order of officers, or the entertainment of such strangers as daily resort unto the same, you shall not find many equal thereunto, much less one excelling it in any manner of wise."

That Harrison goes on for several paragraphs to extol the quality of the administrative nobility and the manner in which the household was run only emphasizes the distinction one needs to recall here because it clarifies what Queen Anna herself was about. There were many stately buildings that could be termed palaces, but in Queen Elizabeth's time there was only one "court": a metaphysical area, wherein only the actual, physical presence of the sovereign brought to life a locale. This place could consequently be termed "the court" solely because the sovereign was physically present. When the sovereign "removed" to another location, then the "court" moved with the monarch, and the vacated building became, politically, an empty shell. It is true that preferences of particular monarchs for certain buildings often suggested that a specific palace was, in fact, housing "the court," but this assumption was based on coincidence. As Harrison notes, Queen Elizabeth had a great liking for the palace at Windsor, spending substantial sums to renovate it. Associated as it was with the bestowal of the Order of the Garter, the palace also became a kind of center where the monarch "held court" on St. George's Day every year. It would thus have been easy, but technically incorrect, to say that the "court" was at Windsor — especially since Elizabeth spent a great deal of time at the palace at Greenwich.

In practice, the disposition of the palaces during the lifetime of Anna of Denmark in England seems to have been as follows. Whitehall Palace served as an appropriate residence for James (and his consort) over All Saints' and All Souls' Days when that palace's central location enabled the sovereign to be close to Westminster Abbey and the houses of Parliament. But because plague ruled London during the first ten months of James's reign, in that year he avoided the City entirely, and in the fall of 1603 both royal court and the legal courts were in the west at Winchester until the slacking off of disease allowed the royal family to spend their first Christmas near, but not in, London. They sojourned at Hampton Court, which was considered to be a goodly distance from the city — "in the country" as it were, with extensive and forested grounds good for deer hunting. But for James, even Hampton Court was presumably too close to the city. As I have observed elsewhere, James had a decided preference for open spaces, spending much of the year at elaborate rustic lodges in Royston and Newmarket in a routine which saw him arising at five in the morning to go hunting with his gentlemen of the Bed Chamber. Thus for much of the year "court" wandered with the king, even though such offices as that of Cecil's were apparently settled in one place. Hampton Court, then, rather than Whitehall, seems to have been the residence that James ordinarily preferred as his "London" location, a preference that had two consequences. The first was that most of the plays by Shakespeare and his fellow dramatists which adorned the Christmas season would take place at Hampton Court, as would the queen's masques. The second consequence, of specific relevance to the subject at hand, was that Queen Anna's physical residence remained at Hampton Court, since the king evidently regarded his many hunting sojourns, paradoxically, not as royal removals but as recreational sojourns in which royal business continued to be transacted.

The practical effect was that unless James went on a summer progress with his queen, visiting the palatial residences of nobles throughout a particular section of England, he and his close circle of advisers were simply "absent" from the company of Anna and indeed of most of his own administrative staff, which was most often to be found at Hampton Court. Thus it will be significant for our assessment of Anna's later activity that the palace at Greenwich, downriver from central London, would eventually become her abode as her court acquired a separate physical space — a local habitation and a name. Indeed, looking ahead to the year in which Somerset married Frances Howard (1613), Anna's expanded activities would prompt her to appropriate Somerset House, rename it Denmark House, renovate it extensively, and make this her own winter palace in central London, thereby effecting a physical separation from the ambience of James's monarchic court. If Denmark House became Anna's space, however, it was because Anna would choose to *reside* there — to convey her queenly presence to that locale. Thus, in studying Anna's "court," the buildings she inhabited are irrelevant; rather, I shall here note how the *persons* of her court found their places around her.

In tracing the origins of Anna's English court, it is reasonable to assume that the accession of a new (and foreign) monarch accompanied by a queen consort with no prior English ties must inevitably have activated a number of ambitious and talented noblewomen. They could hardly hope for royal office under the king, but here, for the first time in decades, was an opportunity for specifically female court activity. It is true that when Elizabeth I had reigned as both monarch and queen, some women nobles, such as Lady Cobham and the countess of Nottingham, had gained unofficial positions of influence if only because a female monarch obviously required female, not male, attendants in intimate quarters. Yet such influence operated outside the customary machinery of state, and for the most part the strictly regnal transactions of Queen Elizabeth involved virtually constant dealings with men.[2] Thus even if Elizabeth shared confidences with certain noblewomen of her Bed Chamber, the male officers of the realm such as the Lord Admiral, the Lord Chamberlain, and the Principal Secretary were also, necessarily, Elizabeth's intimates — perhaps even her best friends — because they, not her ladies, could effect Elizabeth's safety, well-being, and continuance on the throne. Now, with the arrival in England of a queen as consort, but not as monarch, opportunities for strictly female court access suddenly expanded, opening up a new royal sphere peculiar to noblewomen in general.

From remarks made by court figures of both sexes, and from accounts of the participation of noblewomen in Anna's progress south, it would appear that a queen consort was generally regarded as the (social) head of all female nobles in the land. That is, the marchioness of Winchester, all countesses, and all baronesses were, in a theoretical sense, part of Anna's own (women's) "court." This concept was expressed, for example, in the June plans of the Privy Council for a formal meeting of Queen Anna with all the ladies of England, already scheduled to take place at Windsor on 2 July.[3]

Not surprisingly, given the patriarchal power of male nobles over their spouses, the queen's "primacy" in such circumstances might well be regarded as merely symbolic. The earl of Hertford, for example, would later forbid the countess, his wife, the prestige of becoming one of Anna's two chief ladies (a matter taken up in more detail later), requiring her instead to remain at their home estate outside of London, where she spent almost the entirety of Anna's reign. But notwithstanding patriarchal constraints, the principle of a "queen's court" as embracing all of England's female nobility seems to have been in place, providing a social context within which, say, Anne Clifford could come up in 1617 by herself to the royal palace and live there within the demesnes of the queen, associating with ladies of her court, rather than staying alone in some elaborate set of apartments in London. Possibly, too, it was assumed that the queen's social role would give her a degree of moral authority to intercede on behalf of one noblewoman or another, as, for example, in the later case of Frances Howard Somerset, for whom Anna obtained an official pardon years sooner than her husband was able to gain one (see Chapter 5).

Such a notion of a new queen consort's "sphere" in itself was obviously too theoretical, however, to be of any use to the individual noblewoman with ambitions. Moreover, when it came to the control of the sinews of the queen's material power — money and land — it was male officials whom the Crown appointed to administer the resources that were part of the queen's marriage portion.[4] Thus Robert Cecil had a strong voice in the major disposition of Anna's larger assets in England. Yet no matter what males might be appointed by the Crown to serve Anna as Lord Treasurer, or Lord High Steward, a queen consort could, it seems, appoint a formal circle of women whose function was analogous to that exercised by the members of the king's Bed or Privy Chambers. What could be made of such appointments might well be a function of the personality of the new queen and her so-cial design because, for Anna, English precedents would have been as far removed as the time of Henry VIII.

Predictably, then, Anna's own style, early on, was to form her Bed and Privy Chambers herself rather than to allow them to be formed for her, as Cecil and other Privy Council members seem first to have attempted. In-deed, Anna's court was partially and accidentally configured by the circum-stances of a royal funeral. After he was proclaimed king, James desired to travel to England as soon as possible but at the same time to avoid being in London for the burial of Queen Elizabeth, who was not to be interred until 28 April.[5] He therefore began a progress from Scotland twelve days after Elizabeth's death, and situated himself outside of London so that he could enter the city in early May. Anna, however, could not go south at the same time as James because as soon as she crossed into England she would require an entourage of appropriate English noblewomen to accom-pany her to London. But all noblewomen with significant connections were expected to stay in London to attend Queen Elizabeth's remains until the funeral. Anna was therefore required to wait in Scotland until such time as the appropriate English entourage arrived in the border town of Berwick-on-Tweed.[6]

Thus on 15 April 1603, James, now in Yorkshire and having met per-sonally with Cecil and with Henry Lord Howard (the future Northampton), wrote the Privy Council in London to send "some of the ladies of all de-grees who were about the [old] Queen, as soon as the funerals be past,— or some others whom you shall think meetest and most willing and able to abide travel." Robert Cecil, now back in London and apparently directing affairs there for James, complied; this resulted, as one contemporary put it, in the Privy Council's choice of "two countesses, two baronesses, two ladies, and two maids of honor" to ride north to meet the new queen "with an escort of two hundred horse."[7] Significantly, this chosen group that Cecil and the Privy Council were apparently planning to insinuate as the basis of Anna's new English court were all closely allied to the English nobles who surrounded James — a situation that might not, judging from previous events, have been overly congenial to the new queen.[8]

One of the highest ranking noblewomen, for example, was the wife of Edward Somerset, fourth earl of Worcester, who had become Queen Eliza-beth's master of the horse after Essex lost that position.[9] The countess, born Elizabeth Hastings, had long attended the queen.[10] Similarly close to the ruling circle was Frances Howard, countess of Kildare, related to equally powerful men. Her father, Charles Howard, earl of Nottingham, the only baron created earl by Queen Elizabeth in the last ten years of her reign, was now Lord Admiral and had been when the Spanish Armada was defeated in 1588. After her first husband, Henry Fitzgerald, [Irish] earl of Kildare, died in 1597, Frances had married Henry Brooke, eleventh Lord Cobham, who held the crucial position of warden of the Cinque Portes.[11] Lady Kildare had been one of Queen Elizabeth's ladies, too, close enough to the monarch to have reputedly attempted to prejudice her against the wife of Sir Walter Ralegh.[12]

If these two countesses whom the Privy Council intended for Anna were prominent in the old group around Elizabeth, so was one of the baronesses. Lady (Philadelphia Carey) Scrope was another seasoned courtier, married to a nobleman active in border affairs as the keeper of Carlisle.[13] She was, in fact, the countess of Kildare's aunt, sister of Catherine Howard, the earl of Nottingham's deceased wife, and also sister of the outgoing and ailing Lord Chamberlain, George Carey, second Baron Hunsdon. She had attended Queen Elizabeth since 1588 and was present when she died.[14]

The ideological unity of the group extended no further, however, since the other baroness chosen by the Privy Council was probably sent at James's command. This was one of the earl of Essex's sisters, who for many years, and especially since her participation in the 1601 uprising, had been anathema to Elizabeth's court. Long estranged from her husband, Robert, third Baron Rich, Penelope Rich had been living out of wedlock with Charles Blount, Lord Mountjoy, future earl of Devonshire, by whom she had borne several children. But her way of life was probably less objectionable to Elizabeth than her politics, for Rich had written, and perhaps caused to be printed, an aggressive letter to Elizabeth defending her brother Essex.[15] Further, she had been in Essex House in London at the time of the uprising and had actually been named with five earls as one of its conspirators, and thus she was confined to the house of one of the gentlemen of the queen's Privy Chamber.[16] She was, I think, included in the present (conservative) group because of James's interest in making a public point of hailing Essex as "his martyr" and of honoring members of his family.[17]

But the inclusion of Penelope Rich in this conservative group of women powerfully allied to the men of James's circle proved to be a serendipitous indication that Cecil and the Privy Council were not to master events in the question of Anna's entourage. They may have been aware of the new queen's independent nature — of what had happened, for instance, with Chancellor Maitland — but they probably were not able to calculate how

Anna would respond to specific persons. Whatever the Council's intentions, in any event, a rival group of women, good friends of Penelope Rich, seem to have outflanked the Council and Robert Cecil in an independent bid to gain the new queen's favor. As Howes, in his continuation of the Stow *Annals*, respectfully put it long after the queen's new court was a fait accompli: "Before the departure of these personages aforesaid [the official group], diverse ladies of honor went voluntarily into Scotland, to attend her Majesty in her journey into England." This early group was led by Lucy Russell, countess of Bedford.[18] And because this particular noblewoman was destined, in this quick move, to "capture" the new queen, it is important to recall Lady Bedford's own far-reaching connections with the political faction that had surrounded the earl of Essex. Though kept well outside the circle of political power after Essex's execution, members of this social faction and their spouses ranked among the most significant patrons of literature, drama, painting, and music in England, and are thereby central to the artistic history of the early Stuart era.[19]

The countess of Bedford herself, of course, had been involved in the politics of the Essex uprising because she was married to that earl of Bedford who, with the earl of Rutland and the earl of Southampton, had ridden with Essex when he made his bid for power in London. Not surprisingly, therefore, Lucy Bedford was close to both sisters of Essex, that is, to Penelope Rich and Dorothy, countess of Northumberland, who indeed had named one of her daughters Lucy.[20] But Bedford had a range of connections with nobles well known today for their patronage of the arts and for their literary achievement. Her father, Sir John Harington of Exton, was first cousin to Mary, countess of Pembroke, and to her brother, Sir Robert Sidney, aunt and uncle of the young earl of Pembroke and his brother, the future earl of Montgomery. Lucy Bedford was friendly, too, with Barbara Gamage Sidney, wife of Sir Robert Sidney. The late earl of Essex himself had become related to this group when he married Sir Philip Sidney's widow, Frances Walsingham. Later, Sidney's daughter Elizabeth married Roger Manners, earl of Rutland, a lifelong friend of Essex.

In order to follow the countess of Bedford's first association with Anna and to recall the circle of persons she was, by implication, introducing to the new queen consort, it is important to note the long-standing social cohesion of this group (which I shall continue to term "the Essex circle") as manifested during Queen Elizabeth's lifetime. A letter in 1598 conveying news to Sir Robert Sidney in the Low Countries described, for example, a supper at Essex House on 14 February. There the company included "my

Ladies Leicester, Northumberland, Bedford, Essex, Rich: and my Lords of Essex, Rutland, Mountjoy, and others. They had two plays which kept them up till 1 o'clock after midnight." [21] And four years later, during the Christmas holidays of 1602–3, just prior to the accession of James, the countess of Bedford's father, Sir John Harington, again had guests for the holidays: "Sir John Harington means to keep a royal Christmas in Rutlandshire having the Earls of Rutland and Bedford, Sir John Gray and Sir Henry Carey with their ladies, the Earl of Pembroke, Sir Robert Sidney and many more gallants." [22]

This latter celebration indicates not only the intimacy of a group of significant patrons of the arts with the countess of Bedford (herself central to such activity) but also foreshadows the persistence of a faction that would remain coherent even beyond the death of Cecil in 1612. That is, Sir Robert Sidney with his niece, the countess of Rutland, and his nephew, the young earl of Pembroke, were here in Rutlandshire enjoying the hospitality of the father of that countess who would become Queen Anna's most influential lady.[23]

Clearly then the presence of Bedford in the unauthorized party traveling north to meet Anna made the group quite different from — and in many ways more significant than — those politically ensconced women chosen by the Privy Council to serve as escort to the new queen. This explains the great importance of Anna's response to these two delegations of ladies. It is possible that Anna had met Bedford before this occasion. On 16 August 1600, Sir John Carey, deputy governor of Berwick-on-Tweed, had written Robert Cecil discussing the Gowrie Plot, observing in passing that "we look presently for the Earl of Bedford and his countess, my lady Harington, and divers other ladies and gentlewomen to be here with a great train." [24] Whether the strong mutual attraction between Anna and Lucy Bedford had begun during this mysterious trip to the Scottish border — and into Scotland? — in 1600, or whether, as was more traditionally understood, the association began during this trip in 1603, Bedford seems quickly to have established a relationship with the queen, one that would last, despite Bedford's later alienation, until Anna's death in 1619.

It was noted on 31 May 1603 (three days after she had finally left Stirling with the prince) that Queen Anna had attended church in Edinburgh "accompanied with many English ladies." [25] It is important to recognize that this group could not have included the ladies chosen by the English Privy Council because on 30 May these politically acceptable ladies were still in Berwick-on-Tweed. Further, Sir Thomas Edmonds, writing the earl of Shrewsbury less than a month later, Anna now being in England, made a significant observation. He noted that the queen "hath hitherto refused to admit my Lady of Kildare, and the Lady Walsingham, to be of her Privy Chamber, and hath only as yet sworn my Lady of Bedford to that place."[26] Thus the twenty-eight-year-old Bedford must have been immediately attractive to the twenty-nine-year-old queen. Additional evidence of this attraction can be found in the account of the fourteen-year-old Lady Anne Clifford, who to some extent was echoing the sentiments of her mother, the countess of Cumberland, and of her aunt, the countess of Warwick, when she observed on 15 June that "my Lady of Bedford" was "so grand a woman with the Queen" that everybody much respected her—"she having attended the Queen from out of Scotland."[27] And on 25 June, when the queen's progress reached Althorp, the countess of Bedford was still in place as the only English lady yet appointed to the closest position around Anna: lady of the Bed Chamber. Nor was Anna's response to Bedford uncharacteristic, for it is reminiscent of a similar situation shortly after Anna's arrival in another strange country, Scotland, when she was drawn to Esmé Stuart's sister, the countess of Huntly, a young French woman with a sophisticated court upbringing akin to Anna's own in Denmark (see Chapter 2).

Exhibiting at once the independence that was her trademark in Scotland, Anna not only fastened upon an "unauthorized" noblewoman of presumably congenial character but, predictably enough, appears to have ignored—with two exceptions—all of the official escort sent by the Privy Council of England. The most significant of the two exceptions was Penelope Rich, Anne Clifford remarking in late June that the queen showed favor only "to Lady Rich and such like company."[28] In July, Dudley Carleton would reaffirm this, observing that "the ladies Bedford, Rich, and Essex" were especially in the queen's favor.[29] Thus Anna seems already to have been engrossed by women who had never been closely allied to Queen Elizabeth; on the contrary, they were the sister and widow of the earl of Essex, whom Elizabeth had beheaded, and the wife of one of the conspirator earls, Bedford.

But the influence of one of the women chosen by the Privy Council seems nonetheless to have at least partially asserted itself, suggesting how the complexity of court politics can confound single-stranded narratives. Although not selected by Anna for her Privy Chamber, the countess of Kildare quickly attained a position to which Anna would have been highly sensitive—the guardianship of one of her children. As Dudley Carleton wrote Sir Thomas Percy (the earl of Northumberland's younger brother) about

Anna, "Her court is very great of ladies and gentlewomen, but I hear of none she hath admitted to her Privy Chamber or in place near about her, save the Lady Bedford, who was sworn of the Privy [*sic*] Chamber in Scotland, and Lady Kildare, to whom she hath given the government of the Princess."[30] Thus, although Kildare had obviously failed to achieve immediate intimacy with Queen Anna, she was nonetheless the daughter of the earl of Nottingham, the Lord Admiral, as well as the wife of Baron Cobham, still warden of the Cinque Portes. Aggressive early on in her pursuit of Anna,[31] she was awarded the prestigious trust of guardian to Princess Elizabeth, although whether at Anna's or James's instigation it is hard to say. Certainly Kildare's husband, as overseer of England's primary defense against seaborne invasion through Dover, would have been deemed ultimately reliable.

Still, Queen Anna's full acquiescence in this particular appointment would have been surprising, given her personal history in the matter of Henry's governance. Indeed, Lady Anne Clifford's diary suggests a significant modification of this plan when, at some point before July, she added another name in connection with the guardianship. Clifford observed that *both* "my Lady Kildare and the Lady Harington" were the princess's "governesses." Thus Kildare was now sharing the honor with none other than the countess of Bedford's mother.[32] In the end, of course, this proved a timely maneuver, if such it was, because very soon thereafter occurred the "Bye Plot," involving Cobham, Kildare's husband (along with Ralegh and Lord Grey). Cobham was sent to the Tower in August, and in the aftermath Kildare could hardly have been allowed near the person of the princess—a matter on which James would no doubt himself have been adamant. Now, because Anna presumably had once again resisted pressure from the king's side, she was able to capitalize on a fortuitous event. The mother of the countess of Bedford, Lady Harington, together with her husband, Sir John Harington, in fact became the sole guardians of Princess Elizabeth, who grew up under their tutelage.

Having placed her daughter in the household not of a nobleman but of a wealthy (at that time) member of the gentry whose daughter was a countess and chief lady at Anna's own court, she seems to have taken her time assembling the rest of the noblewomen with whom she wanted to be associated. Anne Clifford, who again must have been echoing the sentiments of her mother and aunt, wrote: "The Queen and Prince came to Althorp the 25th of June, . . . my mother, aunt Warwick, and I not till the next day [Sunday]. There we saw the Queen's favor to Lady Hatton and Lady Cecil, for she showed no favor to the elderly ladies, but to Lady Rich and such like company."[33]

What seems clear is that in June the new queen was inclining to ladies from among the former political allies of the earl of Essex and the family of the Sidneys. And because James, for his own political purposes, was honoring and reinstating nobles of the Essex group and the Essex family at just the time that Anna was assembling their spouses and friends to form the nucleus of her court, the queen's behavior toward the old Essex faction can hardly be regarded as politically subversive of her husband's position. Rather, Anna seems at this early point to have been bringing together in her new court a preponderance of women and men from the old Essex group notably associated with high cultural activity. And although, as indicated below, the queen would not choose all her ladies from this group, her later selections of women during the summer suggest that the queen favored women we already recognize as patrons of the arts. Thus we witness a gathering in this new court of noblewomen who, together with the circles that they frequented, may have constituted the closest approximation to an artistic salon possible under the circumstances of the early Stuart court. To view the matter from another standpoint: whether or not there was a conscious group patronage of the arts centered in the queen's court, that is to say, a collective effort, nonetheless individual artists such as John Donne, Samuel Daniel, Ben Jonson, John Florio, George Chapman, and perhaps even William Shakespeare could only have benefited from the highly integrated character of the group whose constituency was already apparent, as we have seen, in the 1602 Christmas gathering at Burleigh-on-the-Hill. Thus the chances were very good that for an artist to be favored by any one figure in Anna's court was a means of access to additional patrons—to the circle itself.

At this juncture, however, it is reasonable to consider whether Anna was indeed her own agent—whether the constitution of her court, given the patriarchal character of the times, reflected Anna's decisions or those of James, despite the king's obvious acquiescence in her ignoring of the ladies designated by the Privy Council. The only case that seems to bear directly on this question, aside from that of Lady Kildare, does, in fact, support the idea of the queen's free agency, for one noblewoman's connections on the king's side do not seem to have greatly influenced the queen. Elizabeth Hatton, one of Robert Cecil's nieces, had actually ridden with the Bedford preemptive party that traveled early to Scotland. Anna had shown her some favor, and Hatton obviously wished not only to become one of Anna's ladies in these early days but to be the keeper of her jewels. Accordingly, she attempted to use influence from the king's side, writing a letter at some point in 1603 to Sir John Stanhope, who assisted her uncle Robert Cecil in his affairs. Stanhope informed Cecil:

I received a letter very lately from my Lady Hatton, wherein she earnestly moved me to interest your lordship to procure for her the King's letter to the Queen, that if her Majesty like of the Lady Hatton's service, he then consent that she have the place with the Queen to keep her jewels and help to make her ready, [Lady Hatton] greatly commending her Majesty's wifely obedience not to do anything without the king's allowance, with further assurance of the Queen's great good opinion of your lordship and her [Anne's] resolute mind to establish you in all Honour and powerfulness. The matter I leave to your wisdom and private resolution. I am pressed to have return of answer with all possible expedition.[34]

But it is significant that despite her status, and despite this letter, Hatton was not to be in the list of those in the two inner circles later compiled by the earl of Worcester. Further, she would not be among the noblewomen appearing in Anna's early masques in which she included her favored ladies. Hatton was absent from the first masque for the Christmas season of 1603–4 and in the Christmas of 1604–5, when Jonson's *Masque of Blackness* was danced, John Packer wrote to Winwood that "the Lady Hatton would fain have had a part, but some unknown reason kept her out."[35]

Further to the point of Anna's free agency, if James himself had claimed the last word in these matters, it is difficult to imagine his denying the wealthy widow of Sir Christopher Hatton and the niece of his first secretary something so insignificant (to his mind) as a place in the entourage of his queen. Thus it seems questionable that Anna's uncharacteristically submissive attitude as conveyed by Lady Hatton in her letter was the true one. Rather, a strong indication to the contrary in this matter of appointing her ladies may be gathered from a later decade, after Anna's death. In 1626 we witness an argument between Anna's younger son, Charles (now king of England), and his consort, Henrietta Maria. At this early point in his new reign, Charles presented his own queen consort with the names of four English noblewomen whom he wished her to receive as ladies of her (exclusive) Bed Chamber. Henrietta Maria responded with reluctance and several days later sent Charles a note with a list of "some whom she desired should have appointments about her." According to Andrea Rosso, the Venetian ambassador to England, Charles, however, seems to have thrown the list aside without reading it, indicating that "he meant to be master and dispose of her officers as he pleased." Several days later, writing in code, Rosso indicated that this matter was not resolved and that differences were becoming more bitter: "It seems that the Queen herself spoke to the King and told him that she desired no more for the regulation of her household than his mother, Queen Anne, had enjoyed. The King replied that his mother was a different sort of woman from her" (*SPV*, 19:494–97). Because Henrietta Maria, in the end, was forced to accept Charles's choice of ladies, the king's recollection of his mother seems to suggest that she herself (whether rightly or wrongly in Charles's view) would not have countenanced such control.

Assuming Anna's own agency in most of these matters, we nevertheless do not find the names of specific persons appointed to Anna's court (beyond those of the countess of Bedford and Penelope Rich)[36] surfacing until 2 February 1604 when the earl of Worcester described the queen's four court groups. He wrote of ladies belonging to the Bed Chamber, the Drawing Chamber, the Private Chamber, and "Maids of Honor" as if in descending degrees of status.[37] Here is Worcester's list of names, in his order.

Bed Chamber:	The countess of Bedford
	The countess of Hertford
Drawing Chamber:	The countess of Derby
	The countess of Suffolk
	Penelope Lady Rich
	The countess of Nottingham
	Susan de Vere
	[Audrey] Lady Walsingham
	[Elizabeth] Lady Southwell
Private Chamber:	"All the rest."
Maids of Honour:	Cary
	Middlemore
	Woodhouse[38]
	Gargrave
	Roper

Most potentially interesting in this list, especially as regards her cultural relevance, is the countess who narrowly missed being elevated as Bedford's counterpart to serve as the only other English lady of the Bed Chamber, a noblewoman whose tastes were evidently as congenial to the queen as those of Lady Bedford. This was the countess of Hertford. In 1603 Frances (née Howard) was twenty-five. The queen "wore her picture" before 1603, and the following September both king and queen visited Hertford's mansion in Savernake Forest.[39] At court long enough to dance in *The Masque of the Twelve Goddesses* of Christmas 1603–4, Lady Hertford was missing from the list of dancers in *The Masque of Blackness* of the subsequent year only because she came down with measles and could not participate.[40] But then, as the earl of Worcester remarked when he sent his 1604 list of ladies to the earl of Salisbury (in the February after *Blackness*), "My Lady of Bedford holdeth fast to the Bed Chamber, my Lady of Hertford would fain, but her husband hath called her home."[41] There, despite her unhappiness at being away from the city, Hertford stayed through Anna's 1619 demise until her own husband's death in 1621 when she returned to court and also married the duke of Lennox.[42]

If James had any influence in Anna's Bed Chamber appointments, there was good reason for him to wish to honor the house of the earl of Hertford. When Queen Elizabeth died childless, the earl of Hertford's son by Lady Catherine Grey became politically significant.[43] He had a conceivable claim to the throne before James VI of Scotland's title to the English crown was finally manufactured by statute,[44] and he was indeed proclaimed heir to the throne in Catholic-oriented Northampton, an event attributed to the machinations of the French. But less than a month after James's accession (2 April), the younger Hertford (styled Lord Beauchamp) yielded to the demands of his father, the earl, that he desist.[45]

The second countess of Hertford having died in 1598, the sixty-two-year-old earl again married.[46] In 1601 he took as his third wife Frances Howard.[47] Although her exalted appointment to the new queen's Bed Chamber might have served as acknowledgment of the earl's loyalty to the new king, we cannot omit the crucial factor of Anna's own inclination here, especially since the earl of Hertford, in effect, would remove his wife from Anna's service—something he might not have done if the appointment had been seen as James's reward to him. Thus, I think that Anna must have preferred her, particularly in view of the fact that after the countess was called home by her husband, Anna (characteristically) never appointed a new lady of the Bed Chamber to take her place.[48] Perhaps then, as with the other ladies around Anna, Hertford's relative youth (twenty-five) as well as her intellectual inclinations were factors that influenced the queen. The countess interested herself in cultural patronage, most notably as patron to Samuel Daniel, an important relationship that has been the subject of recent study.[49]

The women of Anna's second tier, while not of the exalted Bed Chamber that Bedford would continue to occupy alone for the remainder of
Anna's life, was still an important and definable inner circle of women who,
like Bedford, were active patrons of the arts. Among these ladies of the
Drawing Chamber, Penelope Rich — although she too might have been appointed owing to James's policy of favoring Essex's family — seems, nevertheless, to have been congenial to Anna from the outset.[50] At least ten years
older than Anna and most of her other ladies, Rich was considered one of
the "younger ladies" by Anne Clifford, we recall, but, more important, she
appears to have had a decided intellectual orientation. When Bartholomew
Young, for example, translated the *Diana* of George Montemayor in 1598,
he dedicated the translation to her, writing of "that singular desire, knowledge, and delight wherewith your ladyship embraceth and affecteth honest endeavors, learned languages" (*STC* 18044), and noting that, when he
had once given an oration in French, she being there, he had especially
feared her censure because "of your ladyship's perfect knowledge of the
same." "Now once again," he continued, "in this translation out of Spanish
(which language also with the present matter being so well known to your
ladyship)," he was again submitting himself to her censure. For comparable
reasons, Penelope Rich was also one of the nobles to whom John Florio
dedicated his translation of Montaigne's essays. She seems to have been important to a variety of artists — painters and composers as well as writers
such as Henry Constable. Aside from her reputed place in Sir Philip Sidney's
Astrophel and Stella, she was praised by the composers John Dowland and
William Byrd. Indeed, the painter Nicholas Hilliard named his daughter
after her.[51]

Two other women in this circle were sisters: Elizabeth and Susan de
Vere, daughters of Edward de Vere, earl of Oxford. Yet Elizabeth's presence in Anna's circle has not always been acknowledged because of a persistent scholarly confusion. The list for Anna's Drawing Chamber designates
the countess of Derby as one of the ladies. Always present in the queen's
masques, she has often been identified as Alice Spencer Stanley, (dowager) countess of Derby, married by 1603 to Sir Thomas Egerton, Lord Privy
Seal — but this identification is erroneous.[52] It derives in large part from a
1608 comment by a young Italian, Antimo Galli, who said he saw the countess of Derby dancing in Anna's *Masque of Beauty*. Galli identified this countess as "Alicia Darbi," which suggests that the famous dowager countess was
indeed a member of Queen Anna's court.[53] Further, what seems to have
been the natural vivacity of the dowager countess, together with her former

court activities, artistic interests, wide patronage, and possible role as hostess to the new queen at Althorp, might argue eloquently for her presence among Anna's ladies.[54] Indeed, such a conjunction might have joined the microcosm of the literary figures Alice had patronized—John Donne and Ben Jonson immediately coming to mind—with Queen Anna's new court. But because there was a *second* countess of Derby, and because our best understanding of the nature of Anna's entourage is dependent on the identities of her ladies, the two noblewomen must briefly be distinguished from each other.

Alice (dowager) countess of Derby had married Ferdinando Stanley, fifth earl of Derby. After Ferdinando's death without an heir in 1594, his brother, William Stanley, had become sixth earl. William then married Elizabeth de Vere, and she (as opposed to Alice) then became the countess of Derby. Alice retained the right to continue to be known as the (dowager) countess of Derby by virtue of her dead husband's title. It is Elizabeth, countess of Derby, further, who is specifically identified in Worcester's letter describing Queen Anna's newly appointed ladies, for he refers to "my Lady Derby, the younger," distinguishing her, of course, from the dowager countess. Indeed, Elizabeth appears in Anne Clifford's account of events in June 1603, at the time when Anna presumably first met the young countess at Dingley's, where Clifford also saw the queen and Henry for the first time: "Hither also came my Lady of Suffolk, my young Lady Derby and Lady Walsingham, which three ladies were the great favorites of Sir Robert Cecil."[55]

It is certainly no mystery that the younger Derby would have been a great favorite of Cecil, being one of the daughters of Edward de Vere, seventeenth earl of Oxford, and his wife, the former Anne Cecil, sister of Robert Cecil.[56] After her mother died in 1588, Elizabeth came to court at age thirteen to live with her grandparents, Lord and Lady Burghley. Lady Burghley died a year later, and the queen made Elizabeth, whose grandfather was her First Secretary, a Maid of Honor.[57] The young woman remained at court until her marriage at twenty in 1595, and thus from an early age Elizabeth de Vere must have had a rather extensive experience with the political workings of a royal palace, experience which might well have been useful to Anna and her circle during the early days of the accession.

The countess of Derby's own cultural associations, like those of the dowager countess, were various: she was also related to men who were strongly drawn to public drama. Her father, the earl of Oxford, had since

1580 been patron of an acting company that included John Lyly among its playwrights. In fact, in 1602, we recall, this company had merged with the Earl of Worcester's Servants, allowed by Queen Elizabeth at Oxford's own urging, to become one of three companies (Chamberlain's and Lord Admiral's were the others) that were permitted to act in London. Playing at the Boar's Head a year after the accession, they would interestingly enough, become known as the Servants of Queen Anna.[58] Perhaps by coincidence, Elizabeth's husband, William, earl of Derby, was also oriented to public drama. He sponsored a playing company, and there is a record of his wife's intercession for him in this respect.[59] Described in 1599 as "busy penning comedies for the common players," the earl had urged his wife in 1601 to write her uncle Robert Cecil for help in avoiding a ban on playing directed against his acting company, the Earl of Derby's Servants.[60] Elizabeth's own attitude toward the theater is nonetheless ambiguous. Her letter to her uncle concludes: "I could desire that your furtherance might be a mean to uphold them [the players], for that my lord, taking delight in them, will keep him from more prodigal courses."

At the accession Elizabeth was twenty-eight and thus in the general age group of the ladies that the twenty-nine-year-old Queen Anna seems to have favored most strongly—the countess of Bedford and the countess of Hertford, we recall, were both in their twenties. If Elizabeth herself was ambitious for a continuation of the court life in which she had been raised, her position as niece of Robert Cecil would obviously have been a great advantage, and she seems to have been an energetic and capable person. She was a member of Anna's court until the queen's death, dancing in all of her masques. At the time of Anna's funeral in 1619, Derby was designated chief mourner.[61]

Elizabeth's younger sister, Susan de Vere, also became one of Anna's ladies, perhaps at Elizabeth's intervention. Turned sixteen in May 1603, Susan apparently became a great favorite of the queen, in fact, and through her marriage the social ties of the Essex group to the court were strengthened even further. A year and a half after the accession, Susan married the earl of Pembroke's younger brother, Philip, then a Gentleman of James's Bed Chamber (and soon to be created earl of Montgomery), and along with his brother, a great favorite of King James, their uncle, Robert Sidney, also being Lord Chamberlain of the queen's household. The marriage of Susan and Philip, indeed, was referred to as a wedding of two favorites and was the court event of Christmas 1604.[62] Thus, through most of Anna's reign, Susan would be allied to the Herbert circle — to her mother-in-law, the countess of Pembroke, to her brother-in-law, the earl of Pembroke, master of the great house of Wilton.

As the countess of Montgomery, Susan was, like the other ladies of Anna's circle, quite active as a patron of the arts. George Chapman, for example, inserted a dedicatory leaf to her in the 1609 edition of his translation of the *Iliad*, and she was the subject of Ben Jonson's *Epigram* 104. Later, she also served as patron to Donne: in 1619 he preached a sermon at the Cockpit, a group of apartments adjacent to Whitehall occupied by the earl and countess of Montgomery, and the countess asked him for a copy, which Donne sent her.[63] Later she would be the dedicatee of Lady Mary Wroth's *Urania*, written by the daughter of Robert Sidney, who was the uncle of Susan's husband. The countess of Montgomery seems, in fact, to have had an extensive interest in the early forms of the novel we call "romances."[64] In 1619, for example, when Anthony Munday, who had been translating *Amadis de Gaul* through several editions since the 1590s, dedicated his work to the earl of Montgomery, he noted the *countess's* activity. Speaking of how he finished his work at "the urgent importunities of that worthy lady by whom I have thus boldly presumed," he also mentioned that the labor of gathering various editions of the *Amadis* was lightened by the countess, for "by the help of that worthy lady I have had such books as were of the best editions."[65]

But I think Lucy Bedford's cultural activity and her intimacy with Anna are of the greatest importance to our understanding of the new queen's court. Although many of Bedford's acts of patronage are well known,[66] the full scope of her activities has nonetheless been slighted. Her relationship to the arts is succinctly and forcefully indicated by a letter she would write to her good friend Lady Jane Cornwallis in November 1624 (about five years after Queen Anna's death). Lady Jane's father-in-law, Sir Nicholas Bacon, was a collector of paintings, at this time on the point of death, and the countess of Bedford wrote her friend because she had learned that Sir Nicholas "had some pieces of painting of Holbein's which I am sure, as soon as [the earl of] Arundel hears, he will try all means to get." If the paintings were indeed to be sold, Bedford implored her to use her influence with her husband to save them (Bedford called them "pieces") for her. "For I am a very diligent gatherer of all I can get of Holbein's or any other excellent master's hand; I do not care at what rate I have them for price." She also asked Lady Jane to commission her husband, whose judgment Bedford apparently admired, to procure her any other paintings "if he know any such thereabouts" and "upon any conditions." Some of the paintings that she herself owned, Bedford continued, "I found in obscure places, and gentlemen's houses, that, because they were old, made no reckoning of them; and that makes me think it likely that there may yet be in divers places many excellent unknown pieces for which I lay wait with all my friends." "Dear Madam," she concluded, "Let me hear by this bearer whether I have not been misinformed concerning these pictures, and if I have not, make them sure either for me or nobody. And be not curious to think I may pay too much, for I had rather have them than jewels." [67]

Bedford's interests, of course, were not confined to painting. In 1600, the composer John Dowland, in Denmark, had dedicated his *Second Book of Airs* to her. Her influence on letters, however, was more extensive. The poet Michael Drayton had begun dedicating work to Lucy when she was thirteen,[68] and in the years before Queen Elizabeth's death, Bedford was active enough to occasion George Chapman to write a sonnet to her in the preface to the earliest (1598) edition of his translation of the *Iliad*, while Ben Jonson, in 1601, presented Bedford a printed copy of *Cynthia's Revels* in which was inserted a leaf containing a set of verses to her. Jonson also mentioned the countess in an ode which was his contribution to "The Phoenix and the Turtle." [69] Further, toward the end of Elizabeth's reign, John Florio (who had dedicated his first publication, an Italian dictionary, to Bedford after she was married) finished his famous translation of the *Essais* of Montaigne as a resident in her house, observing that the countess had introduced him to the scholarly Theodore Diodati and Matthew Gwynne, his collaborators in the project. Yet another well known translator, Philemon Holland, dedicated his 1606 translation of Suetonius's *History of the Twelve Caesars* to Bedford. Moreover, beginning late in the Elizabethan period and continuing after the accession of James, Lady Bedford was also patron to Samuel Daniel and John Donne — indeed, she stood as godmother to Donne's second daughter — and, significantly, Florio and Daniel would both become gentlemen of Queen Anna's Privy Chamber.

Most suggestively, in light of her relationship to Queen Anna, the countess of Bedford also intersects with Shakespeare in various ways. A member of the same social circle as the earl of Southampton, Shakespeare's patron of the early 1590s (if the long poems are any indication), Bedford can be connected to matters Shakespearean, if not to Shakespeare directly, through the activities of Christmas 1595 at Burleigh-on-the-Hill, the opulent residence of her father, Sir John Harington. According to Jacques Petit, tutor to the countess of Bedford's younger brother, John Harington, and servant to Anthony Bacon (secretary to the earl of Essex and a good friend of Penelope Rich), there was a holiday entertainment there of two hundred guests.[70] Writing to Anthony Bacon, Petit observed that this holiday featured the presence of the countess of Bedford, who showed great liberality. And on New Year's, Petit reported, professional actors, possibly the Lord Chamberlain's Servants, Shakespeare's group, performed the tragedy of *Titus Andronicus*.[71]

In fact, the relationship of Queen Anna's circle to the biography of Shakespeare is an intriguing subject that cannot be fully explored here, although one or two further instances may be revelatory. The earl of Southampton, well known as the dedicatee of Shakespeare's early poems, and the earl of Rutland were both members of the Essex circle and close to Bedford's husband. Thus, in addition to the performance of *Titus* at the great house of Bedford's father, we may also note that at Christmas in 1604–5 Southampton entertained Queen Anna at his house in London, using Shakespeare's company, the King's Servants, for the occasion, on which they were scheduled to present *Love's Labor's Lost*.[72] Later, in 1613, it was for this earl of Rutland's brother and heir that Richard Burbage and William Shakespeare together would execute an Accession Day Tilt *impresa*.[73]

The complex topic of Shakespeare aside, the activity of Southampton suggests that the male nobles and their wives with whom the ladies of Anna's Bed Chamber and Drawing Chamber associated were also influential artistic patrons. Both the older earl of Rutland, Essex's companion, and the earl of Southampton had supported John Florio in his translation of the *Essais* of Montaigne, but apparently Rutland's wife, Sir Philip Sidney's daughter Elizabeth, was also generous in these areas.[74] Ben Jonson's *Forest* XII is a hundred-line epistle to her, suggesting Jonson's appreciation of her patronage: "With you, I know, my offering will find grace."[75] Another male member of the Essex social circle, Charles Blount Lord Mountjoy, was also inclined toward high culture. Well known as a patron of Samuel Daniel, Devonshire was, according to Sir Robert Naunton, "much addicted" to reading and "a good piece of a scholar."[76] One of his retainers, Fynes Morison, observed that he "could read and understand the Italian and French, though he durst not adventure to speak them" and that his "chief delight was the study of divinity, and more especially in reading of the Fathers and the Schoolmen." For "recreation," however, Morison observes, Devonshire delighted in "reading play-books." Thus, it is highly significant that when we consider Devonshire's reading preferences in conjunction with the activities of Southampton, Rutland, Bedford, and the family of the countess of Derby, there were at least five peers in this group around Queen Anna with specific and documented interest not only in the arts in general but specifically in public plays.

Further, a sixth such peer in the group who seems to have a special relevance to the public drama of the time was William Herbert, earl of Pembroke. Nephew of Queen Anna's new Lord Chamberlain and of Sir Philip Sidney, and brother of Philip Herbert, the future earl of Montgomery, who would soon marry Susan de Vere, Pembroke was clearly involved in a wide range of cultural activities.[77] For example, he helped Inigo Jones travel and study in Italy, gave Ben Jonson £20 a year for books, befriended the great actor Richard Burbage, and was a dedicatee of the Shakespeare First Folio of 1623, in which he and his brother, then earl of Montgomery, were described by Heminges and Condell as having shown much "favor" both to Shakespeare and his plays.[78] To quote Margaret Hannay, to Pembroke

were dedicated over 100 literary works, more than to any other peer of his time, including the First Folio of Shakespeare and the works of Ben Jonson. His own poetry was praised by such writers as William Browne, Ben Jonson, and John Donne and was set to music by Nicholas Lanier and Henry Lawes. To him were dedicated also important translations, such as George Chapman's *Homer* and the works of Joshua Sylvester. Like Robert Sidney, Pembroke helped Thomas Bodley establish his library; he paid for 251 Greek manuscripts for the Bodleian Library.[79]

This good friend of the countess of Bedford, and probable lover of his accomplished niece, Lady Mary Wroth, was thus preeminently important as a cultural figure. Further, his involvement with the persons in Anna's entourage is not only unquestionable but indicative of the ambience of arts patronage (including public drama) that seems to have surrounded this group.

Queen Anna's own specific relationships with these nobles are, of course, difficult to ascertain, but her inclination to the arts strongly suggests a commonality of interests, especially if we recall the attitudes she shared with the countess of Bedford. Like the countess, Anna favored John Florio, from whom she learned to speak Italian with great fluency, appointing him as "reader of the Italian" and groom of the Privy Chamber.[80] She also favored Samuel Daniel, who held the same position as groom and wrote at least four masques and pastorals for her. But there is some reason to think that Anna was most drawn to music and the visual arts. Certainly, her inclination to masquing is not inconsistent with this premise. Further, Graham Parry has noted that she not only provided Inigo Jones with his first full-scale monumental commission but she also patronized Isaac Oliver and in 1617 drew into her service Paul van Somer, the most advanced painter in England before the coming of Mytens and Van Dyck. At the same time, Constantino de'Servi was reported by the Florentine ambassador Ottaviano Lotti as standing in high favor with Anna, "who takes pleasure in the portraits from life he has painted for her," while the great garden designer Salomon de Caus (who later dedicated his *Institution Harmonique* [1615] to the queen), laid out her gardens at Somerset House and Greenwich.[81] Under Anna's influence, too, as Oliver Millar has noted, the Royal Collection began once more to expand.[82]

Anna's taste for music (shared by her son Henry) is suggested by the remark of a contemporary that she kept "more than a good many" French musicians.[83] Indeed, the experience of one English composer is interesting to follow here for a moment in that it indicates how any artist of the time might have prospered by means of his association with the queen's network. John Dowland is described by scholars of the music of this period as the best lutenist of his time as well as its most gifted composer, his *Lachrimae*, a series of seven pavannes, being the best-known such composition of its day in all of Europe. In 1598 Dowland had been appointed lutenist to the court of Anna's brother, Christian IV of Denmark, from which, in 1600, he sent to his wife residing in England the manuscript of his *Second Book of Songs*, dedicated to Lucy, countess of Bedford. In July 1603, after the accession, Dowland came to England where he stayed until the summer of 1604. In the autumn of 1603 Queen Anna was in Winchester where the court was taking refuge from the plague in London, and there she had a masque performed for Prince Henry (see Chapter 4, below). Dowland must have visited the court then, for he mentions that he "had access" to Anna in Winchester. When, a number of months later, he published the famous *Lachrimae* (entered in the Stationers' Register 2 April 1604), he inscribed them to Queen Anna, who was thus the dedicatee for one of the most famous music collections that the period produced: music written for five viols and lute.[84]

In this general context, those court masques that so occupied Ben Jonson and Inigo Jones professionally seem to hold somewhat smaller relevance to the broader rhythms of Anna's court life and cultural activities. These spectacles lasted (not counting rehearsals) for the space of only one night a year and were not even performed every year of her reign. Thus although surveys of the period define James's queen via these masquings, they were, in the end, only the tip of the iceberg. For Anna's network of artistic associations was complex; indeed, a common thread of interests connects her with other figures best known for their patronage of painting—with Prince Henry, the earl of Arundel, Buckingham, and Charles I, a topic that in itself warrants further study.[85]

But from another viewpoint Queen Anna's masques do have a relevance to the subject of Anna's new court, because the lists of those ladies who danced in these spectacles serve as an important indicator of the composition of the circles around the queen. Generally arranged to be danced by twelve women including the queen, these masques involving a core of eight ladies were then supplemented by the "guest appearances" of four other young noblewomen who were not "regulars." More than half of Anna's dancers were thus invited for only one masque, as opposed to that much smaller nucleus of noblewomen who almost always danced. A constant presence in the masques that Anna gave between 1603 and 1612 (when she stopped masquing), it is this group of eight noblewomen (more or less) which seems to have been tied most closely to the queen. Thus, since the masque texts or the records of court gossip name the noblewomen who danced in most of her seven masques, we can not only identify what was probably Anna's inner circle but, over the period of the seven masques, infer changes in it as some names drop out or first appear.

In the masque lists actually available by way of various documents for five of the seven masques (1603–10), the following noblewomen were constants: the countess of Derby (all five); her sister, the countess of Montgomery (all five), and the countess of Bedford (four), she being absent from *Tethys' Festival*.[86] Such figures seem to point to the high standing of these women with Queen Anna, although two others emerge as comparably important even though they danced less frequently. Penelope Rich appeared in Anna's first two masques; she died before Anna presented her third masque; it seems clear that Rich enjoyed the same kind of access.[87] Another woman, Althea Talbot, daughter of the earl of Shrewsbury, who married the young earl of Arundel (Northampton's great-nephew) in 1606, was a late arrival. But she appeared in the first court masque following her wedding to Arundel—this was Anna's third masque (the 1608 *Masque of Beauty*)—and then was present through all subsequent masques (two) until the lists fail. For this reason, one might well consider her a late-coming member of Anna's inner court circle. If so, she fit the pattern of Anna's preferences here in the sense that the countess of Arundel also patronized the arts.[88]

In addition to selecting her ladies during the first months of her reign, Anna's appointment of one prominent official who had to be male was especially noteworthy. He warrants comment here not only by virtue of his position but also because of his own arts patronage. The court of the queen consort, as previously suggested, was considered separate from the king's, at least socially, and in many cases it had officials who were often counterparts of officials in the court of the monarch. Anna's court, for instance, required a Lord Chamberlain. At the court of the king, this official—the earl of Suffolk in James's early reign—was a close political adviser as well as the man who regulated access to the sovereign and was responsible for all matters pertaining to the king's physical and ceremonial comfort, duties obviously offering opportunity for much political power. And as far as artists were concerned, it is important to recall that one of the minor officers of this Lord Chamberlain was the Master of the Revels, the official who controlled and dealt with the London actors and theaters, and who also summoned particular companies of players for performances at the Christmas court revels every year. That the *queen's* Lord Chamberlain may have had similar if far less extensive responsibilities in her own court can now be inferred from fragmentary documents that show this official signing warrants of payment to professional acting companies (specifically Shakespeare's) in 1615.[89] Hence the identity of Anna's Lord Chamberlain and the process of appointing him in the summer of 1603 provide a final intimation of the probable "atmosphere" of Anna's court as well as a reminder of the strength of her own will.

Her Lord Chamberlain indeed became the first controversial issue of Anna's new reign. As early as 15 June, when Anna was midway in her progress south, Sir Thomas Edmonds wrote to the earl of Shrewsbury informing him that King James was extremely irritated at the queen "for conferring the place of her Chamberlain (to the which Sir George Carew was recommended) on one Mr. Kennedy, a Scottish gentleman, of whom the King hath very ill conceit."[90] Anna could be expected to represent his interests with her characteristic strong-mindedness, but pitted against her in this matter was Robert Cecil, who supported the candidacy of Carew. Cecil's advocacy, coupled with James's anger about Kennedy, represented formidable opposition to Anna's plan, especially in view of the fact that George Carew was no mean person. He had served as Mountjoy's second-in-command in the final suppression of Tyrone in Ireland, but perhaps more important, he corresponded often with Cecil, under whose influence Carew's career prospered until he was eventually created earl of Totnes.[91] But although Anna did replace the Scottish Kennedy, she did not acquiesce in Cecil's preference for Carew in the position. On 28 June, Dudley Carleton wrote that "Sir George Carew who posted before in hope of some special place about her hath not found the welcome he looked for."[92] Instead, waiting for several months, she followed a different course. On 14 August, Sir Robert Sidney—created Lord Sidney of Penshurst 13 May 1603—was rumored, and in October 1603, confirmed as the queen's Lord High Chamberlain and Surveyor General.[93] Sir George Carew became, instead, Sidney's second—Anna's Vice Chamberlain and Receiver.[94]

Thus Anna chose the brother of the countess of Pembroke and of Sir Philip Sidney, the uncle of the young earl of Pembroke and of his brother, the future earl of Montgomery, and the father of Lady Mary Wroth, as her Lord Chamberlain. His entrée to Queen Anna must have been effected through the countess of Bedford because, we recall, he was close enough to her and her family to have been part of the Christmas celebration at Burleigh-on-the-Hill in 1602. Lady Essex and Penelope Rich were also very fond of him.[95] Penelope Rich and her brother Essex backed him in his futile competition with Cobham to be Warden of the Cinque Ports in the 1590s.[96] Sidney's integration with the Essex group is also attested to by the godparents of his offspring: the earl of Southampton, the countess of Bedford, and Penelope Rich all stood in this capacity, while Rich and Mountjoy together acted as godparents of a son born in 1594.[97]

Sidney's own high cultural orientation is well known, his great house, Penshurst, being celebrated in the poem by Ben Jonson for its hospitality to the arts and its practitioners. Another recipient of this patronage, George Chapman, dedicated the 1609 edition of his translation of Homer's *Iliad* to Sidney. Himself a writer of poetry surviving in an autograph manuscript of thirty-five sonnets and twenty-four other poems, Robert Sidney was also quite fond of music. In 1598 the earl of Southampton procured songs for him in Paris from the music seller Léon Cavellat, and Robert Dowland, whose godfather Sidney was, presented to him *A Musical Banquet* in 1610, noting in the dedication "the love you bear to all excellency and good learning (which seemeth hereditary above others to the noble family of the Sidneys) and especially to the excellent science of music."[98] And, to offer a final example, Sidney was one of the nobles who helped Thomas Bodley establish his now-famous library at Oxford, donating £100.[99]

In the end, the cultural significance of Queen Anna's court is perhaps best exemplified in the conjunction of Robert Sidney, her Lord Chamberlain, with the countess of Bedford, her chief lady. For they, along with their relatives and the persons in their circles, could connect Queen Anna, in a way that James's Gentlemen of the Bed Chamber and Privy Chamber could not connect him, to a remarkable group of the most active and influential supporters of artists and writers of the time. That this group itself was a recognizable entity and that it did wield important patronage power at the beginning of the reign will be clear from a final episode, one that will also lay groundwork for repositioning Ben Jonson, writer of many of Anna's masques, not at the center but at the periphery of the queen's court.

A defining moment during Anna's progress into England in June 1603 was her visit to Sir Robert Spencer's great house Althorp in Northamptonshire. At this time she would have experienced a prominent aristocratic counterinfluence to that of the countess of Bedford and Penelope Rich, who by then seem to have been included among her familiars. Part of the welcome extended to Anna at Althorp was an outdoor show scripted by Ben Jonson and now known as *The Entertainment at Althorp*. Traditional literary narrative goes so far as to identify this elaborate three-day show as that which first drew Anna to masquing and to Ben Jonson himself, who, of course, subsequently wrote five masques for her.[100] But this assumption about the influence of *Althorp* on Anna ignores what followed over the course of the next few months, when events would suggest not only that the queen had already sketched the lines of her interlinked network but also that she had delineated the nature of her own space. For if her new entourage defined her arts patronage and where, in general, it would be directed, Anna's own choices also demonstrated a clear break with traditions deriving from the former queen of England.

Located twenty-one miles northeast of Stratford-upon-Avon, Althorp was the red brick manor that served as the palatial home of one of the richest men in England, Sir Robert Spencer. His great-great-grandfather, Sir John Spencer, had turned the raising of sheep into a highly profitable business handed down with careful attention from son to son, so that by 1603 Sir Robert's house, six miles northwest of the walled city of Northampton, could serve as an appropriate stopping place for royalty. But even though the queen's visit was expected—Sir Robert's account book lists detailed preparations—he himself was not present.[101] This absence, furthermore, lends a special relevance to the events attendant on Anna's visit, since she there encountered the particular atmosphere of arts patronage that was to define her by her seeming rejection of it.

As previously observed, a formal meeting of Queen Anna with all the ladies of England had already been planned by the Privy Council to take place at Windsor on 1 July. But Anna's stopping at Althorp on 25 June, without James, seems to have been regarded by many of the female nobility as a major social occasion, whatever the Council's plans. Indeed, it was in the days of hastening to and attending this event that the young Anne Clifford, accompanying her mother and other female relatives, began to keep a diary. And it is Clifford who alludes to the throng of nobility traveling with haste to Althorp to view the queen for the first time. Nor was she naively exaggerating, for Ben Jonson himself commented on "the multitudinous press" of people. It was this press that, on the third and last day of Anna's visit, hindered the parting address to the queen attempted by a youth accompanied by "divers gentlemen's younger sons."[102] Indeed, when that (Monday) part of Jonson's *Entertainment* brought forth the folk figure Nobody, his speech of greeting began: "Queen, Prince, Duke, Earls, Countesses" — an indication of the composition of the large audience.[103]

What is important to consider here is that since the Althorp visit was obviously to be a large and complex affair, and since Sir Robert himself was a widower and his thirteen-year-old son was too young to assume the ceremonial burden and stature of greeting and escorting Queen Anna as her host at Althorp, some persons had to substitute for the absent host. Indeed, his very absence must have been made possible by the fact that Spencer did have female relatives in the peerage who could do the entertaining for him. There can be little doubt that it was they who welcomed the new queen, and indeed it is their putative presence that makes the occasion relevant to the general point under emphasis in this chapter. Robert had at least three aunts who had grown up at Althorp and who would have been appropriate for these royal welcoming duties. Their substantial marriage portions, provided by the wealth of the Spencer family, had enabled them to join that very interesting and largely unstudied group of rich and educated young women in the landed gentry who married into the peerage, thus importing both money and culture into various earldoms.[104]

Robert Spencer's aunts were not in their twenties, as were Queen Anna and the countess of Bedford. They had all married in the 1580s, and they and their husbands played significant roles in the high cultural history of that period, as the younger countess of Bedford would later. Anne née Spencer, widowed twice, was now a baroness, married to Robert Sackville ("Lord Buckhurst"), the son of Richard Sackville, earl of Dorset (himself best known to literature as a contributor to *Gorboduc* and to *The Mirror for Magistrates*).[105] Anne's husband had a reputation for "singular learning" as well as a great facility in Latin and Greek, such inclinations presumably prompting him to leave money in his will to found Sackville College in Sussex.[106] Anne was also a distant kinswoman of Edmund Spenser, and she may have acted as his patron, since in 1591 the poet dedicated his "Mother Hubbard's Tale" to her.

Elizabeth née Spencer, another baroness, was married in 1574 to George Carey, second Lord Hunsdon, Queen Elizabeth's Lord Chamberlain (now ailing and soon to die). It was, in fact, Elizabeth's sister-in-law who was one of the group picked by the Privy Council for the trip north to greet Anna at the border. Generous to such writers as George Chapman, Abraham Fleming, and Edmund Spenser, Lord Hunsdon is best known as the titular patron (as was his father) of Shakespeare's acting company even before he became Lord Chamberlain in 1597.[107] Elizabeth herself was remembered by Edmund Spenser in "Muiopotmos," which was dedicated to her, and in one of Spenser's sonnets written in the dedication section of *The Faerie Queene*. But other artists paid tribute to Elizabeth as well, including Thomas Nash, who praised her for her hospitality, and John Dowland, who made note of her in his *First Book of Songs*.

The youngest of these three sisters, Alice (about forty in 1603), most probably acted as hostess at Althorp.[108] In 1579 she had married Ferdinando Stanley, earl of Derby, before his assumption of his father's earldom—when he was styled "Lord Strange." Ferdinando had been the titular patron of Lord Strange's Servants, the acting company whose members were to serve as the nucleus of Shakespeare's own group, the Lord Chamberlain's Servants, Shakespeare contributing to the repertory of Lord Strange's Servants in 1592 and perhaps in 1593.[109] Six years after Ferdinando's death in 1594 (he was then the earl of Derby), his widow Alice, still known, as mentioned above, as the (dowager) "countess of Derby," married Sir Thomas Egerton, Lord Keeper of the Great Seal of England, who later became Baron Ellesmere and then Viscount Brackley. To students of literature he would become known because of his famous secretary, the poet John Donne, and because of his patronage of the arts.[110]

Like her sisters, the dowager countess of Derby sponsored Edmund Spenser, who dedicated his "Tears of the Muses" to her, praising her "excellent beauty" and her "particular bounties" to him.[111] She seemed particularly fond of staged spectacles. For example, the *Ashby Entertainment*, written by the dramatist John Marston to be presented in August 1607, would, when printed, be entitled "The Honorable Lord and Lady Huntingdon's Entertainment of their Right Noble Mother, Alice Spencer, Countess Dowager of Derby, the Last Night of Her Honor's Arrival at the House of Ashby," which was the Huntingdon residence. Twenty-seven years later, another masque would be given for the countess, when she was seventy-five. It was entitled *Arcades: Part of an Entertainment Presented to* [Alice Spencer] *the Dowager Countess of Derby at Harefield by Some Noble Persons of Her Family Who Appear on the Scene in Pastoral Habit*, by John Milton.[112] At that point Alice would, as a patron, have encompassed the lifetimes of the poets Edmund Spenser, John Donne, John Marston, and John Milton — and have been a source of largesse for them all.

I have mentioned three of these Spencer sisters because any of them would have been appropriate nobility to greet the visiting queen in Sir Robert's absence, especially Alice and her husband, Sir Thomas Egerton. This is because, six months previously, they had entertained Queen Elizabeth at their great house, Harefield Place in Middlesex (the future site of Milton's *Arcades*), for four days. On that occasion, she had arranged an elaborate entertainment for Elizabeth involving such figures as a mariner, satyrs, nymphs, the spirit of Time, and so forth.[113] Sir Robert Spencer had been on hand, presenting the queen with nineteen sheep and two bucks.[114] It may therefore have occurred to him, widower as he was, to ask his aunt to provide a similar reception for the new queen at his Althorp.[115]

The relevance of this discussion about hosts for the Althorp visit to the topic of Anna and the organization of her own new court is to establish a new atmosphere to which Anna was now being exposed — the persons who would most probably have chosen both the entertainment and its arranger. At Althorp, Anna was meeting a different group of women, not members of the Essex group but noblewomen apparently no less interested in patronizing the arts. Indeed, if the dowager countess of Derby was the Althorp hostess, she can easily be envisaged choosing Ben Jonson, who as Aubrey noted was a favorite of Sir Thomas Egerton, for whom the poet was writing flattering epigrams before 1603.[116] The potential bridging of artistic influence here, then, seems obvious. Since Ben Jonson wrote most of Anna's court masques, some commentators see the Althorp episode as introducing Jonson to the queen's attention and thus as explaining her choice of Jonson as her masque writer.[117]

I have, however, described the social importance of the Althorp reception to make a different argument — to emphasize the continuing influence of the countess of Bedford and her circle in matters of artistic patronage by the new queen early in the reign. Two consequences of the Althorp reception make the point. First, none of the Spencer sisters became a member of Anna's court, despite the countess of Derby's experience in royal matters. Second, Ben Jonson did *not* write Anna's first masque, given six months later at Hampton Court. As to the first consequence, Anna's previous and subsequent behavior suggests that she preferred to be surrounded by women of her own age—in their later twenties—Penelope Rich being the highly significant exception.[118] The Spencer women were of an earlier generation as well as of different allegiances.

The choice of someone other than Jonson as Anna's first masque writer is also indicative of the general situation. One can hardly assume that the queen was consciously exercising her own artistic prerogatives this early in her English reign. Nor can it be said that Ben Jonson was any kind of a "failure" at impressing Anna at Althorp. The *Entertainment* is lively, amusing, graceful, and appropriate—but sociopolitical situations are never simple. Thus, for whatever reason, Jonson simply was neither an exclusive, nor an immediate, nor a permanent favorite as an artist, either as regards the queen or those in her circle, however popular the playwright may have been with King James. Nor was he necessarily an important issue. What is most significant for the present discussion is that when Queen Anna decided to present her first Christmas masque, she did not act unilaterally but took someone else's advice as to the choice of writer—the suggestion of the countess of Bedford.

Despite much literary history to the contrary, events do not necessarily revolve around writers and their competitions. Further, it is relevant that the countess of Bedford was herself hardly an enemy to Ben Jonson, while the earl of Pembroke, socially friendly with many in the Essex circle, was a generous patron to the great poet. Jonson had also dedicated work to the countess of Bedford during Queen Elizabeth's reign, especially *Cynthia's Revels*. Nevertheless, the fact is that at the moment another writer, Samuel Daniel, was enjoying much largesse from the countess of Bedford and was in good standing with many in the old Essex circle as well. Having secured the patronage of Sir Philip Sidney's sister, the countess of Pembroke, as early as 1592, he had gone on to gain that of Fulke Greville, Sir Philip Sidney's friend and biographer, by 1595. Perhaps because Greville had also been close to the earl of Essex since 1587,[119] Daniel, by 1596, had begun to benefit from the patronage of others in Essex's circle, notably Charles Blount, Lord Mountjoy and future earl of Devonshire.

Indeed, the importance of a "gentlemanly" aura, as suggested in Chapter 1, may have rendered Daniel more desirable than Jonson, a public dramatist. By 1599 Daniel was also a member of the household of Margaret Russell, countess of Cumberland, becoming tutor of her daughter, Anne Clifford, well before the accession.[120] And, remarkably, Daniel was in other networks as well. His sister had married John Florio in the late 1580s,[121] and in 1599 Florio had become a temporary member of the countess of Bedford's household where he finished his scholarly translation of Montaigne.

All this being so, the countess of Bedford's favor to Daniel in 1603 had been publicly apparent before she met Queen Anna, for when King James, in his own progress south on 23 or 24 April, had stopped at one of the houses of Sir John Harington, the countess of Bedford's father, Daniel, was actually part of the ceremonial welcome extended there to the new monarch. Obviously chosen for this purpose by the hosts, Samuel Daniel was thereby the first English poet to read a formal welcome to James, delivering the long "Panegyric Congratulatory" (printed also in 1603).[122] Thus, although Ben Jonson's traditional identification with Anna's masquing is so pervasive in the cultural history of this period that Graham Parry in *The Golden Age Restor'd: The Culture of the Stuart Court* assumed *The Masque of Blackness* (Christmas 1604) to have been Anna's initial court presentation, the first was actually a different piece — *The Vision of the Twelve Goddesses*, written by Samuel Daniel. Bedford's own instrumentality in this matter, furthermore, is indicated by Daniel's prefatory epistle to the 1604 octavo of *The Vision* where, inveighing against a previous unauthorized quarto, he dedicates the masque to the countess, adding that his publication of the masque script was an effort to explain the actual plan of the masque "whereby I might clear the reckoning of any imputation that might be laid upon your judgment for preferring such a one to her Majesty in this employment as could give no reason for what was done."[123] It was Bedford, in other words, who had recommended him to the queen.

The decisive direction of Anna's patronage — or of the patronage she allowed exercised in her name — would be emphasized by Daniel's additional fortunes at this time. William Shakespeare and his fellows were the first dramatic troupe to have received a new patent (May 1603) at the accession as the acting company known as Servants of the King (although almost certainly not at the behest of James himself).[124] But later in this same year, even though Daniel's experience with play performance was merely as the writer of one closet drama, *Cleopatra*, while Ben Jonson or other poets (such as Shakespeare) were proven theatrical professionals, Daniel was awarded an acting company himself. In this regard, it is not generally noted that although the other two adult dramatic companies (the Queen's Servants and the Prince's Servants) were also allowed the names of royalty, their appointments to these titles occurred eight months later than that of Shakespeare's company. Moreover, their own written patents to this effect were not to be delivered to them until several *years* after the fact.[125] Thus, in point of time, the *second* dramatic company actually to have in hand a new royal patent after the accession of King James was the Children of the Chapel Royal. Their patent, dated 30 January 1604, newly designated this popular group as "The Children of the Queen's Revels." Further, one clause in the patent (issued, of course, as if from the monarch) foregrounded Samuel Daniel again. It gave him authority over the company, the patent permitting playing "provided always that no such plays or shows shall be presented before the said Queen our wife by the said Children or by them anywhere publicly acted but by the approbation and allowance of Samuel Daniel who her pleasure is to appoint for that purpose."[126]

Thus it appears that early in the new reign, royal artistic patronage that in any way benefited individuals (as opposed to a group such as Shakespeare with his fellow players) was emanating not from the court of the king but from the court of the queen. Indeed, she would later appoint two men of letters, Samuel Daniel and John Florio, as grooms of her Privy Chamber. Significantly, James made no comparable appointments of literary personages, nor did he directly favor individuals in positions involving artistic activity.

However, in light of the foregoing, it could be argued that it was not Anna but the countess of Bedford who was controlling royal patronage — that Anna was simply being swayed by others. But given Anna's Scottish history and her subsequent artistic choices, as far as they can be ascertained, it would seem, rather, that either the countess of Bedford and the queen had similar tastes or that Bedford was extremely perspicacious in gauging Anna's own preferences. The queen's loyalty specifically to Samuel Daniel in later circumstances, for example, argues the individuality of her own mindset. It was indeed Ben Jonson, not Samuel Daniel, who wrote the majority of Anna's masques, replacing Daniel in this office by the second Christmas of the new reign. But granting Jonson's unquestionable talent in this genre, critical arguments that urge a failure of Daniel's own *Vision of the Twelve Goddesses* as the reason for Jonson's accession to the post ignore two points. The first is that there is no evidence of Daniel's failure, court criteria being as yet unknown, since masques had not been a staple at the court of Queen Elizabeth.[127] Rather, it would seem that Daniel was actually rewarded with another position connecting him with the giving of shows: his role with the Children of the Queen's Revels. The second point is that political factors, worth brief pursuit here, may have had as much to do with Daniel's subsequent disappearance from the masquing scene as did artistic ones.

At some time between Daniel's *Vision of the Twelve Goddesses* in the

Christmas of 1603–4 and the following Christmas season of 1604–5 — the season of Jonson's debut with *Blackness* — Daniel oversaw a performance of his own closet drama, *Philotas*, by those newly patented Children of the Queen's Revels of which he was certainly the censor and probably the general manager.[128] Evidently this play about Alexander the Great's abuse of power in killing his outspoken adviser and friend Philotas was taken by a member or members of the Privy Council as an apology for the Essex conspiracy (a line of thought made at least plausible by the patronage Daniel had received from more than one member of the old Essex circle). After one or more performances, the play was apparently forbidden through the instigation of one or another member of the Council and Daniel was summoned to defend himself.[129] The poet may have compounded his problems by involving Mountjoy (recently created earl of Devonshire by King James) in the affair. Devonshire was still living with and would soon marry Essex's sister Penelope Rich, herself previously indicted as a conspirator in the Essex Plot, but now, of course, a lady of Queen Anna's closely held Drawing Chamber.[130] Thus the halt in Daniel's career as writer of Christmas masques for the queen may well have been occasioned by pressure from the anti-Essex English circle around James but also by the sensitivities of several in the circle around the queen. Since Devonshire, a patron of Daniel, was annoyed to have been mentioned in connection with *Philotas*, suffice it to say that Daniel was intimidated.[131] He may even have been sincere when he wrote Cecil that he wished to withdraw from the stage.

Because it is clear that the *Philotas* script existed by 29 November 1604, the play may well have been performed by this date and thus, by late autumn, have precipitated Daniel's troubles. Therefore, by the time rehearsals would be needed for a queen's masque in the Christmas holidays of 1604–5, Daniel might already have been perceived as inappropriate as its author, and Ben Jonson was then offered the opportunity. But, if so, even this substitution could not have been effected independently of the queen's circle. Again, one looks primarily to the influence of the countess of Bedford, for in 1601 Jonson had presented to her one of the two known copies of his *Cynthia's Revels* with intercalated dedicatory leaves. These copies had special poems printed with the dedications, the countess receiving one such copy and William Camden, Jonson's distinguished teacher, receiving the other.[132] Jonson also mentioned Bedford in his poem to the countess of Rutland (Sir Philip Sidney's daughter, Elizabeth),[133] and he enjoyed enough hospitality at Sir Robert Sidney's Penshurst to write about this great house of Queen Anna's Lord Chamberlain. Thus it is not surprising that in the

Christmas season following the *Philotas* problem, Jonson was newly ensconced as the queen's masque writer, initiating his own brilliant court presentations with *The Masque of Blackness.*

Even so, to make the point about Anna's own role in artistic appointments, the long-range consequences of Jonson's success certainly did not
include the eclipse of Samuel Daniel on the court scene. Daniel seems to
have been the continued recipient of more "favor" from Anna than was Jonson. In August 1605, for example, when the queen visited Oxford, she and
her ladies were presented with a pastoral, *The Queen's Arcadia,* enacted by
the men of Christ Church College, and John Chamberlain noted that compared with the other dull entertainment, this pastoral "made amends for all,
being indeed very excellent."[134] The writer of *Arcadia* was Samuel Daniel.
Four years later, Anna, who had a very strong bond with her son Henry, deferred her 1609–10 Christmas season masquing because she wanted to celebrate Henry's installation as Prince of Wales in June 1610. She thus planned
to dance in a masque especially prepared for this celebratory occasion. The
writer she chose for this masque, *Tethys' Festival,* was Samuel Daniel. Again,
four years later, in 1614 (two years after the queen had stopped masquing
entirely), during the Christmas season in which Somerset's marriage was
celebrated at Hampton Court, the queen sponsored her first entertainment at her own palace in London—the renovated Somerset House, renamed Denmark House—into which she had recently moved. This new
venue—the queen consort's court—was a place where the king and his
nobles were entertained as *visitors,* and suitably enough, Anna's Christmas entertainment in 1614 was a lavish pastoral and counter-celebration
of the marriage of her only Scottish lady of the Bed Chamber (Bedford's
counterpart), Lady Drummond, to the Scottish Lord Roxborough. This
work, *Hymen's Triumph,* enacted by young unmarried ladies not of the
queen's close circles, was also written by Samuel Daniel. Further, though
Daniel was made a groom of the queen's Privy Chamber in 1607 and a
gentleman-extraordinary of the same chamber in 1613, Ben Jonson, despite
his successes, was never so appointed—nor did James do him the honor.
Thus, if politics may have initially suspended Daniel from court masquing,
and if Jonson's brilliant successes justly maintained him in his newly won
position as substitute scriptwriter for the queen's masques at court, Anna's
continued treatment of Daniel—even if at Bedford's instigation—hardly
shows him as disgraced. Rather, in the end, one is reminded of the kind
of persistence on the queen's part that characterized her behavior in Scotland and, now, in England where, as with Mr. Kennedy and the countess of

Hertford, she never rested when her will had been crossed. In the first case, she appointed her own Lord Chamberlain. In the second case, she never appointed a replacement for the countess of Hertford as her second English lady of the Bed Chamber. By the same token, she never ceased honoring Samuel Daniel even if exterior circumstances forced his removal as writer of her Christmas masques.

A person of definite cultural tastes, Anna apparently discovered compatible intellectual leanings in members of the old Essex circle, particularly the noblewomen. Establishing a circle during the first several months in England almost wholly through the countess of Bedford's contacts, Anna speedily passed over the noblewomen and noblemen who had stood well with Queen Elizabeth. And as we have seen, Anna entrusted to Sir Robert Sidney the influential management of her court in those presumably social areas outside of the purview of the king's ministers, and in resistance to the combined support of James and Cecil for another candidate, a Howard. Further, the queen largely entrusted the countess of Bedford's parents, the Haringtons, with the ideological development of her children. Although at first the Haringtons shared the guardianship of Princess Elizabeth with Lord Cobham's wife, they eventually became her sole educators. And Prince Henry became best friends with John Harington, the countess of Bedford's younger brother.

But even though Queen Anna entrusted much to the Harington family and their Essex-Sidney network of contacts and kin, she does not seem to have granted Robert Sidney or Lucy Bedford exclusive access and influence. She also chose for her court women of comparable intellects but of different political and familial ties, such as the countess of Hertford. Moreover, Anna had no qualms about cultivating the two nieces of Robert Cecil, Elizabeth and Susan de Vere. As countess of Derby, Elizabeth had been one of the former queen's courtiers, but this did not prevent Anna from favoring both her and her sister. When Susan, in a love match, married the brother of the earl of Pembroke, who himself was kin to Anna's own Lord Chamberlain, the queen's court thus came to comprise nobles with wide-ranging ties.

Indeed, this court seems to have cast a far wider net within the English nobility than did that of James. The king's court was heavily populated with Scots, so that, for example, the only English Gentleman of the Bed Chamber was Philip Herbert, earl of Montgomery, the earl of Pembroke's brother and Susan de Vere's husband. And, for the most part, James's English appointees were drawn from two families—that of Cecil, and that of the Howards, represented by Suffolk and Northampton.[135] But the more catholic construction of Anna's court, although dominated by the so-called Essex faction, also included relatives of Cecil (the aforementioned Elizabeth and Susan de Vere, although another niece, Lady Hatton, had been rejected), as well as at least two Howards. The wife of the earl of Suffolk, Northampton's nephew and Lord Chamberlain, seems to have been included in Anna's circle from the outset, either because of her affinity with Anna or for political reasons; and later the wife of the earl of Arundel, great-nephew and sole heir of the childless Northampton, would also join this circle. Thus Anna's court was not completely defined by the countess of Bedford's network, although in time — as Prince Henry matured and as James himself began to develop favorites — the Howard/Essex duality between the two courts became more pronounced with, as we shall see, far-reaching consequences.

At the beginning of Chapter 1, I spoke of the influence of Queen Anna's court as like that of a yet undiscovered mass in space whose presence for a long time can only be deduced by the gravitational forces it exerts on the orbits of the other planets. To nothing is this metaphor more relevant than to recent criticism that attributes the cultural efflorescence of the early Stuart court neither to King James nor to Queen Anna, but instead to their son Henry, Prince of Wales. Praised for his broad sponsorship of arts and letters before his death at the age of eighteen, and celebrated for his precocious sense of a political destiny and his vision of an imperium, Henry has been perceived as a figure whose death brought an abortive end to a magnificent, prospective renaissance of the arts in England. But before centering the young prince as a cultural icon for the early Stuart period, it is well for us to remember that it was Anna who brought Henry to England, possibly by the violent means of her own self-induced miscarriage. Indeed, that she wrenched him away from what may have been a definitively Scottish emotional orientation was suggested by an account of his painful parting from his erstwhile protector, the earl of Mar,[136] after which Anna reasserted her claim to the nine-year-old boy, introducing him into her own English circle. Accordingly, we might well reformulate Roy Strong's conclusion to his *Henry, Prince of Wales, and England's Lost Renaissance*. Commenting on how remarkable it is that in Renaissance England "the crown stands quite apart, under both Elizabeth and James, from these major thrusts forward in the arts," Strong offers as exception the activity he attributes solely to Henry. What is striking, he writes, is how many figures around the Prince had links either directly or indirectly with the Essex circle. Southampton, who danced in *Oberon*, was one of the prince's most loyal supporters. Sir Thomas Chaloner, Henry's Lord Chamberlain. had been his agent both in Italy and in France. Sir John Hayward, the Prince's historiographer, looked to Essex as his patron. . . . Inigo Jones and Robert Dallington had been members of the household of another devoted follower, the Earl of Rutland. Samuel Daniel, who wrote the installation masque [*Tethys' Festival*], was a protégé of Philip Sidney's sister, Mary, Countess of Pembroke.[137]

The relationship of Southampton and Essex to persons in the countess of Bedford's social circle is now well documented, and it is therefore highly significant that Bedford became Anna's lady of the Bed Chamber when Henry was only nine and a half. It was at this time too that Sir Thomas Chaloner was appointed his teacher. The prince was ten when Samuel Daniel wrote his first masque for Anna. Moreover, there was one person who, when Henry was ten and a half, finally gained complete control over Henry's education and the selection of his companions. That person was his mother.

Through this repositioning of Henry, Prince of Wales, we have, then, come full circle. Between the ages of nine and sixteen, Henry was under the aegis of Anna and her court, so that the influences on the young prince cited by Strong originated in the queen's venue. Clearly, it was Anna, not Henry, who, concealed by critical misrepresentations, was the hidden influence not only on the trajectory of Henry's life but also on the formation of a Jacobean court nucleus.

I have been arguing here that Anna of Denmark, shortly after arriving in England, succeeded in focusing attention on a phenomenon not seen since the reign of Henry VIII — the court of a queen consort. In populating this space with nobility renowned for their patronage of the arts, Anna was able to provide Jacobean high culture with a local habitation and a name. But the queen's own court came to have an emblem as well. This was the Christmas season court masque. Inaugurated during her first year in England, this spectacular presentation was to evolve under Anna's direction into a signature event that embodied the queen's own regnal identity, at least for a short time, as the cynosure of Jacobean artistic production.

1. Anna, Queen of
Scotland. Portrait
attributed to Adrian
Vanson, 1595.
Courtesy of the
Scottish National
Portrait Gallery.

2. Anna, Queen of
Scotland. Copy by
unknown artist.
Courtesy of the
Scottish National
Portrait Gallery.

3. Henry, Prince of Wales. Oil on canvas by Marcus Gheeraerts the Younger, 1603. Courtesy of the National Portrait Gallery, London.

4. Henry, Prince of Wales, and John Harington. Oil on canvas by Robert Peake the Elder, 1603. Courtesy of the Metropolitan Museum of Art. Purchase, Joseph Pulitzer Bequest, 1944 (44.27).

5. Henry, Prince of Wales and the third earl of Essex. Oil on canvas by Robert Peake the Elder, 1603. By gracious permission of Her Majesty Queen Elizabeth II. Copyright reserved. Figures 4 and 5 are reproduced without comment on the coincidences in Roy Strong, *The English Icon* (New York: Pantheon Books, 1969), figures 210 and 222.

6. Sir Robert Sidney, first earl of Leicester. Oil on canvas by unknown artist, 1588. Courtesy of the National Portrait Gallery, London.

7. Lucy, Countess of Bedford (?). Oil on canvas by unknown artist, ca. 1603. Courtesy of the National Portrait Gallery, London.

8. Design by Inigo Jones for *Love Freed from Ignorance and Folly*. From the Devonshire Collections. By permission of the Trustees of the Chatsworth Settlement.

9. Anna of Denmark. Watercolor on vellum by Isaac Oliver, 1612?.
Courtesy of the National Portrait Gallery, London.

10. Anna of Denmark. Oil on panel attributed to Marcus Gheeraerts the Younger, ca. 1612. Her attire presumably indicates that she was in mourning for Prince Henry. Courtesy of the National Portrait Gallery, London.

11. Princess Elizabeth. Oil on canvas by Robert Peake the Elder, ca. 1610. Courtesy of the National Portrait Gallery, London.

12. Anna of Denmark. Oil on canvas after Paul Van Somer, ca. 1617. According to Diana Scarisbrick in *Tudor and Jacobean Jewellery* (London: Tate Gallery, 1995), 67, the monogram "S" on her ruff at the left signifies her mother, Queen Sophia, and "C4" her brother, Christian IV of Denmark. The crossbow in her hair is an emblem of the superiority of brains over brute strength. Courtesy of the National Portrait Gallery, London.

13. Lodovick Stuart, first duke of Richmond and second duke of Lennox.
Oil on canvas by Paul Van Somer, 1620. Courtesy of the National Portrait
Gallery, London.

4. THE STUART MASQUE AND THE QUEENLY ARTS OF CEREMONY

The Stuart masques associated with Anna of Denmark have traditionally been historicized not as expressions of the queen's own court programs but as richly tapestried instances of an early modern form of art created for patriarchal agendas. According to this view, these shows served as vehicles for exhibiting major English artists such as Ben Jonson, Samuel Daniel, and Inigo Jones, who invested these spectacles with learned iconography, elaborate scenery, and symbolic dance figuration not only to emblematize their own views of art and state politics but also to enhance the regnal programs of King James I. Accordingly, the role proposed for the queen in the Stuart masque has conformed to this tradition. She and her ladies, oblivious to the serious allegorical representations and political statements of the scripts, scenery, and even of their own costumes, served as unwitting agents in these serious presentations, themselves busied and satisfied with their dancing and their pretty clothes.[1]

But we have observed the queen in the early years of her English reign developing her own creative agenda for self-display. Anna located many aristocratic patrons of the arts within her circle, and by including, in several cases, more than one member of the same family, she established a network of noble alliances strengthened by certain important family kinships. And because the queen's masquing inevitably involved ladies drawn from this group, we should expect that such shows, rather than having been configured to celebrate James I, might well have served a more obvious purpose, that of reaffirming Anna's own treasured identity as a queen of substance, not of shadows.

As observed in Chapter 3, Anna already did have a financially and legally defined "court," but it was her masques that reified it as something more than an elaborate bookkeeping item in the Crown's provenance. Because masquing involved noblewomen, it had the effect of distinguishing and culling out from the general palace culture of King James a second and specifically female ambience of "court"—the "atmosphere" of a court of the queen consort. In this regard, far from being designed as structured political commentary in dialogue with the king (although Jonson's masque scripts may well be interpreted in accordance with such intention), Anna's masques attempted to shape a queenly royal "identity." Indeed, this kind of masquing, new to the English court in 1603, so transformed a hitherto marginalized court recreation that by 1613, when Anna herself had stopped masquing, its firmly established function as a politically significant court display goes far in explaining King James's own appropriation and transformation of the revivified genre. In fact, although the subject lies beyond the purview of this study, the king introduced a form of masque suited to his own purposes, a species of display that he maintained beyond Anna's death in 1619 to the end of his own reign in 1625. And although James's design for the masque was very different from that of his consort, his ends were similar in that he used these spectacles in ways that Anna herself had invented.

It is important to bear in mind, however, that while the relationship of the early Stuart court masque to Queen Anna herself has often been ignored or underestimated, it is possible to emphasize its importance to the exclusion of the queen's many other opportunities for centering herself. Accordingly, the narrative offered here discusses Christmas masquing in conjunction with other activities—such as the ceremonies attending childbirth—that the new queen deployed as her means of royal self-expression. Although of paramount importance, her masques occurred once a year (and sometimes not that often), but since Anna reigned throughout the remaining 364 days, she had other opportunities to celebrate her royal status. I shall allude briefly in the course of this chapter to several of these activities in order to suggest that Anna's ceremonials as queen, taken collectively, all helped to reshape the cultural ambience of the early Stuart court.

In deciding to focus considerable creative energy in reconfiguring the masque—her single most original endeavor—the new queen consort was undoubtedly aware of preceding tradition. In fact, it has not been sufficiently emphasized that in Queen Elizabeth's court these shows had been associated with men, not women.² References to masques surviving from Elizabeth's later years suggest this male prerogative, which is also reflected in the drama of the period. For example, the masquing in *Romeo and Juliet* is presented as a pastime for rich young men of good gentry families who could playfully invade the homes of other gentry such as the Capulets to present their show. In fact, this carnivalesque convention of masqued invasion from outside the household (nostalgically recalled by Capulet from his own younger days) was behavior obviously available only to men, for it was they, not the young women of their social class, who could wander through the streets of Verona *en masque* and unchaperoned; or, to take another example, through Venice, where Gratiano, Lorenzo, Salerio, and Solanio, on the way to visit Antonio, could parade to the accompaniment of a "wry-neck'd fife" past Shylock's house in order to abduct Jessica, disguised as her lover's page-*boy* (2.7, 2.8).

The court masques during the latter part of Elizabeth's reign seem to have been similarly gendered. In 1589, Arthur Throgmorton wrote to Robert Cecil about a masque he and other gentlemen hoped to offer at court, and in 1595 and 1599 two of the all-male Inns of Court — Gray's and the Middle Temple — presented masques from their own annual revels before Elizabeth during the holiday seasons.³ In Scotland, too, the court was accustomed to masques as a male activity. Before his marriage to Anna, James helped to embellish the wedding he had arranged between the earl of Huntly and the duke of Lennox's sister (Anna's friend) by writing for the occasion a dialogue that featured men impersonating such figures as Zani, Nymphs, and Mercury and that referred to the coming of "strangers in a masque." James also helped William Fowler, Queen Anna's secretary, to devise some sort of male show for the banquet honoring the baptism of Prince Henry on 23 August 1593.⁴ Thus, at James's accession in 1603, if masques were to be arranged at court, English custom and Scottish precedent might suggest that they would be masques of men. And since their own revels were an annual affair, young men from the Inns of Court might again have been obvious and available candidates to present such upper-class shows during the time of Christmas court celebrations — Inns of Court men would, after all, present masques at court for the wedding of Princess Elizabeth to Frederick in 1613.

But despite male monopoly, noblewomen in England before 1603 had not been strangers to masquing. They seem to have organized such shows as private, patriarchally supervised entertainment. For example, in the summer of 1600, Anne Russell, one of Queen Elizabeth's maids of honor, married the heir of the earl of Worcester with festivities at Lord Cobham's house in Blackfriars. There the other seven maids of honor presented a masque to celebrate the marriage, even persuading Queen Elizabeth to dance.[5] Indeed, thirteen years later, a few months after the accession, Queen Anna showed herself to be familiar with such female, in-house festivity. When the royal family had removed to Winchester because of the plague, they were joined there by the nine-year-old Prince Henry, and between 11 October 1603, when Henry arrived, and 17 October, the queen and her ladies privately presented for him the first known masque of the reign.

This small domestic event, in fact, produced two interesting reactions. One helped found the strong narrative tradition of frivolity so often associated with England's new queen. That is, although Thomas Edmunds had written the earl of Shrewsbury from Winchester that "the Queen did the Prince the kindness at his coming hither to entertain him with a gallant masque," the other report was less lenient.[6] Lady Anne Clifford (fourteen at the time) described what I believe is the same masque in a diary entry (before Christmas 1603) not previously associated with this occasion: "Now there was much talk of a masque which the Queen had at Winchester and how all the ladies about the Court had gotten such ill names that it was grown a scandalous place, and the Queen herself was much fallen from her former greatness and reputation she had in the world."[7]

So soon? Clifford's mother, the countess of Cumberland, and her aunt, the countess of Warwick, had both been close to Queen Elizabeth but were not included even among the ladies of Queen Anna's new Drawing Chamber. As for what was "scandalous," it may not have been the masquing itself that was shocking but that the queen and her ladies — rather than men — took part in it. In any event Clifford's comments, enshrined in history, may even be the original basis for the traditional legend of Anna's "frivolity."

More important to my purposes, however, both Clifford's and Edmunds's reports suggest that Anna had taken an early interest in masques. Indeed, at the same time she was arranging this show for Prince Henry in October, she was making plans for her own first Stuart masque. The comte de Beaumont, French ambassador to England, noting the show for Prince Henry in a letter to Paris, remarked that the queen proposed "d'en faire d'autres plus beaux cet hiver." Indeed, he continued, in significant retrospect to the matter of Chapter 2, it seemed that the king and his principal ministers, constantly concerned about Anna's "esprit," were quite content to see her so absorbed, as these activities would presumably divert her from those political self-assertions so characteristic of her Scottish reign. Ironically, however, these masques were not to be diversions from, but expressions of, this "spirit" about which the king and his closest advisers had learned to be wary.[8]

Thus, two months later, the royal couple having returned to celebrate at Hampton Court the first Christmas of the reign, Anna used this season of revels to launch, in effect, the Jacobean court masque. I should like to pay some attention to this first Christmas season in order to establish the context and manner of Anna's masquing, for although the queen's spectacles must surely be contextualized within the plethora of other ceremonials available to her, there is no doubt of her masques' importance to her own royal agenda. Further, this particular activity is, unlike many others, recorded and can thus illuminate the function of Anna's circle in developing a regnal presence for the queen and her cultural circle at the Jacobean court.

As a concept, of course, "court," as mentioned above, existed only in the physical proximity of the sovereign himself. The onset of Christmas season, however, seems to have dictated a fixed royal residence, either at Whitehall in the city or at Hampton Court, very near the city but accessible to deer hunting. In one of these palaces, beginning in Advent and moving through Christmas to Twelfth Night, much of the ambitious nobility gathered to celebrate the holiday season. And although the process does not seem to have galvanized King James, he was punctilious about appearing at Whitehall or Hampton Court to observe these holidays. They often featured formal entertainment as the heritage of the last several decades under Elizabeth, when the Crown had even begun paying for professionally executed stage dramas to enhance the festivities.

But professional plays were, again, only the tip of an iceberg whose bulk consisted of weddings, dinners, and other elements of the general Christmas atmosphere anciently termed "revelry"—the sum of activities that gave the Master of the Revels, a subordinate of the Lord Chamberlain, his theoretical reason for being as a court official. Further, during the festive Christmas season, hospitality was extended throughout England from the great houses of earls who opened their doors to all comers as a form of noblesse oblige to the king's own analogous special entertainment of ambassadorial "strangers" at the English court. As Ottaviano Lotti, secretary to Count Montecuccoli, the Florentine ambassador-extraordinary, explained it in a dispatch at this time: "That which in Italy is commonly called '*il*

Carnovale' runs its course in these parts from the birthday of Our Lord until Twelfth Night, or in other words, according to our usage, until the day of Epiphany. At this time, even more than at other seasons, all the people turn their minds to festivities and pleasures, but their Majesties' courtiers in particular show themselves all the more ardent in this because of their capacity to spend money, and because it is proper for them to entertain one another."[9] From the ambassadorial perspective then, Christmas served two purposes. The season of revels required celebratory activity by the court; conversely, activity that required celebration, such as the entertainment of ambassadors, could be used to enhance the annual Christmas revels.[10]

The revels of Christmas 1603–4, which saw Queen Anna's first masque, were especially elaborate not only because they were the first of the new reign but also because the new ruler of England had been, as was customary, the recipient of a number of mandatory first visits. James then had to receive at this time not the various ambassadors-in-ordinary residing in London but extremely distinguished foreign nobles sent by the continental states as ambassadors-extraordinary for the specific purpose of congratulating him upon his accession to the English throne. In James's case, the 1603 plague had forced him (and thus the court) to move between Oxford, Southampton, and Winchester, preventing even the king's annual visit to London at the end of October when a brief period of court revels usually honored All Saints' and All Souls' Days (Shakespeare's "All-Hallondtide") and saw the opening of Parliament. Thus a great many ambassadors-extraordinary had not yet even been officially welcomed and conducted through their special receptions, which, in the end, proved quite suitable settings for such elaborate entertainments as masques.

The specified ritual for the welcome extended to an ambassador-extraordinary was elaborate but adaptable. Upon arrival, the ambassador-extraordinary was usually accorded an initial, highly ceremonious audience with the king. This was followed by a brief or extended series of less elaborate but more substantive meetings (not necessarily involving the monarch himself), which culminated after an unspecified number of days in a final personal royal interview, known among the ambassadors as the "audience of farewell." In the ceremony attendant on this final encounter (in such a case the entire day was wholly given over by the Crown to the one embassage concerned), there was a personal interview with the monarch after which the ambassador-extraordinary and his party were "feasted" in a highly formal midday dinner with the king, intended as an elaborate gesture of respect to the state that this particular emissary represented. Quite often, therefore, the "farewell-process" extended to inviting the ambassador-extraordinary on this same day to supper and then to some kind of late-evening spectacle.

In 1603, the persistence of plague, beginning almost with the accession itself, had caused the absence of James from his Hampton Court and Whitehall palaces. Thus ambassadorial farewell feastings had suffered so many postponements through the latter half of the year that eliminating the backlog became a necessity; indeed, by Christmas James had not yet had audiences of farewell for the ambassadors-extraordinary from Spain, France, Poland, Tuscany, or Savoy. Not surprisingly, then, these obligatory events served simultaneously as a means of embellishing the first Christmas revelry of the new reign.

"The King will feast all the ambassadors this Christmas," wrote Arbella Stuart to her uncle, the earl of Shrewsbury, on 18 December,[11] and it seems that the 1603–4 Christmas season was indeed arranged in this spirit.[12] Juan de Taxis, count of Villa Mediana, the ambassador-extraordinary from the king of Spain, would be feasted on 26 December (St. Stephen's Day) in the Great Chamber at Hampton Court, after which he would be further entertained by hearing a play (by Shakespeare and his fellows). On 27 December (Childermas, or the Feast of the Holy Innocents), Stanislaus Cikowski de Voislanice, vice chamberlain of Cracow, ambassador-extraordinary of the king of Poland, was to be feasted and entertained with a professional stage performance (again by Shakespeare and his fellows) scheduled to conclude the evening's revels. Then on 6 January, Christophe de Harlay, comte de Beaumont, ambassador-extraordinary from Henri IV of France, was to be feasted and entertained by "a masquerade of certain Scotchmen" as well as a play "in the Queen's presence."[13] Finally, on 12 January and 2 February (Candlemas), the ambassador from Savoy and Alfonso, Count Montecuccoli, ambassador of the Grand Duke of Tuscany, were scheduled for equivalent revels.

I have detailed this diplomatic context for the first Jacobean Christmas because it suggests the elaborateness of these revelry rituals, which were repeated every year, providing the celebratory atmosphere that Queen Anna now proceeded to appropriate for her own uses — for masquing. In this regard she won for the masque, hitherto merely a sometime event that most often accompanied weddings, a secure place in the annual Christmas revels at court so that, in James's reign, this particular kind of spectacle came to be an inseparable part of the court holiday revels, a position it had never held in the days of Elizabeth. Further, the change and achievement attendant on

Anna's introduction of her own version of the masque in this Christmas season is indicated by the very first such spectacle in this same season — one offered not by the queen but by a group of noblemen.

Serving perhaps as a paradigm not of Anna's innovations but of the Elizabethan masque tradition that she was to overshadow, this traditional masque of *men* has not hitherto formed part of the canon of Stuart masque documents, despite the fact that it was organized by an important noble and described by courtly onlookers. Yet the emphasis to be found in this particular description on almost everything about the masque *except* its written script serves to foreground the viewpoint I shall be adopting in my own examination of Anna's first two masques. In all instances, contemporary comment indicates that it was not the written script, or the lavish scenery, or the dancing, or the music of the masque that most interested most courtiers. It was the participants.

The 1603 masque of men was to serve as a showcase for the younger courtiers whom the king favored, and in the eyes of the courtly onlookers, it was they who were, in effect, the text. Accordingly, it seems best to follow the lead of Dudley Carleton, who focuses not only on the participants of this first court masque of James's reign but also on the basis for their selection. Significantly, Carleton identifies the duke of Lennox as *rector chori*, which means that the noble who organized this show was James's second cousin, the Scotsman presumably closer to the king than any other: at this time, Lennox was described by the Venetian ambassador, Giovanni Carlo Scaramelli, as "the person deepest in the King's confidence, and has some time ago been named nearest to the crown" — that is, during the minority of the princes.[14] To be included, then, by the organizer in this masque either validated one's own current court status or, at the very least, augured well for one's court future, as we may guess from what is known of the subsequent careers of the seven dancers chosen here by the duke of Lennox. According to Dudley Carleton's order, these men were the earl of Pembroke, Monsieur d'Aubigny, Sir Thomas Somerset, Philip Herbert, James Hay, Richard Preston, and Sir Henry Goodyere (54). Because these identities are crucial in providing a sense of the "flavor" of such an event as it would exist at the early Stuart court, I think it relevant briefly to describe the status of each of these persons. Why were they chosen for this first Stuart masque by the duke of Lennox?

In this group were two sets of brothers. One set was Lennox and his younger brother, "Monsieur d'Aubigny," Esmé Stuart. Now twenty-four, Aubigny had succeeded their father as seventh Seigneur d'Aubigny in France and, at some point between James's accession and this Christmas, and probably through Lennox's influence, had also become a gentleman of James's Bed Chamber.[15] The second set was the earl of Pembroke and his younger brother, Philip Herbert. Pembroke's inclusion was obviously a function of the early appeal that he held for King James, who had made him a Knight of the Garter during the first Garter feast of his reign in the previous summer.[16] Herbert was also in high royal favor just now, since he was about to be appointed to the Bed Chamber. Indeed, he seems to have become a favorite in a style of special relationship accorded such future nobles as Somerset and Buckingham.[17] And within the year Philip would marry Susan de Vere in a prestigious court wedding at Christmas and would be created earl of Montgomery by James.

Thus four of the dancers were obviously in high favor with the king himself, while the remaining four enjoyed only slightly less access to the monarch. Two of these courtiers, James Hay and Thomas Somerset, were beginning to build brilliant careers. Hay, who had been a gentleman of the Bed Chamber in Scotland, would make a marriage which, like Philip Herbert's, would be celebrated as a major court event (Thomas Campion writing the wedding masque). Being described in the next several months as a prime favorite, Hay had an assured future.[18] And Somerset, third son of the earl of Worcester (Elizabeth's and then James's Master of the Horse), had been one of the two nobles selected by the Privy Council to travel to Scotland officially to inform James of Queen Elizabeth's death after Hunsdon's brother, Sir Robert Carey, had made his unauthorized gallop north with the news. Now twenty-four, the future Viscount Somerset of Cashel had been named Queen Anna's Master of the Horse; thus he sat with Robert Cecil, Robert Sidney, the earl of Southampton, and others as an officer of the Queen's Council.[19]

A full appreciation of the status of participants is crucial to our understanding of the Stuart court masque. Although the nobles dancing may have been amateurs from the artistic point of view, the least influential of these rising court figures could easily—if they thought about it at all—have made or ruined the personal lives of any of the actual artists connected with the masque.[20] The composers, painters, designers, and choreographers, the inventor of the idea and writer of the lines, and the paid actors (hereafter designated in these discussions as "professionals") who themselves uttered those longish descriptive speeches some readers today take for the whole of a masque—all these were individuals who might at the time have well been dismissed as merely the artisans. So one might speak of the scenery, costume, and dance as they reinforced the intellectual plan of the symbolism (such iconology being a consideration only crudely relevant to this particular pre-Jonsonian masque), but the true "structure" of such a court spectacle organized by a duke of Lennox for the viewing of other nobles and courtiers was constituted by the identity of the participants. The asset they brought to the masque was not their skill as actors, dancers, or musicians. It was their status. Thus it is from their viewpoint—that of the dancers of this scriptless and untitled *Masque of the Orient Knights* (my name for it)— that we need to follow the normal course of expectations: what generally was supposed to happen in such a show.

This precursor of Anna's masquings was to be the culmination of revelry planned for New Year's Night at Hampton Court. On that evening there was first a play presented by the King's Servants ("Robin Goodfellow": presumably *A Midsummer Night's Dream*),[21] and then, the common players now dismissed, the court set itself to enjoy the main and intime business of the evening, the aristocratic masque. Now those who, unlike Arbella Stuart, were not privy to the secret could look forward to discovering the identity of the vizarded young participants of this elaborate midnight spectacle.

As is well known, early modern masques were visually organized according to a central motif that determined the scenery, costume, and even the figuration of the dances, this motif being termed the "device." In the case of *The Orient Knights*, the device was the idea of eastern Asia. At the lower end of the great hall a "heaven" had been built from which first descended a magician from China. After "a long sleepy speech" (*pace* literary criticism) comparing China to England, this professional interlocutor—the figure dressed as a magician—announced that through his great powers he had transported certain masked knights all the way from China and from India to pay homage to King James, new ruler of England. A traverse then opened to reveal a vaulty place where were seated the eight masked, armed, and costumed knights with their torchbearers and other lightholders. The knights wore loose robes of crimson satin embroidered with gold and bordered with broad silver laces, and under these robes they showed silver doublets basted with cloth of silver. With buskins, swords, and hats all alike (decorated with an Indian bird feather and jewels), each of the eight masquers had by his side a shield painted with a distinctive design and motto. All this, in the eyes of Dudley Carleton, "was no unpleasing spectacle." And of course this viewing of nobles is what he reported, not a *précis* of the written script.

After several minutes of this display, each masked knight, then, to a background of music produced by two professional singing boys and two professional instrumentalists, individualized himself by advancing out, probably with a torchbearer on each side.[22] Holding his shield so that James could view the impresa, he moved toward the throne of the king. Then, in the course of presenting this shield, the "knight" recited a speech explaining the relationship of the impresa to himself and of himself to his king, a description rendered also for the benefit of the audience of noble onlookers. Some notion of the manner of these painted motifs is available from Carleton's description of one of them: "The rest in their order delivered their escutcheons with letters, and there was no great stay at any of them save only at one who was put to the interpretation of his device. It was a fair horse-colt in a fair green field, which he meant to be a colt of Bucephalus' race and had this virtue of his sire that none could mount him but one as great at least as Alexander." [23]

It is important to understand, however, both in this spectacle and later in the queen's own masques, that this individualizing walk-through by each gorgeously costumed courtier (tokenly masked but now hardly unidentifiable) was only the first phase of the presentation. Yet, curiously, it is for this first phase that the writer of the masque's script penned those *words* which have usually survived (although not in this case) in printed or written form as the exclusive entity we term "the masque" when today we prepare to read, say, *The Masque of Blackness.* Thus those initial descriptions, the "parts" spoken by the professional interlocutors, have acquired a deceptive metonymy. Composed by a Jonson or a Daniel or a Campion, they have come misleadingly to define the entire masque as a "literary" or, more sophisticatedly, as an iconological impersonation.[24] But what most often has not survived in written scripts, except in some of the more elaborate directions of Thomas Campion, are the remaining four-fifths—the succeeding and much longer phases of these court masques, which comprised activity not expressed or expressible in words alone. Thus it seems appropriate, at least for the purposes of this present discussion, to correct the imbalance resulting from critical emphasis on the *word* by shifting the analytical focus to the masque's five distinct stages of organization. Accordingly, I shall be designating what I have just described in *The Orient Knights*—the initial costumed display with the procession of each individual masquer to perform a symbolic "task" on stage (here the showing of one's shield to the king)—merely as "Part 1" of what was actually a five-part structure.

Part 2 began here when the masquers of *The Orient Knights*, their display processions concluded, organized themselves for dancing. Still in full view, they betook themselves to execute the conventional early modern English and continental dances, here probably choreographed for unusual convolutions and for figuration — squares, circles, diamonds, letters. In this dancing, furthermore, although all masquers were of the same sex, gender differentiation was implied by the requirements of the form, which was executed by couples. In fact, it is important to note that participants in Stuart court masques — whatever the politics of individual selection — were almost always chosen not only to make up an even number but, it seems, to make up increments of four.[25]

This Part 2 was usually referred to simply as "the measure," a name, however, with specific implications: the English "measure" was a slow and stately dance.[26] Executed by couples, this particular dance usually began as one of the dancers held the partner's left hand in his right; facing the onlookers, both made obeisance to the throne and then to the onlookers. Then, turning to each other at an oblique angle, they executed that mutual reverence which began every dance and was performed before the dance music itself started; however, musicians often played an opening chord or four bars of introduction to accompany this preliminary gesture. (An exemplary instance may be noted in 1618 when Prince Charles, dancing in the measures of *Pleasure Reconciled to Virtue*, "excelled them all in bowing, being very formal in making his obeisance both to the King and to the lady with whom he danced.")[27]

One figure of "the measure" performed by a couple suggests how the four couples of *The Orient Knights* may each have been moving, although the complexity of masque dancing probably lay in the fact that four or more same-sex couples were simultaneously executing some larger dance structure choreographed by the dancing-master. In the "sideways single," for instance, one dancer holding the hands of the other (the partner always doing a mirror-image of the action) stepped apart sideways, inside knees bent, outside feet flat on the ground but rising to the toes by the close of the beat. The second beat moved the inside leg away from the partner to join the other foot, both feet now on tip toes but sinking to the heels at the close of the beat, partners continuing to hold hands, now slightly lowered. On the third and fourth beats, the sequence was reversed to move the couple back together, the joined hands lifted slightly as the hip of each dancer was gracefully raised a little to the side when stepping.

Other convolutions included in the "measure" were the double, the backward single, the succeeding double, and the reprise, and one entire piece — the particular "measures" referred to here as Part 2 — were presumably rehearsed sequences of such steps. Thus, Part 2 was designed to allow the participants, often well rehearsed by the dancing master, to show their command of grace and movement in those little sallies of medium talent characteristic of such aristocratic affairs. In the present instance, however, according to the attentive Dudley Carleton, the knights of the Orient were perhaps underrehearsed. "The first measure was full of changes and seemed confused, but was well gone through withal."

When, after a number of rehearsed sequences, this exhibition ended, a new and quite different phase in the masque began. I term it here Part 3, and it was often referred to by Jacobeans as "the ordinary measures." Sometimes including the pavanne (another slow measurelike dance with connotations of stateliness), Part 3 now expanded the focus of the event away from the exhibition of the masquers to include certain of the courtly, seated onlookers.[28] In this sequence, each of the principals of the masque invited persons of the opposite sex in the courtly audience to dance, the process being known as "taking-out." However, this taking-out did not represent a general dissolution of the formality of the presentation. Indeed, the eight initial takings-out by the eight dancers of *The Orient Knights* could by no means have been a casual affair dependent upon impulse. Judging from the results, at any rate, it would seem that the duke of Lennox, the *rector chori*, had this phase well in hand. Indeed, that the details survive is itself telling, Dudley Carleton being careful to report these takings-out. He wrote here that the eight masquers chose the following eight ladies (this is his order): Queen Anna, the countess of Derby, the countess of Hertford, the countess of Suffolk, the countess of Bedford, Susan de Vere, Lady Southwell the elder, and Penelope Rich.

It is important to note that here was no courtship ritual. "Ceremonial politics" seems a more apposite phrase as we note that although the duke of Lennox, who probably took out the queen, was the only married man of the eight masquers, only two of the ladies taken out were themselves *unmarried*: Susan de Vere and Lady Southwell. Thus the invitations had almost everything to do with nonmarital considerations. And in choosing the noblewomen taken out, Lennox was paying a compliment to the court of the queen, since the countesses of Bedford and Hertford were the two members of the queen's exclusive Bed Chamber, while all the other ladies, except for Lady Southwell, were of the queen's inner circle.[29] Therefore, the initial taking-out was highly political and carefully deferential, suggesting its usefulness for determining the interplay of court alliances or political overtures.

I am not certain how long a Part 3 might continue, but at some point the tempo of the music changed definitively, as did the complexion of the dance coupling. As Part 4 began, those courtly audience members who had been taken out were "empowered" to take out other courtly onlookers; at the same time, the eight masquers selected a second set of partners.[30] Thus in Part 4, participation in the dancing inevitably became more general. Because now the musical mode adopted the faster tempi of the galliards and corrantoes (always characteristic of Part 4),[31] it seems to have been the younger, more energetic, but less exalted courtiers who were invited to join an activity that probably led to new sets of takings-out. "In the corantoes," Carleton punned, "they ran over some other of the young ladies." In this connection, apparently, the clothing of the Orient knights had not been well thought out, for Carleton noted that "their attire was rich but somewhat too heavy and cumbersome for dancers, which put them besides their gaillards."

No matter how lively, however, and no matter how crowded the floor may now have been (especially if the previous invitees remained), Part 4 by no means signaled the outbreak of a general dancing that dispersed the unity of the overarching presentation. Instead, the galliards and corrantoes were eventually halted as the professional, costumed, main interlocutor gave a rehearsed speech (again usually now part of the verbal remnant of the masques we have) to recall the masquers. In the present case, the magician from China who had first descended from the clouds reminded the masquers that time was fleeting and he called them to a close. All male and female courtiers taken out were returned to their seats and the last phase, Part 5, featured the finale that the *ballet de cor* of the French court referred to as the *sorti*. This was a final dance by the masquers, alone again, a dance that culminated in their formal exit, after which they unmasked and joined the courtly audience, which now followed the king toward the refreshments. Carleton elliptically describes this final phase in the presentation of *The Orient Knights*: "They . . . so ended as they began, with a song; and, that done, the magician dissolved his enchantment and made the masquers appear in their likeness to be the Earl of Pembroke, the Duke etc."[32]

If the foregoing constituted the bare bones of the usual social form of the Elizabethan masque, with noblemen the dancers, then Anna, if only because she was queen consort, raised the masquing stakes dramatically. *The Orient Knights* had featured young nobles perhaps nimble enough to perform male dance steps energetically—certainly such powers as the earl of Worcester and the earl of Northampton or the earl of Mar were not among the celebrants here. But when Anna chose to present a masque, everything changed. Royalty was dancing. Indeed, that Anna's own first masque of this first Christmas of the Stuart court, scheduled for 8 January, was already being anticipated as a major occasion may be gathered from the activities of the foreign ambassadors. They vied to be present. But some were left out, and even though the greater part of both their respective entourages was to be admitted, neither the Savoyard nor the Florentine envoy himself was invited because they were in "so strong competition for place and precedence that to displease neither it was thought best to let both alone."

But the envoys from Spain and France were even more problematic and had to be handled with particular care. As representatives of the two foremost continental powers at the English court, these emissaries required careful, even-handed treatment. Accordingly, the French ambassador-extraordinary had been invited for New Year's evening to *The Orient Knights*, while the Spanish ambassador was now coming to the queen's masque. With respect to the question of court prestige, however, it appears that it was the Spanish envoy, as Carleton observed, who thought he had gained the advantage. "The Spaniard thinks he hath carried it away by being first feasted (as he was the first holiday and the Polack the next) and invited to *the greatest masque*" (italics added). Further, although the French ambassador, himself anxious to attend the queen's masque, made "unmannerly expostulations with the king and for a few days troubled all the court," this problem, very significantly, was settled by Queen Anna herself. She "was fain to take the matter upon her, who as a masker had invited the Spaniard as the Duke [of Lennox] before had done the French." Thus the French emissary was "flatly refused to be admitted," and it was the Polish and Spanish ambassadors who attended the queen's masque "with their whole trains." Even at this early stage in the reign, then, it seems that Queen Anna had found a way to insinuate herself into sensitive areas of international diplomacy by reviving the court activity of masquing as means of showcasing herself. Clearly the mere prospect of her first masque pitted the French ambassador against the Spanish—France against Spain—not in a space bounded merely by the circle of her attendant countesses and ladies but in the larger theater of what she had apparently managed to configure as the most prestigious evening of the entire holiday season.

Exclusiveness had, in effect, become a kind of tool that the queen could employ not only with ambassadors and with the nobility of her own circle but also as a mode of defining her relationship to the court of the king. Thus an entertainment that had occurred infrequently at the court of Queen Elizabeth was suddenly elevated into a matter of status. Indeed, in the case of this first of Anna's masques, the "influence" stakes were raised further—if not by design then by fortune—by the elaborateness of the set. Dudley Carleton, a courtier himself, pointed out that the sheer amount of scenery required for this masque took up considerable room. The great hall in Hampton Court was, in fact, "much lessened by the works that were in it, so as none could be admitted but men of appearance." "Be it art or hap," as Shakespeare's Antony might put it, the queen's masque was thereby rendered much more exclusive and more prestigious than the masque presented by the young courtiers of *The Orient Knights*, most of whom were members of the king's Bed Chamber.

Ben Jonson's stature in English letters has led some commentators tacitly to assume that Stuart court masquing actually began with his own work. Yet the vehicle for Queen Anna's court debut was, in fact, Samuel Daniel's *Vision of the Twelve Goddesses*, the poet being chosen as "deviser" by Anna's only lady of the Bed Chamber, the countess of Bedford.[33] Thus it is Daniel's court masque that must claim attention as the model for that mode which Queen Anna would use to inscribe a new concept of queenship on the Stuart court, a model to which Jonson basically adhered, despite his own brilliant innovations.

Not surprisingly, *Twelve Goddesses* differed in significant ways from the structure represented by *The Orient Knights*. The dancers in the occasional masques of Queen Elizabeth's later years, and in *The Orient Knights* as well, were young, mostly single males. And although a masque at court, by courtiers, could doubtless involve the peerage (as would the occasional palace wedding masque in Elizabeth's time), in general *The Orient Knights* featured men whose age and marital status accorded with a tradition of participating nobles who, with the exception of Lennox, were more to be distinguished by their youth or wealth than by their political power (see the cases of Esmé Stuart, Philip Herbert, and James Hay). That is, despite the fact that the dancers were gentlemen of the Bed Chamber and thus special favorites of James—lending luster and excitement to the masque—they could hardly compete in the political arena with the likes of Salisbury, Northampton, Suffolk, Worcester, or Mar, the king's close political circle. Indeed, it is significant that none of the Orient knights (Lennox, of course, excepted) was a member even of the enlarged English Privy Council. Further, the only earl dancing, young Pembroke, would wait years before attaining any powerful office. To a great extent, then, *The Orient Knights* was furnished with single young men of brilliant prospects but no formal power — the cast of Romeo's masque writ large.

In an age when wedding and kinship represented wealth and power, and masques could serve as elaborate reminders of young men's marriage-ability, Queen Anna's first masque — featuring women instead of men — departed unquestionably from any such emphasis. Those dancing in *Twelve Goddesses* were married women in the peerage who were therefore not masquing because of their marital availability. Quite simply they were dancing because they were noblewomen in the prestigious circle around the queen consort of England. This said, however, it would be inaccurate to suggest that Anna did not consider marriage itself to be an important political and social mode of forging alliances, or that in revising the masque conventions, she provided no place for marriage brokering.

Rather, what Anna did was increase the number of dancers from the eight of recent tradition to twelve. Actually, it is more accurate to think of this number as "eight plus four" because of the composition of each group. The eight women of Anna's closely held Bed Chamber and Drawing Chamber furnished the core membership of her masques and rarely changed. But the additional four "openings" that the queen created by designing her masques for twelve persons seem to have been reserved for young marriageable women favored either for themselves or for their first families, the latter case also accounting for the occasional presence in her masques of married ladies whose husbands were of undistinguished rank. When attempting to gauge the court prestige or influence of women appearing in Anna's masques, therefore, it is important that we reckon the occasional nature of their appearances: when such ladies were merely among the "outside four." For example, although Lady Mary Wroth and Lady Anne Clifford, both literarily significant as authors, are often described by commentators as "having danced in Anne's masques," the implication is not quite what it seems. It is true that these women made appearances as members of a year's visiting quartet, but these infrequent invitations are not necessarily indicative of any special favor, friendship, or influence that they may have enjoyed with the queen.[34] They were invited either to honor their relatives or because they happened to be at court for other reasons in a given Christmas season.

Hence the most dramatically visible difference a courtly audience would have noticed between the men's masque of *The Orient Knights* and the queen's first masque was that eight of the twelve dancers in *The Vision of the Twelve Goddesses* were the queen herself and a group of countesses who were married to some of the most powerful and prestigious nobles in the kingdom. These were the countess of Suffolk, Lady Rich (the mistress of the new earl of Devonshire, conqueror of Ireland, and sister of the dead earl of Essex), and, for this first Christmas, the countess of Nottingham. Since the other ladies dancing were also either countesses or soon to become so by marriage, the "population" of this new masque was politically more electric than that of its immediate predecessor, which had been composed for the most part of younger men with far less influential political networks. As I now describe *Twelve Goddesses*, then, I do so to suggest a structural paradigm for Anna's six other masques as well (they not being described here in equivalent detail). The structure will demonstrate how Anna succeeded in developing an agenda that called attention to herself and her ladies and at the same time honored and complimented important noblemen.

Significantly, the device that Anna approved for this masque was not the kind of allegorical scenario in which intellectual qualities (such as Patience) might be impersonated. Rather, the masque featured mythologically powerful female figures—specifically, twelve classical goddesses. Because Samuel Daniel was careful to write a full description of his masque, and also because a contemporary list yields the identities of those ladies who appeared in it with the queen, the noblewomen's roles and their order of presentation may be identified as follows.

Juno	The countess of Suffolk
Pallas Athene	Queen Anna [35]
Venus	Penelope Rich
Vesta	The countess of Hertford
Diana	The countess of Bedford
Proserpina	The countess of Derby
Macaria	Lady Hatton
Concordia	The countess of Nottingham
Astraea	Lady Walsingham
Flora	Susan de Vere
Ceres	Dorothy Hastings
Tethys	Elizabeth Howard

Thus the foremost goddesses of the Roman pantheon were impersonated by countesses, appropriately hierarchalized. The countess of Suffolk, for example, wife to James's new Lord Chamberlain, was shrewdly honored as Juno, while the lower-ranking or younger ladies, whose number could be increased, reduced, or invented as the occasion demanded, represented minor classical/allegorical figures, such as Flora and Astraea.[36] Further, because there are several "cast lists" of Anna's later masques, we can even sort out those ladies who, appearing continually, must have enjoyed Anna's particular favor. These included the (then) *two* countesses from the Bed Chamber (Bedford, Hertford) and certain women from the Drawing Chamber (Derby, Rich, Nottingham, Suffolk, Susan de Vere, Lady Walsingham, and Elizabeth Howard). Of all these ladies, however, only the countess of Bedford, the countess of Derby, her sister Susan de Vere (the future countess of Montgomery), and Lady Walsingham constituted a permanent core of women whom Anna always placed in her masques; over the nine years in which Anna gave masques, she only occasionally added to this exclusive group.

But the dancers for *Twelve Goddesses* also included the first of the occasional ladies invited for a one-time-only compliment to them or their families. One such here, for instance, was Lady Hatton, who had written her uncle, Robert Cecil, in an unsuccessful effort to effect her appointment to Anna's Drawing Chamber (see Chapter 3). Hatton's inclusion in this first masque (and once again in the 1608 *Masque of Queens*) could well have been a gesture to Cecil, despite the fact that two of his other nieces were already in this Drawing Chamber. Another such rarely chosen dancer was the young countess of Nottingham, whom Anna had known since childhood. Born Margaret Stewart, she was one of the two children of the second earl of Moray, James Stewart, killed at the age of twenty-five. Her mother also dead, Margaret had been brought up at the queen's Scottish court, and at the age of twenty-three she accompanied Anna to England. During the summer of 1603 she had attracted the aging and prestigious Lord Admiral, a recent widower, in a quick courtship. When the earl married Margaret, he catapulted her upward into the English nobility. How Anna felt about this may be adumbrated by her own words in a letter to James that I think describes this situation, since it was written early in the first year of the new reign.

> I have been as glad of the fair weather as yourself and the last part of your letter, you have guessed right that I would laugh — who would not laugh — both at the persons and the subject but the more at so well chosen Mercury between Mars and Venus? You know that women can hardly keep counsel. I humbly desire your Majesty to tell me how it is possible that I should keep this secret that have already told it, and shall tell it to as many as I speak with, and if I were a poet I would make a song of it and sing it to the tune of Three Fools Well Met.[37]

Anna's response may well have proceeded from resentment that her ward had made this very prestigious match with a Howard and one of James's circle without first consulting her. Nonetheless, to exclude the new Lady Nottingham in this first Christmas would obviously be offensive to the earl of Nottingham, who had been a key participant in organizing the English earls for their unanimous acceptance of James as king of England in the days after Elizabeth's death. It seems significant, however, that the new countess never danced in a second masque.[38]

Dorothy Hastings and Elizabeth Howard, on the other hand, are good examples of the kind of young woman Anna would customarily include in a visiting quartet. Daughter of the earl of Huntingdon, Hastings would make a marriage within several years to Sir James Stuart, the eldest son of Lord Blantyre, and subsequently the earl of Roscommon. Elizabeth Howard, who dressed as Tethys, was seventeen and the daughter of the countess of Suffolk. Possibly making her first appearance at court, she would be invited back in the following year for *The Masque of Blackness*, perhaps again through her mother's influence or because Anna liked her and wanted to congratulate her. She had in the interim married William Knollys (uncle of the late earl of Essex) who became a baron at James's accession.

As regards the masque itself, the queen's presentation differed considerably, both in scope and solemnity, from the eight-man *Orient Knights*, which had preceded it by several weeks. For example, *The Vision of the Twelve Goddesses* conducted Part 1, the important exhibition of the dancers, in a much more formalized manner than did *The Orient Knights*. *Vision* opened with a Temple of Peace in the foreground, in front of which was to be seen the figure of the Sibyl. (Unfortunately, Daniel's own account, from which my description is inferred, was not overly concerned with scenic details.) In the background was a mountain with broad steps leading up to a shadowy height where could be discerned a host of dim forms. Iris, goddess of the rainbow (probably a professional and a boy), descended these steps, moved up to the Temple of Peace, and informed the Sibyl of the coming of goddesses, proffering a list with brief descriptions of each deity. According to Daniel's account, the Sibyl was to read out each four-line description first so "that the eyes of the spectators might not beguile their ears" and so that "at their descending there might be no stay or hindrance of their motion which was to be carried without any interruption to the action." [39]

Daniel's (and the queen's) emphasis on such theater was borne out by what followed. Trumpets and cornets, played by the king's musicians disguised as satyrs lurking in the dark among the rocks around the broad steps, began to sound a stately march. With this accompaniment a procession slowly materialized: flickering torchlights shadowed figures descending the stairs in ranks of threes. Holding aloft white torches, the Three Graces in their silver robes led this procession. Then, hair and robes decked with stars, three more torchbearers followed, these preceding the first rank of three goddesses: the queen and two of her ladies. Behind these goddesses, another rank of three torchbearers, then three more goddesses, and so on in alternating groups of threes until the full number of twelve divinities had completed their descent—"which being all seen on the stairs at once," wrote Dudley Carleton, "was the best presentation I have at any time seen."[40]

The first rank of goddesses were Lady Suffolk, the queen, and Penelope Rich. Thus the queen honored both the Howards and the Essex circle. The second rank of three goddesses were the queen's favorites, Hertford and Bedford together with the countess of Derby (Elizabeth née de Vere and niece of Robert Cecil), who would several years later be well enough established in the queen's favor to hold Princess Mary in her christening ceremony. The next triad was Hatton, Nottingham, and Walsingham. Significant here was the placement of the new countess of Nottingham, whom the queen was ranking not with other countesses but with the now unmarried Lady Hatton and Lady Walsingham, the latter the wife of a knight, Sir Thomas Walsingham, Chief Keeper, along with his wife, of the queen's Wardrobe. But unlike the other two ladies in this group, Walsingham was a member of the queen's Drawing Chamber and would appear in two more masques with Anna.

The last triad was Susan de Vere, Hastings, and Howard. These were the younger ladies of the group, their place dictated not by their standing in the queen's favor but probably by their age and unmarried status. Indeed, Susan de Vere, sixteen, would be described as a favorite of the queen when she married the future earl of Montgomery during the next Christmas season.

I spoke of a difference in solemnity between the two first masques of the season. Part 1 of *The Orient Knights*, for instance, had featured each knight approaching the king to exhibit a blazoned shield with its motto, and in this way James himself had been structured into the spectacle. But there seems to have been enough of a mood of informality that when the young Philip Herbert, James's current favorite, had presented his shield with Bucephalus on it, the king had "made himself merry with threatening to send this colt to the stable, and he [the masquer] could not break loose till he promised to dance as well as Banks his horse."[41] But Part 1 of

Twelve Goddesses foregrounded its female participants, so that James was not structured into the situation at all. Each goddess in her elaborate costume approached not the king but the Temple of Peace. To the accompaniment of music and the singing of the Three Graces, she offered her gift to the altar there. To quote Daniel, the author of the masque script: "One after another with solemn pace ascended up into the temple and delivering their present to the Sibylla (as it were but in passing by) returned down into the midst of the hall, preparing themselves to their dance, which, as soon as the Graces had ended their song, they [the Goddesses] began to the music of the viols and lutes placed on one side of the hall."

Daniel's description usefully recalls the basic purpose of a Part 1, as well as its relationship to a Part 2, "the measure," but this queen's masque, with twelve persons involved, differed from *The Orient Knights* in that the dancing exhibition itself seems to have been much more complex and accomplished. As the goddesses danced with each other, the music moved in "divers strains framed unto motions circular, square, triangular, with other proportions exceeding rare and full of variety." [42]

Part 3 — the taking-out — began here when the goddesses now formed a large circle. The Three Graces held aloft their white torches and sang a summons, for here, presumably, the women broke out of the circle to make their politically significant dance invitations for the "common measures" (measures sufficiently conventional that the unrehearsed noble onlooker now taken out by a masquer could participate without disgracing himself). Carleton followed these takings-out of *Twelve Goddesses* closely, his account indicating that the noblemen chosen by the goddesses were not their own husbands, and thus that the invitees must have been persons whom the queen had determined to distinguish as the first takings-out of her court. Carleton lists these invitings in the following order: the earl of Pembroke, the duke of Lennox, the earl of Suffolk, Henry Lord Howard (future earl of Northampton), the earl of Southampton, the earl of Devonshire, Sir Robert Sidney, the earl of Nottingham, the earl of Northumberland (brother-in-law to Penelope Rich and participant in the secret correspondence with King James of Scotland before Elizabeth's death), Lord Knollys (future husband of Elizabeth Howard and now Lord Treasurer — was Elizabeth directed to take him out?), the earl of Worcester (who had succeeded Essex as Queen Elizabeth's prestigious Master of the Horse and retained that office under James), and Lord Monteagle.

With two exceptions, then, these invitings were not submissions to spouses, since the husbands (the king, the earls of Bedford, Derby, and

Hertford, as well as Sir Edward Coke and Sir Thomas Walsingham) did not dance at this juncture. The takings-out then obviously being political, any-one who was omitted is significant. For example — and perhaps it should be expected, in light of the Scottish events depicted in chapter 2 — the only one of James's Scottish lords to be taken out was the duke of Lennox. Not only did he hold the highest rank at court next to the king, but he was the only Scottish noble in England whom Anna seems to have trusted. In two other instances, however, the queen consort did honor James's English political inner circle (Northampton and Worcester) and simultaneously acknowl-edged the Stuart Crown's new approach to Essex Plot conspirators. Two of the initial invitees were Southampton (newly re-created by James as earl after his release from the Tower in the previous spring) and Lord Mont-eagle, heavily fined (£8,000) by Elizabeth and put in the Tower for partici-pating in the Essex Plot, but also freed at James's accession.[43] Thus though partly composed of nobles favored by James, those others first taken out here showed that the queen in effect had also appropriated the power to add — at least in these circumstances — half a dozen other nobles to those favored by James. That is, nobles chosen by the queen now shared, how-ever briefly, the physical space in the dance occupied by the nobles closest to James. Such a fleeting, perhaps intangible, association cannot be said to have *worsened* the status of Pembroke, Sidney, Devonshire, or Northum-berland. Years later, in fact, James would seem to have taken the point when he used a Christmas masque as the mode of suggesting the status of a new favorite, George Villiers, future earl of Buckingham.

Part 4 of a masque extended the "taking-out" process to less presti-gious persons — or perhaps it should be said such persons were defined as less prestigious, at least in Anna's framework, by having been consigned to these "common measures." But in the particular case of *Twelve Goddesses*, the takings-out for the corrantoes and galliards of Part 4 seem to have been as carefully designed as those for Part 3. The particular requirements of this first Christmas season had, in fact, made the queen's masque politically relevant owing to the struggles for precedence among the crowd of am-bassadors in attendance to congratulate the new English king. This social tension had occasioned the exclusive invitations only to the Spanish and Polish ambassadors to attend *Twelve Goddesses*. Honoring them in Part 4 of the masque seems, then, to have been deemed an appropriate gesture: a kind of gesture — the invitation to dance — that could, in fact, be proffered to a male emissary only by a woman. And while this compliment might, in the end, have meant little politically, the queen could withhold it and thereby exercise a negative power, creating resentment. But in the present situation, withholding seems not to have been in Anna's mind. Carleton followed events: "For galliards and corantoes they [the queen's ladies] went by discretion, and the young prince [age nine] was tossed from hand to hand like a tennis ball. The Lady Bedford and Lady Susan [de Vere] took out the two ambassadors [Spain and Poland], and they bestirred themselves very lively." [44]

Toward midnight *Twelve Goddesses* moved into Part 5 (the *sorti*) as the figure of Iris appeared ceremonially to summon away the goddesses, presumably as a dance ended. They now bowed farewell to those nobles with whom they had been coupled in dance, the male nobles withdrew, and the goddesses again commanded the scene alone. When the music resumed, they performed a final short, rehearsed dance before they departed, evidently in the same kind of procession as marked their entrance, escorted by torches, nymphs, and music, moving up the wide stairs to the upper reaches of the mountain where they disappeared. Shortly thereafter, the ladies returned unmasked and the king left his specially constructed throne to signal a general exodus. The dancers of the masque and, significantly, the ambassadors followed behind James to a banquet which was, as Carleton wrote, "dispatched with the accustomed confusion. And so ended the night's sport with the end of our Christmas gambols." [45]

Anna's masque broke a long-standing tradition at the English court by presenting not noblemen but noblewomen and by preempting Twelfth Night — a traditional occasion of high revelry at the acme of the Christmas season — to do so. It would appear then that this calculated ceremony of display was intended to establish the importance of her presence and that of her ladies at the center of a new royal court, the court of the queen consort. Notwithstanding this intention, however, it must again be emphasized — in contradistinction to traditional narrative — that Anna was not therefore "addicted" to masquing: it was hardly her sole activity. Rather, the queen seems to have been concerned with establishing a particular principle at the outset of her English reign: *Twelve Goddesses* marked Anna's preemptive move to distinguish her female court from its surrounding patriarchal context. She did this by appropriating the masque itself.

There is, I think, justification for stating matters in this way. During the years that Anna gave masques, there were never any other court spectacles comparable to *The Orient Knights*, that is, offered under the auspices of the king or of male members of his circle. Such masquing did resume after

Anna apparently lost interest in the form, but the first decade of the Jacobean reign reflects a new court dynamic. Because the queen was the wife of the monarch, it was she who in effect was the most powerful "courtier," or at least one of the most powerful, around the king. In this respect, events, if not theory, suggest further that there was room for only one flashily visible "courtier" group apart from the monarch and his ruling circle of older earls. Such a visible group apparently was not to form around the young men of the king's Bed Chamber, who might have given masques wherein the young dancers might be pleased to "take out" the queen and her ladies. Rather, such self-centering was to be the provenance of the queen herself and her circle, whose masques would take out persons of far more *gravitas* than the young men of James's Bed Chamber.

To dispel any inadvertent misstatements about my general intent here, I must certainly stress that there were, of course, a number of court masques written by Jonson and Campion (several with surviving scripts) in which the queen and her ladies did not participate at all. But I consign them to a different class of display. Although their written scripts might present poetry and imply display (especially in the case of Campion) literarily superior to some masques in which the queen danced, the auspices under which such other masques were produced differentiate them *socially* from the queen's shows. For notwithstanding the most lavish expense, none of these productions presented royalty. Instead, these were all-male masques allowed at court to celebrate the weddings of nobles. Those invited to participate were most often relatives of the groom, because such spectacles seem to have been the responsibility of his family. Thus the dancers were chosen not by the king or queen but by the leading member of the particular family concerned in the marriage.[46] Indeed, for literature and the history of art, costume, and music, some of these masques might be considered more interesting than one or another particular masque given by the queen, but prestigious sociopolitical events are not necessarily determined by the aesthetic excellence of their theater. Thus, however many wedding masques survive in text and might even have been produced during the nine years that Anna was interested in masquing, they could hardly have "overshadowed" the queen in any respect, whatever their literary merits.

In practice, then, when the Christmas season was at hand, Anna of Denmark often used the holiday revelry as the context for mounting a masque, such spectacle being, after all, traditional at continental courts and traditionally led by their queens.[47] But it is significant for our sense of Anna's general influence on the high culture of the early Stuart court that even at the outset of her reign, masques were not for her an inevitable annual event. Instead, the queen seems to have masqued when she saw fit, just as she would *cease* masquing when masques no longer seemed to suit her. Mere statistics make the point. Anna reigned through sixteen holiday seasons in England before she died at age forty-five in 1619. During this time she planned only seven masques, the seventh masque being cancelled out of deference to the death of the queen of Spain shortly before the beginning of the 1611–12 holiday season.[48] Thus Anna's sixth and final masque occurred only halfway through her reign in the holiday season of 1610–11 when she had just turned thirty-seven, and the fact that she never resumed masquing after this season emphasizes the limits of her relationship to this particular activity.

In the end, to appreciate any cultural contribution to the art of the period inherent in Anna's masquing, we must situate it in the context of her general approach to the problem of her role at court as queen consort. Thus, instead of viewing the rationale of her masques as the fulfillment of the theories of Samuel Daniel, Ben Jonson, and Inigo Jones, we should regard them as art in service of the queen's attempt to solidify a nebulous royal role. Consequently, it is interesting to note signs from the early years of the reign that James found this masquing to be useful for his own purposes. Commentary to this effect surfaces in the year after the presentation of *Vision*—that is, during the winter holiday season of 1604–5, famous in masque history as the occasion of Jonson's first effort in this kind, *The Masque of Blackness*. This occasion, in fact, serves to clarify further the inherent political advantages in the matter of masquing that Anna herself had been exploiting so skillfully.[49]

At some point after 7 December 1604, the king, hunting at Royston, wrote to the Privy Council observing that the absence of a masque during this second Christmas of his reign might, after the elaborate presentation of the year before, connote some "ominous presage." This move might have been at Anna's behest, but whatever the initial impulse, it was James who now apparently suggested that a masque by the queen might feature "fine ballets or dancing," his words seeming to some commentators to underscore the traditional portrait of the superficial Anna busied with festive pastimes. But since James could hardly have forgotten the ten years of hard political Scottish experience with his consort, he may simply have hoped that these masques, the queen's innovation, after all, would thus continue to absorb her attentions. Whatever the case, the Privy Council responded to James by informing him that another masque would cost £4,000. This financial figure apparently caused James to pause, for he wrote back to suggest to the Council that the queen herself could finance a masque by using the funds of her own court and also by requiring her ladies to pay for their own costumes. If this wasn't possible, the king continued, then let other Christmas plans be made — for "jousts or barriers" perhaps — male activities, incidentally, involving the younger noblemen.

The Privy Council's response to these suggestions, in the only one of its letters surviving from this interchange, serves to define, by its disagreement with the king, those expectations that Anna had already managed to establish by late 1604 anent her masquing. It begins by indicating the Council's (Elizabethan) concept of when court masquing was appropriate: "Many Christmases pass without any such note; dancing, comedies, plays, and other sports having been thought sufficient marks of mirth, except some great strange Prince or extraordinary marriage fall in that time."

This point conceded, the Council goes on to offer some contrary observations that James then seems to have taken seriously. The Council notes that if there is indeed to be a queen's masque, then James, rather than trying to think of ways to avoid paying for it, had better "resolve beforehand that the expense must be your own." Drawing perhaps on the experience of those Scots who now formed part of the English Privy Council, the letter to James opines that the queen will "think it a scorn to draw such as are fit to attend her Majesty and suffer them to be at charges." More important, as an indicator of how Anna had already politicized the masque, the Council also observes that abandoning the idea of a Christmas masque merely "for the saving of £4,000 would be more pernicious than the expense of ten times the value." For if foreign ambassadors noted that an event at the English court had been cancelled merely because it cost the sum of £4,000, then "the judgment that will follow will be neither safe nor honorable."[50] That is to say, opinions might be formed regarding either a hidden financial weakness in the kingdom that might tempt aggressive international exploitation, or a lack of appropriate "greatness" — of magnanimity in the quality of England's monarch himself.

This analysis was apparently accepted by the king, which suggests the increased political relevance of royal masquing. As a result, *The Masque of Blackness*, Jonson's own first script for Anna, made its appearance. *Blackness* has attracted much attention recently regarding its suggestions of colonialist and racist conceptions in early modern England,[51] but the focus of the present discussion is how Anna used these spectacles to concentrate court attention on herself, her ladies, and their relationship to other members of the nobility. Thus, *Blackness*, for my purposes, is mainly relevant in that it shows the same seven noblewomen—generous patronesses of the arts themselves—dancing with Anna for the second successive year: the countesses of Suffolk, Bedford, and Derby, and the ladies Susan de Vere Herbert, Penelope Rich, Audrey Walsingham, and Elizabeth Howard. And again we note a "visiting quartet" in the persons of four ladies (three of them married) selected to make up the twelve. Because these visitors might have been invited for any number of reasons, those offered here are merely possibilities illustrative of the use to which the masquing of the queen could now be put.

One visitor was a Howard, Ann Lady Effingham, married to the earl of Nottingham's heir. As daughter-in-law of the prestigious Lord Admiral, who was about to travel to Spain to sign the Spanish Peace for King James, she was an appropriate substitute for Nottingham's young wife. The countess may not have danced this year because of a growth on her face, or perhaps because the queen did not like her, but Anna could nonetheless have decided to honor the Lord Admiral through Lady Effingham.[52] The three other visitors were from the Essex group. One was Frances Lady Bevill, sister-in-law of the present earl of Rutland, who was one of the old Essex circle, close to Bedford and Southampton. Lady Bevill was married to Rutland's brother (who succeeded him to the earldom). Another was Lady Mary Wroth, the daughter of Queen Anna's Lord Chamberlain, Sir Robert Sidney. The third visitor was the unmarried Lady Anne Herbert, the sister of the earls of Pembroke and Montgomery.[53]

The presentation of *The Masque of Blackness* seems to have taken care to indicate the status of these women vis-à-vis each other even at the outset when the black daughters of Niger were first revealed as seated in a great concave, four-tiered shell. The front tier was occupied only by Queen Anna and the countess of Bedford. The countess of Hertford was herself still a lady of the exclusive Bed Chamber, a rank she shared with Bedford, but she had measles this Christmas and could not appear; otherwise, one presumes, the front tier would have held three, not two figures. That the other ladies were parcelled out into the last three tiers,[54] and that Anna did, in fact, restrict this first tier to herself and Bedford emphasizes how the physical deployments of masquing were revelatory of court status. Accordingly, we are presumably viewing Anna's (not Ben Jonson's!) order of preferences when, as Part 1 unfolded, the twelve daughters of Niger advanced in couples toward the courtly onlookers.

The Queen and the countess of Bedford
Anne Herbert and the countess of Derby
Lady (Penelope) Rich and the countess of Suffolk
Frances Bevill and Anne Effingham
Elizabeth Howard and Susan (de Vere) Lady Herbert
Mary Wroth and Audrey Walsingham

Since the queen, three countesses, and a baroness constituted the first three couples, it seems reasonable to guess that the unmarried Anne Herbert was being shown great honor in her placement here as a compliment to the countess of Pembroke, her mother, and to her brothers, the earl of Pembroke and Philip Herbert (married to Susan de Vere). That the subsequent takings-out of the masque extended the social and political statement is a reasonable assumption, although little specific information concerning choices of partners is available except for a reference to the taking-out of the ambassador from Spain, who, in turn, danced at some point with the queen.[55]

There was, however, considerable commentary on court activities throughout this Christmas season, the sensation of *Blackness* being no small part of an extremely crowded social calendar. The de Vere–Pembroke wedding on 27 December, as one contemporary noted, was not only a wedding of two favorites but also the symbolic bonding of the Pembroke and Oxford houses. Thus the bride was led to church at Whitehall between Prince Henry and Queen Anna's visiting brother, the duke of Holstein, and King James stood in for Susan de Vere's father, who had just died. As was the case with Anna's masques, all the leading nobles and ambassadors expected to be among the guests and vied for invitations.[56] Further, the following Sunday (the same day as *Blackness*), in a far more significant ceremony, the four-year-old Prince Charles was invested as duke of York — the first English duke to be created since the execution of the duke of Norfolk. The royal child was carried by nine earls to the elaborate investiture; moreover, eleven new Knights of the Bath, lodged and feasted at court for three days before the ceremony, were created at the same time (*SPV*, 12: 472).

It does not appear, however, that Anna's masque was in any way eclipsed by these events, since it prompted strong if contradictory responses. Writing disapprovingly to Winwood, Carleton provides graphic images of the noblewomen's makeup and apparel: "Their apparel was rich, but too light and courtesan-like for such great ones. Instead of visards their faces and arms up to the elbows were painted black which was disguise sufficient, for they were hard to be known but it became them nothing so well as their red and white, and you cannot imagine a more ugly sight than a troop of lean-cheeked Moors. . . . [The Spanish ambassador] took out the Queen and forgot not to kiss her hand, though there was danger it would have left a mark on his lips." [57]

But in his report to the Doge of 27 January 1605, Nicolo Molino, ambassador from Venice — a city-state that Shakespeare's *Othello*, given during this same Christmas season, depicts as more familiar with blackness than was Hampton Court — had a very different impression: "[I was] conducted to the King's chambers where his majesty appeared about the seventh hour and moved on to the place where they gave the masque, which was very beautiful and sumptuous" (*SPV*, 10: 213).

Moreover, more than two weeks earlier, on 10 January, Ottaviano Lotti, secretary to the Florentine ambassador, had written his own government: "Her Majesty the Queen's masque was performed on Twelfth Night, in truth with much more magnificence and rarer invention than the other [Susan de Vere's wedding]. Also it was staged in a larger room which was most richly adorned, quite apart from the assembly of so many of the nobility, which made a lovely sight." [58] The French ambassador, M. de Beaumont, concurred. Omitting any mention of blackness, he wrote on 12 January to Villeroy in France about "ce superbe ballet" (*superbe* being an adjective that could mean both "splendid" and "arrogant"), with, as the Privy Council had hoped, no imputations of poverty to the Kingdom of England.

In sum, *Blackness* seems to have been the same kind of vehicle — no matter the differences effected by a Jonsonian script — as *Vision*, in that for both masques Anna devised a structure in which she and her court became a spectacular presence in a glittering and politically symbolic social season. Like the queen's future masques, these early spectacles fulfilled a new set of grandiose expectations at court, expectations which Anna herself, with the help of her carefully chosen circle of nobles, deliberately shaped.

But no matter how much it has misled commentators about the interests (and hence, perhaps, the negligible court presence) of the new queen, Anna's Christmas masquing can hardly be taken as even the defining metaphor of the queen consort's potential effect on the assemblage of delicate balances which are the sum of any royal court situation in the late sixteenth and early seventeenth centuries. Rather, any intangible prestige accruing to her royal position through ceremony could manifest itself in more compelling ways than Christmas masquing with her cultured noblewomen. Indeed, though this has not been remarked, *The Masque of Blackness* itself actually heralded Anna's temporary cessation from presenting these elaborate shows. The time elapsed between *Blackness* and Anna's next masque, not presented until Christmas 1607–8, suggests that such spectacles — if it were a question of enhancing the status of England's queen consort through ceremony — could be heavily reinforced by more solemn ritual and ceremony. Masques, in fact, yielded, after *Blackness*, to quite a different kind of theater.

Anna had been six months pregnant when she danced *Blackness*, so the ceremonial splash achieved by an evening's masquing was quickly eclipsed by a new queenly figuration: Anna as Consort, Spouse, and Progenitrix, soon to give royal birth surrounded by such ceremony as that which was pertinent to a queen's pregnancy, lying-in, and delivery of a new child — ceremony denied Elizabeth I. Given the statistics of mortality in the period, in fact, the bearing of an infant who might indeed survive as potential heir (*vide* the birth of Charles) to the throne was always fraught with a suspense that dwarfed any masque.

Anna would undergo this experience — this display? — twice in England before 1610. Soon after her first English baby was born, Anna would again become pregnant. The first time around, the thirty-two-year-old queen consort, in the three months after *The Masque of Blackness*, was the center of ceremonials that were achieved at considerable expense and demonstrate dramatically that a queen was by no means wholly dependent on Christmas masquing for riveting the attention of the court upon her person. The "lying-in," for instance, was an important process. Samuel Calvert wrote of the "great preparation of nurses, midwives, rockers, and other like offices to the number of forty or more" as the queen, her "great ladies," and the young princes removed in the spring of 1605 to her palace at Greenwich. There the earl of Suffolk, as the *king's* Lord Chamberlain, was personally responsible for ordering the lying-in chambers, including the actual bed in which Anna would give birth. This bed was so elaborately wrought and decorated as to cost £15,593.14.8, almost four times the amount of one of Anna's masques. Further, there was "great preparation for the Christening Chamber, and costly furniture provided for performance of other ceremonies." [59]

Six midwives stood by, although the queen did not speak with any of them nor would she indicate which she would employ "until the easiness or hardness of her travail doth urge her to it." The queen "expects her delivery every hour," continued Calvert on 6 April, "and prayers are daily said everywhere for her safety." Finally, Anna's delivery of a baby girl on 8 April set in motion a political theater extending beyond Anna herself. James seized the opportunity to name this new English princess after his mother, Mary, whom Queen Elizabeth had executed. Two days after the birth, James ordered the building of "two stately tombs," one for Queen Elizabeth and one for his decapitated mother.[60] Such political symbolism was followed by events of greater practical importance to courtiers, since such a royal birth was most often the occasion of the drawing up of an honors list. Significantly, this list seems to have been determined by the queen herself.

Roland White, for example, wrote the earl of Shrewsbury that "against the christening, at her Majesty's earnest desire, these shall receive honor by creation." He then named the nobles who were to be elevated in a great ceremony to be held on 4 May and witnessed by the greater part of the nobility of England. Thus, although it is not generally recognized, three of the better-known earls of the period came to their titles at this time, and quite possibly nominated by the queen herself—even though James cannot have greatly objected to any of these persons.[61] Robert Cecil, already Viscount Cranbourne, became earl of Salisbury, and his brother, Baron Burleigh, their father's heir, became earl of Exeter. The earl of Pembroke's younger brother, Philip Herbert, was created Baron Herbert of Shurland and then immediately earl of Montgomery. Finally, the birth of Princess Mary also brought the queen's Lord Chamberlain, Robert Sidney—whose original appointment had been made against the wishes both of James and Cecil—new status as he was created Viscount L'Isle: not quite an earl, but no longer a baron.[62]

These celebratory creations of 4 May were followed, on the next day, by an event which more specifically foregrounded the queen consort, even though Anna was absent from the proceedings. I refer to Princess Mary's christening, which took place as Anna herself remained in that conventional forty-day seclusion that preceded her churching. Yet it was Anna's, not James's, palace that occupied center stage at this time. On this Sunday all three courts at the palace at Greenwich were railed in and hung about with broadcloth. Then, between four and five in the afternoon, the infant made her appearance. She was carried down from the queen's apartments, through both of the great chambers, through the hall where the king was, and then down the winding stairs into the conduit court. There, at the foot of these steps, around a canopy borne by eight barons, was assembled the crowd of the peerage and higher clergy: barons, earls, and bishops. With the baby now under the canopy, the nobles led a procession to the chapel.[63] I omit account of the subsequent christening ceremonies here to emphasize what would follow as concerns Anna. Her absence from the christening only sharpened anticipation of the ceremony of her own reappearance. She finally returned to public view on Whitsunday, 19 May. This event was celebrated as the theater of her churching—that ceremonial enactment of her spousal significance as queen consort—as "one flesh" with the king.

Six days before this event, on 13 May, the Florentine ambassador, Lotti, had noted that "from next week her Majesty will let herself be seen in public, and beautiful tilts will be held in those days as is the custom, along with other festivities of mirth."[64] And when that Sunday arrived, it was Anna who held center stage, for in the elaborately symbolic ceremony of churching, James assumed the role merely of precursor. Accompanied by most of the peers of the realm, he had proceeded by barge down the river to the queen's palace at Greenwich. He moved to the royal chapel of the palace to occupy the same elevated stall from which he had previously looked down upon the christening of Princess Mary, and again he listened as the bishop of Chichester preached a sermon to the assembled peers. Afterward James moved down into the chapel where he offered his besant (the gift that the monarch traditionally presented to God when taking the sacrament) at the altar. Then, withdrawing to the side, he closed himself off behind a rich "traverse" or curtained-off area to the right of the altar and waited.

Queen Anna, with a great train of ladies, had been moving down from her apartments in procession and was now escorted to her private stall overlooking the assembled nobles. She remained there until King James's cousin, the duke of Lennox, and Anna's brother, the duke of Holstein, the godfathers of the new princess, accompanied her to the chapel floor and up the aisle between the stalls of the assembled nobility to the main altar. Once there, she made a low reverence, offering her own besant. This done, she moved aside to her own traverse at the left of the altar, on the side opposite to that where James was secluded. The service continued, but at its conclusion, both king and queen moved out from behind their separate traverses, meeting at the altar and "embracing each other with great kindness." Hand-in-hand and led by a procession of earls and barons, the royal couple then came down the aisle, out through the portals of the chapel, back through the conduit court, and up the steps to the palace. Moving through the great hall they continued up the stone steps until they arrived at the portals of the king's presence chamber. There, doing great reverence to each other, the royal couple separated. Having, as his subject, escorted the king to his chambers, Anna now moved to her own rooms.[65]

If the cost of the whole royal childbirth sequence — almost three times that of a Christmas masque — indeed inhibited queenly spectacle for the Christmas season of 1605–6, the symbolic trade was obviously — and would continue to be — well in the queen's favor as regards the effect on her relevance and thus on her court "presence." Further, in November 1605 she must have known that she was again pregnant and could anticipate another royal birthing drama for the late spring. The arrival of a second royal child in fourteen months would coincide with another reminder of Anna's significance: the long-anticipated visit by her brother, Christian IV, king of Denmark. Because she had danced in *Blackness* when six months pregnant, appearing in another masque when only four months pregnant may not have daunted her. But she may have abstained from masquing in that 1605–6 Christmas season because of the expected expenses of another childbirth sequence added to the pomp of the royal Danish visit.

Again, though, the omission, from the viewpoint of self-presentation, would seem to have been well worth a missed masque. In January 1606, Mary was eight months old. The new princess would be joined by another, almost coincidentally with the visit of Christian. And thus Anna, after her next churching, would be appearing with James and with Christian IV as the wife of a king, the sister of a king, the mother of the future king with two infant princesses to add to the three royal children she had already produced. In the end, however, 1606 proved not a happy time. Sophia, born on 22 June and named after Anna's mother, died the next day. So this time there were no honors and, of course, no elaborate christening ceremony. Instead, the ceremony of Sophia's burial was held on the following Thursday during which she was conveyed on a barge covered with black cloth up the river from Greenwich and buried in the presence of the Privy Council and "all the lords."[66] Although Anna undoubtedly gained an emotional respite when Christian visited her privately, she could not join him in the public festivities of his visit until 3 August, when she was again churched.[67] But then on 23 September, Princess Mary also died. Thus it seems understandable that, for the second consecutive Christmas, and perhaps for many reasons other than cost, Anna did not offer a masque.

This double hiatus is not overly obvious to the casual glance because it would seem as if Christmas masquing at court continued unabated. In each of these seasons (1605–6, 1606–7), a wedding masque furnished entertainment that was not in the class of the queen's presentations because, essentially, they were "family" affairs with the groom's family usually paying most of the bill.[68] In January 1606, Ben Jonson's *Hymenaei* celebrated the crucial union between the young earl of Essex and Frances Howard, daughter of the earl of Suffolk, an alliance advocated by Robert Cecil, whose own son and heir had married Frances Howard's sister. This was a futile attempt to effect a reconciliation between the Howards, implicated in the execution of the earl of Essex, and the extensive network of the dead earl's own relatives and supporters.[69] By the same token, the 1606–7 Christmas following the deaths of the little princesses was marked not by Anna's masquing but, again, by a noble court wedding, the scant critical attention accorded it suggesting how strongly the towering literary reputation of Ben Jonson (who did not write this script) has virtually identified him with the very existence of these presentations. But Sir James Hay, one of King James's earliest and favorite young gentlemen of the Bed Chamber, was married this Christmas to the heiress Honora Denny. It was Thomas Campion who was commissioned to write the wedding masque, which was danced by nine men, including Theophilus Howard, Lord Walden, son and heir of the earl of Suffolk (to whom, in fact, Campion dedicated the printed script of the masque). Perhaps for the same reason that she did not masque this year, or because of her continued coolness toward the Howards, Anna declared herself ill and did not attend.[70] The event again makes the point, however, that though masques in some form seem now to have been an annual fixture for the Christmas revels at court, Anna of Denmark herself masqued more sparingly than is generally assumed.

Indeed it was not until the Christmas season of 1607–8 that Anna staged the third of her six masques, *The Masque of Beauty*. It was received by the court in a manner emphasizing that the queen's own spectacular shows had come to be viewed as especially significant court occasions, highly relevant to the display not only of the queen but of the general European significance of the English Crown. In this particular case, for instance, the new banqueting house at Whitehall now having been completed, James himself seems to have been intent on a particularly emphatic display of English regal magnificence. On 4 January the king dined "in great pomp, with two rich cupboards of plate, the one gold, the other that of the House of Burgundy pawned to Queen Elizabeth by the states of Brabant, and hath seldom been seen abroad [out of the cupboard], being exceeding massy, fair, and sumptuous." John Chamberlain continued: "I could learn no reason of this extraordinary bravery, but that he [the king] would show himself in glory to certain Scots that were never here before."[71] Whatever the specific reason for such display, but seemingly in consonance with it, Anna's *Masque of Beauty* in this same season featured her ladies wearing jewelry said to be quite out of the ordinary. "Whatsoever the device may be," as Chamberlain noted, "and what success they may have in their dancing, yet you should have been sure to have seen great riches in jewels, when one lady, and that under a baroness, is said to be furnished for better than an hundred thousand pounds; and the Lady Arbella goes beyond her, and the Queen must not come behind."[72]

Zorzi Giustinian, the Venetian ambassador, suggests a rationale for the impact intended by James and Anna, both working here perhaps for different but parallel purposes. We recall the English Privy Council warning James not to cancel the masque of Christmas 1604 lest it make the English court seem short of money. Now, reporting to the doge, and having previously observed that it was at James's request that the queen and her ladies were preparing to give a magnificent masque" (*SPV*, 11: 74), Giustinian described the present season's festivities in a highly adulatory manner: "I must touch on the splendor of the spectacle which was worthy of her Majesty's greatness. The apparatus and the cunning of the stage machinery was a miracle, the abundance and the beauty of the lights immense, the music and the dance most sumptuous. But what beggared all else and possibly exceeded the public expectation was the wealth of pearls and jewels that adorned the Queen and her ladies, so abundant and splendid that in everyone's opinion *no other court could have displayed such pomp and riches*" (italics added).[73]

Giustinian's subsequent summary has, finally, much to suggest about his estimation of Anna herself: "So well composed and ordered was it all that it is evident the mind of her Majesty, the authoress of the whole, is gifted no less highly than her person. She reaped universal applause."[74]

"No other court" may speak to the *general* effect purposed both by queen and king, especially by Anna as she displayed for James—through herself and the noblewomen of her court—the magnificence of the English state. But the fact that the masque was Anna's allowed her, it seems, to manipulate it again as an instrument for awarding prestige to others.[75] Traditional accounts of court activity smile at the concept of squabbling ambassadors competing in contests of vanity for invitations to Stuart court masques, but it is difficult to believe that foreign nobles and professional emissaries, products of complex political and aristocratic processes in their own countries, were merely engaged in pluming their own egos. No matter how personally vain any particular emissary may have been, clearly they all understood that these masques had been fashioned as highly selective and significant court occasions, exclusion from which could reflect badly on the position of one's own state vis-à-vis England and thus with neighboring states of the Continent as well. If England, for example, placed less value on the emissary of Henri IV than on the ambassador from Venice, even in as trivial an event as a masque, then perhaps the English perceived a weakness in France that might just bear looking into. Thus, given the growing social prestige her masques seemed to be acquiring, Anna's own control of them may have made her at least obliquely relevant to the interactions of international diplomacy—as indeed had been the case before the first masque of her English queenship.

The recorded reactions of Antoine de la Boderie, the ambassador from the court of Henri IV, aptly indicate Anna's control of these masquings as well as the prestige that she caused them to accrue. In this particular season of *The Masque of Beauty*, La Boderie had complained to the duke of Lennox that Queen Anna intended to invite the Spanish ambassador, but not him, to the masque. But La Boderie had also not been invited to Anna's previous masque (*Blackness*), which the Spanish ambassador had attended. Now La Boderie understood that King James had told Anna that her inviting the Spanish ambassador might again offend the French, but, La Boderie wrote, James's cautioning apparently carried no weight with the queen. It was for this reason that La Boderie was now writing the next highest member of the aristocracy, the duke of Lennox, to observe that King James did not seem to be master in his own house. Lennox, of course, promised to look into the matter, and he went so far as to consult the First Secretary, the earl of Salisbury, and the earl of Dunbar (two of James's closest and most influential political advisers), returning to La Boderie with what was obviously intended as a placating response. Apparently the king was highly grieved (*marri*) at how blithely the queen seemed to have made a commitment to the Spanish ambassador, but there was nothing that could be done about it after the fact. Instead, and in compensation, James now invited La Boderie to dine with him alone.

As regards the prestige accrued by Anna's masquing events, it is extremely significant how La Boderie responded to this special compensatory effort by James to honor him (and France). The ambassador sent word back to the king of England that this royal invitation, rather than ameliorating the situation, made it worse. There was simply no comparison, La Boderie pointed out, between an occasion in which the king might have dinner with La Boderie personally and alone, and the kind of honor that had been accorded the Spanish ambassador by an invitation to the queen's masque! The dinner with the king was merely private activity; the latter—the invitation to the queen's masque—was an opportunity to be part of "un spectacle et une solemnité publique."[76]

It was the obverse of this view, however, that La Boderie—and some commentaries today on James's court—seem not to have grasped. That is, if the spectacle held such leverage, then so did she who was its center: the queen. In the end, we gather from the letter of the French emissary, although James was said to be quite vexed with the queen, she herself had made such an issue of her own prerogative (*prenoit ceci si haut*) that none of the advisers, nor the king himself, dared say anything further to her about the matter. La Boderie apparently could draw only two conclusions from this outcome: that Anna had great partiality to Spain, and that no one could deal with "le pouvoir qu'elle avoit sur son mari." What he apparently did not fully understand—at least according to his correspondence with Henri IV—was that the queen consort, by developing elaborate royal masques as her occasional signature events at Christmas, seems to have created *ab ovo* a complex ceremonial featuring female courtiers, male courtiers, and foreign ambassadors to which she alone was the key. Thus there was more to be considered in connection with a queen's masque than merely a spectacle of ladies dancing in jeweled dresses whom any nobleman, native or foreign, had the inherent right to watch with the king. Rather, overtures had to be made to a different figure, equally royal.

Finally, this same masque indicates some significant changes in the group around Anna by 1606. The queen, perhaps to add to the calculated splendor, had increased the size of the group presenting *Beauty* by another increment of four, inviting not twelve but sixteen ladies.[77] The "regulars" remained the queen and four nobles of her inner circle: the countesses of Derby, Bedford, and Montgomery as well as Lady Audrey Walsingham. But on this occasion the queen also made a generous overture to the earl of Worcester, James's Master of the Horse. Worcester and his countess had seven daughters, four of whom now danced for the first time in *The Masque of Beauty*. What is interesting to note, however, is they too proved not to be temporary visitors. Rather, these four women also danced in two of the three remaining masques of the queen for which the names of dancers are listed, and I am assuming that they probably appeared in the last one, too.

Interestingly, these were not extremely young women. Two of the Worcester daughters had come to Elizabeth's court as maids of honor in 1593, and all four had been married since the middle 1590s.[78] Nor did any of them have politically influential husbands, a fact significantly aligning them with most of Anna's intimates (with the exception of the countess of Montgomery and now the countess of Arundel). Yet, possibly reflecting further on the ambience of Anna's court, two of these ladies (like the countess of Arundel) had superficial connections with the arts that bear further investigation. Whatever the cause, it is important to note that it was the countess of Arundel and the daughters of the earl of Worcester, together with Bedford, Derby, Montgomery, and Lady Walsingham, who after 1606 constitute the core group of women to be found in Anna's remaining masques.[79]

The Masque of Queens, the last of Anna's masques for which there is extensive information available concerning its political deployment, is finally relevant to my point about the role of these spectacles in Anna's addressing of the question of her royalty. Planned for the 1608–9 Christmas season, it included, finally, as a guest the French ambassador La Boderie, who seems to have felt that a full report of the event was necessary. While I shall not attempt a *précis*, I am particularly interested in those of his observations which concern how the masquing occasion manipulated the interaction of political valences. We can infer from La Boderie's comments, for example (as in the case of Zorzi Giustinian in January 1605), that, again, an invitation to the masque was only the first part of the entertainment "package" designed to pay special honor to this ambassador on his designated "day." La Boderie makes clear that, before the entertainment that evening, King James invited him to dinner with only the king and the two princes, Henry and Charles, present, while Mme. La Boderie was privileged to dine with Princess Elizabeth. Later, during the masque itself, La Boderie was seated near the king while Mme. La Boderie, who might be considered as the special guest in the princess's party, was asked owing to the crowding to sit on a bench nearby together with the members of the Privy Council. The Council's coherence as a group in this instance suggests, in fact, the extent to which the seating of the masque audience was itself arranged ceremonially, suggesting the whole affair as a type of state occasion.

La Boderie also offers a new glimpse of how Anna integrated the very form of the masque into her own social and political agenda. I have previously suggested that masques are to be viewed as segmented into five parts. La Boderie's comments suggest that these parts themselves either were, or came to be, separated by short intervals. Indeed, La Boderie thought these pauses were too numerous and dull, but it appears that Anna utilized these *intermèdes* for her own social purposes. At one point, during one such pause, she, though a "performer," actually left the dancing place and, in her costume, approached La Boderie's wife to engage her in conversation with many shows of familiarity ("mille démonstrations de privauté").

The amplitude of La Boderie's report also reveals how carefully calculated the "takings-out" may have been. For example, on this particular occasion, after the nine-year-old Prince Charles had been taken out by a lady of the masque, Mme. La Boderie was again honored when the prince took her out. Further, from one of the French ambassador's other remarks, it seems that Anna had arranged matters here so that she herself planned to honor La Boderie by taking *him* out. Further, and indicative again of the care with which these matters were planned, Anna had that morning evidently sent one of her ladies to La Boderie's chamber in the palace to inform him of her royal intention. But the French ambassador, not considering himself a particularly good dancer and afraid of being laughed at, had asked the queen's lady to consult with Anna about his reluctance. As a result, a different member of the French party, Baron de Bressieux, was taken out by one of the queen's ladies ("fut mené danser") so that he could subsequently ask the queen to dance (necessarily knowing in advance that she would accept), and in this manner the queen was able to honor France by dancing with a representative of that state.[80]

It is not La Boderie, however, but Ben Jonson who leads us to the part of *The Masque of Queens* that Anna calculated most carefully. Although the "device" for the masque had all the five countesses and six other ladies of Anna's court impersonating such historical queens as Bonduca and Zenobia, Anna chose not to represent any such historical female. Rather, she represented herself. That is to say, for the first time she employed the court masque not to symbolize but to *signify* her queenship. Jonson's prefatory remarks to the masque quarto published in the same year (1609) describes the queen's pervasive role here: "The twelfth and worthy sovereign of all I make Bel-Anna Royal Queen of the Ocean, *of whose dignity and person the whole scope of the invention doth speak throughout*" (italics added).

The device unfolded accordingly. Heroic Virtue introduced the House of Fame filled with famous queens of history now resting upon a throne erected in the form of a pyramid. And it seems that, while in this Chaucerian House of Fame, these historical figures were hourly hearing the praises of a Bel-Anna. So they yielded her first place among them as the most queenly of them all.

> The glories of Bel-Anna so well told
> Queen of the Ocean, how that she alone
> Possessed all virtues for which, one by one,
> They were so famed, and wanting then a head
> To form their sweet and gracious pyramid
> Wherein they sit — it being the sovereign place
> Of all that palace and reserved to grace
> The worthiest queen — these without envy on her
> In life desired that honor to confer
> Which with their death no other should enjoy.
> She this embracing with a virtuous joy
> Far from self-love, as humbling all her worth
> To him [James?] that gave it, hath again brought forth
> Their names to Memory, and means this night
> To make her, once more, visible to light.

Anna rested at the top of the pyramid, playing herself, and emphasizing her position of honor by being the last queen to appear in the initial procession-and-exhibition (Part 1) of the masque. In one sense, then, 1609 marked a culmination. The masque was "entertainment," but there was, we may grant, a political achievement to be measured by the fact that, barely six years earlier, the structure of the English court had yielded no vehicle through which a queen consort could have made a comparable symbolic gesture, one most often reserved for the monarch.

Thus, although the confusion of surviving documents might seem to obscure this matter, it is nonetheless possible to discern two agendas in Anna's program of ceremonials. The first — the focus of this chapter — seems to have been aimed at symbolically establishing the very fact of her queenship at a court long accustomed to a monarch without a royal companion. But this agenda connects to another, which contextualizes other masques to be discussed in my final chapter. In this second framework, Anna's ceremonials emerge not simply as opportunities for self-configuration but as part of a long-range program through which she would be allied with the person thought to be England's future king, Henry, Prince of Wales. Here, I would emphasize once again that Anna of Denmark's activities, though enhancing the prestige of a number of peers well known for the importance of their arts patronage, cannot be easily grouped and polarized as "political" in some cases and "arts-oriented" in others. Rather, Anna's contributions to the high culture of the court were complicated by the likelihood that her chief aim, despite her patronage and masquing, was not necessarily the nurturing of the arts. Certainly the patronage networks that Anna consolidated through her court reflected her own artistic sensibilities, but she also seems to have valued the group of noble women — and men — around her as they might help her to attain something more than a utopia for individual creativity in writing, music, and the plastic arts.

In the end, Anna of Denmark thus offers us something of a paradox in the Stuart court situation as it relates to the arts. Her circle was defined by the presence of many of the most active patrons in England, but these same nobles were, as Anna seems to have been, political enemies of one of the most powerful ruling families, the Howards. As such, those earls and countesses in Anna's circle seem therefore to have figured in a different set of projections — Anna's plans for her relation with Henry, Prince of Wales, plans which affected not only the deployment of her last two spectacles but also her engagement with members of her circle who were concerned both with politics and with the arts.

Thus, the last phase of the short-lived Anna's Jacobean career, as well as her last years, cannot adequately be understood except, on the one hand, in the retrospective light of her past behavior in Scotland and, on the other, in her anticipation of Prince Henry's future maturation and ascent to the throne of England. Even after Henry's death, when Anna's engagement with the arts abruptly declined, she still maintained a hand in the play of political influence and counter-influence at court, adjusting once again to altered circumstances. In short, if Anna's *modus operandi* in England shifted more than once, it seems that her fundamental aim — already apparent in her Scottish years — never wavered: to assert a meaningful royalty into the role of queen consort. And it is just this resolution that was so important to artists seeking the patronage of nobles in Anna's circle, because any enhancement she imparted to her queenship inevitably helped empower that circle of cultured peers around her, female and male.

Indeed, although it is difficult to analyze (and outside the purview of this study) the precise degree to which Anna's influence — her distinctive style in appropriating the arts for more complex purposes — affected the larger scene of Jacobean politics, it is at least reasonable to wonder how far this influence did help shape the careers of that period's most famous patrons. To cite one particularly interesting example: Anna had very close ties across a range of common interests with the earl of Pembroke, nephew of her Lord Chamberlain, who, as the dedication on the opening pages of the First Folio tells us, "prosecuted," along with his brother, both the plays of Shakespeare "and their author living, with so much favor." This was an earl — now the king's Lord Chamberlain himself — whom Heminges and Condell hoped would "use the like indulgence toward" Shakespeare's plays as "you have done unto their parent." Given the long-standing involvement of Pembroke with Anna and the members of her court, it is tempting to wonder whether the organizers of the First Folio — and the author that their volume represented — might have been indirect beneficiaries of Anna's queenly insistence on her own royal identity.

5. MASQUING
AND FACTION
PRINCE HENRY
AND AFTER

I have saved for this final chapter my discussion of the masquing with which Anna of Denmark is associated in her later years because those presentations cannot be situated outside of the rather convoluted context of her other court activity. Throughout the first decade of her English reign, when Anna was attending to the composition of her inner circle and her quasi-annual masquings, and the deaths of two of her babies, Anna's focus on protecting and promoting a particular kind of role as an active queen consort seems to have remained constant. Accordingly, her subsequent activities—not only the mounting of a masque such as *Tethys' Festival* but also her presence at several well-known celebrations, such as *The Barriers* and *Oberon*, both featuring Henry Prince of Wales—take on a certain hue when viewed through the prism of Anna's predominating concerns. And so too does Anna's complete cessation from masquing in 1612, which placed her in a different position as regards such culminating spectacles as Samuel Daniel's *Hymen's Triumph*, on the one hand, and Ben Jonson's *Golden Age Restored*, on the other. Indeed, that this latter masque was to feature the newly created earl of Buckingham turns the prism full circle to illuminate an Anna who, as death approached, seemed concerned first and last, as in Scotland, with what it was to be the queen.

A very important object of Anna's attention, it seems clear from the outset of her English sojourn, is indicated by the signs that she intended to exert considerable influence of her own through the agency of Prince Henry, the future king of England. Given her fiercely proprietary attitude toward Henry in Scotland, where she was prepared to go to extraordinary lengths to claim her eldest son, it is hardly surprising that once in England,

Anna moved quickly to strengthen her position. In fact, she sought to increase her relevance to her son's own maturing political position in a manner reminiscent of the single-mindedness of her contestations in Scotland. And though in the period immediately after James's accession, the life of a very young boy, even a prince, was not likely to generate any especially revealing written records, there are two crucial texts that shadow Anna's hand.

The first text is actually a portrait, existing in two states, of the prince and a companion, one state presumably deriving from the influence of James and the other from that of Anna. I suggest this because during his progress from Scotland, King James, making several public gestures of goodwill toward the Essex family, had shown much favor to the earl of Essex's young son, whose title he would restore from its prior attainder after Essex's treason against Elizabeth. Appointing in these early days the boy to be a lifetime companion to Prince Henry, James may also, therefore, have ordered that this companionate relationship be expressed by the portrait of Henry now in the royal collection. Painted by Robert Peake the Elder, it depicts Henry in hunting costume standing over a slain deer: at the left kneels the twelve-year-old earl of Essex in attendance. But if this painting was indeed ordered by the king, its counterpart seems very much to have been, if not in purpose, then in effect, a function of the activities of the queen. Also by Peake, it is actually the *original* from which the former was copied. Now in the Metropolitan Museum of Art, New York, it depicts the youth at the left in attendance on Prince Henry not as Essex but as the fifteen-year-old John Harington, the younger brother of the countess of Bedford, who was the one English lady of Anna's exclusive Bed Chamber.[1] Thus this placement of Harington within the portrait in a position that only a favorite with the prince could have enjoyed, clearly foregrounds a youth closely attached through his sister to the queen's circle.

Because, as mentioned in Chapter 3, John Harington and Henry would remain friends throughout the prince's life, what gives the painting even greater significance is the relevance of this Harington's (and the countess of Bedford's) parents to the royal family. We have seen that the countess of Bedford figured importantly in the English disposition of Princess Elizabeth, the only daughter of Anna and James. Not only did the future queen of Bohemia grow up with the Haringtons, but great affection seems to have resulted (as between Henry and John Harington's son) from the association. When Elizabeth married Frederick V, the elector Palatine, in 1613 and made her new home on the continent, for example, she continued to correspond with Lady Harington, who eventually left England with her husband to visit their former charge.² Yet while these strong emotional bonds united Anna's two older children with the family of her own highest ranking lady, the countess of Bedford, no comparable relationships were generated between these royal children and any person in the circle of King James.

Moreover, after 1604 Anna seems actually to have achieved some unspecified but official custody over Henry of far greater significance than James probably intended when he finally permitted Anna, against his better judgment (see Chapter 2), to travel from Scotland to London in the company of the heir apparent with the earl of Lennox. Once in England, in some benign replication of the Scottish situation, Henry seems not to have been situated in the queen's immediate vicinity at all. He was moved into his own household at Oatlands (the background in the two paintings mentioned above) to live under the governance of Sir Thomas Chaloner.³

But this patriarchally structured situation wherein a Crown-designated governor presided over Henry surrounded by a small court of noble boys did not last long. Only a year later, in 1604, Elizabeth Darcy (wife of John sixth Baron Lumley) sent the countess of Shrewsbury significant news that possibly involved her own husband:

The Prince's house is dissolved, and I perceive there will be great industry used to get Mr. Murray [out] of his place: Sir Thomas Chaloner's board is quite taken away, and the young youths about the Prince go most of them to the university except the two earls [Essex and Dorset?], and Mr. Harington. . . . There was speech that the Prince should have an able man to look to him in Court, whereto my Lord of Shrewsbury was named; but now I hear the Queen will look to him herself.⁴

Anna had obviously assumed virtual control of the young prince's circumstances, with Henry's friend, John Harington, surviving the drastic dissolution of the group of noble boys who had made up the court at Oatlands. The implication is that Henry would no longer remain at one location, removed from the queen; instead, with the king often absent at his hunting lodges, Henry would accompany the queen, traveling with her wherever she established royal residence. Thus by 1604, as opposed to the alienating situation in Scotland, the queen may have had almost constant access to Henry from the time he was ten until his accession as Prince of Wales at the age of sixteen when he acquired his own palace.

Clearly it is impossible to ascertain the extent of intimacy between an early modern mother and her son, especially in aristocratic circles (*vide* Lady Capulet and Juliet), but indications are that the queen was constantly solicitous of Henry's very presence. Zorzi Giustinian, the Venetian ambassador to England, writing the doge in late June 1607 (Henry now being thirteen) that, as instructed, he would pay a call on the prince, put it this way: "I will do so when I go to visit the Queen who is devoted to him and never lets him away from her side" (*SPV*, 11:10).⁵ Nor was Henry ever estranged, it seems, from John Harington. Two years later, in 1609, when Prince Henry was fifteen, the English ambassador residing in Venice gained an audience with the doge to inform him, among other things, that Harington would be requesting access to the Venetian ruler, and the English ambassador took some pains to make Harington's status clear. He described him as "a youth but little over sixteen, son of Lord Harington. . . . The sister of this young gentleman, the Countess of Bedford is the Queen's favorite maid-of-honor; and the Princess, Her Majesty's only daughter, is brought up at the house of Lord Harington, father of the youth, whose mother is governess to the Princess. Add to this that it is thought certain that the young man will marry Lord Salisbury's only daughter, and being the right eye of the Prince of Wales, the world holds that he will one day govern the Kingdom."⁶ Expanding on Harington's friendship with Henry, the ambassador recalls to the doge that "when the Prince with tears in his eyes" took John to the king "to ask [for Harington's] leave of absence [from England], his Majesty said to him [Harington,] 'What hast thou done John'—that is his name—'that thou art so master of the Prince's favor—tell me what art thou hast used?' "

Needless to say, Harington secured his audience with the doge, and it speaks well for the young man's perceived status that during the interview, the English ambassador himself apparently remained standing, the more to honor Harington.⁷ After he had talked with young Harington, the doge himself commented, "We do not wonder the Prince loves him; he deserves it" (*SPV*, 11:389).

Continuing to describe the prince's attitudes as they illuminate Anna's own potential role at court, we should note that the prince was not such putty in all hands. At a time rather closely preceding this—16 December 1608—Henry had complained to King James that he was living too far from significant court activity. After James told his son he might make whatever arrangements he liked, Henry, according to Marc'Antonio Correr, sent word to no less personages than the earls of Southampton and Pembroke (both inducted into the Order of the Garter by James in 1603) to move their households and their horses so that he himself could occupy their lodgings at the palace. The earls both refused, so "the prince had them removed by his people to the indignation of these gentlemen who are of very high rank.

This is a great proof of spirit on the part of the Prince who, though only fifteen years of age, gives the highest promise in all he does" (*SPV*, 11:206).[8]

Thus, in 1610, when the time came for Henry's installation as Prince of Wales, the attendant ceremonies and Henry's response to them suggest the nascent influence with which Anna was leaguing herself. Twenty-four Knights of the Bath, created only at coronations and installations such as this, had been chosen for this solemn occasion in the life of the state, and among these knights (usually young nobles who had not yet come into their future titles) were several earls and barons. In fact, Correr remarked that Henry, "who wishes this solemnity to prove as magnificent and pompous as possible," paid special attention to the list of these knights, crossing out the names of those who were not to his liking. Further, after his installation, he would spend the fall settling his household and ordaining his officers, as gentlemen vied for these appointments, "and yet there is not one who dares to attempt the way of favoritism, for although his highness does nothing without the King's permission, yet he is extremely particular that everything shall be the result of his own choice."[9]

The distortive effect of premature deaths on historical narration is thus nowhere better exemplified than in this case. In those two years following Henry's installation, courtiers were seriously reckoning with Henry's attitudes, present and future. These were relevant to the possible influence of persons especially attached to the strong-willed heir apparent, but Henry's death precluded these same persons — young John Harington and his sister, the countess of Bedford — from figuring in the political chronicles of a future that subsequently belonged not to Henry but to Prince Charles.[10] And the same situation governs, I think, our received historical sense of Anna of Denmark. There are important indications of the developing relationship between Henry and his mother as he moved into his manhood — a relationship that may, in the end, as easily have sprung from similarity of temperament as from the queen's careful planning. "Developing" is, in fact, a particularly appropriate word, because it is possible that Henry resisted being snatched from Stirling at the outset of the Jacobean reign by a mother who may have been a virtual stranger. But the elaborate court entertainments that took shape two years before Henry's death in November 1612 can be fully appreciated if we view it, too, as an expression of the relationship with her son that Anna had carefully cultivated for almost a decade.

The date of Henry's installation as Prince of Wales was set for June 1610 — after which time he would have his own palace, court, and courtiers in a sphere of influence destined to become increasingly powerful as the time approached for Henry's coronation as Henry IX of England. In anticipation of this momentous event, the revels of the Christmas season 1609–10 featured Henry in "barriers," an elaborately scripted and stylized medievalist tournament involving fifty-eight "defenders." This year the barriers preempted the Twelfth Night date that Anna usually appropriated for her masques, though she would scarcely have objected to this substitution and may indeed have encouraged it. This spectacle, which marked the future king's first public court appearance as a man in arms, was, in costly show, fully equal to a masque, and judging from what the prince was exposed to and what was expected of him, the affair indeed much resembled the masque in that the ceremony was almost more important here than the immediate activity.[11]

The whole began on Saturday, "before ten o'clock at night," and the visual impact of this ritual must have been impressive. To begin the event, the ambassadors from Venice and Spain being present, and to the accompaniment of speeches following scripts written by Ben Jonson, the prince and his party proceeded into the middle of the hall in the new banqueting house at Whitehall, all on horseback.

There the Prince performed his first feats of arms, that is to say at Barriers against . . . six and fifty brave defendants consisting of earls, barons, knights, and esquires who in the lower end of the room had erected a very delicate and pleasant place . . . from whence in comely order they issued and ascended into the middle of the room where then state the King and the Queen and ambassadors to behold the Barriers with the several shows and devices of each combattant.[12]

The bouts continued into the next morning, each "bout" consisting of two "pushes" with the pike on horseback against a similarly armed opponent, and followed up with twelve sword strokes. The prince gave or received thirty-two pushes and about 360 sword strokes, but after this demonstration of masculine strength, there followed ceremony of a different kind. On Sunday, the day after the barriers, the prince feasted all the combatants at his palace, St. James, giving rich prizes to the three best contestants.

As for the queen, she had deferred her own celebration of Henry to the time of his investiture in June, preferring to mark this premier event, rather than the preceding Christmas, with her masquing. It is thus significant of her personal tastes that she chose Samuel Daniel, the script writer of the first masque of her reign, for this occasion. For although Ben Jonson, of course, continued to script her Christmas masques, Daniel was obviously the writer she called on when she wanted to mount a spectacle of great personal significance.[13] Accordingly, preparations began as early as 26 February, the masque obviously designed not only to honor the son over whom she had fought so many battles in Scotland but also, I think, to accentuate her own relationship to him.[14] Thus, although Daniel may have written the words of the script and Inigo Jones imagined and designed the scene, it was the queen who chose the dancers in *Tethys' Festival* and who would give final approval as to how the whole mode of presentation was to be configured. The result was a spectacle that not only glorified the new Prince of Wales but also celebrated Anna as queen of England and as the creator of a royal race. With the new Prince of Wales watching the masque as Chief Auditor with his father, *Tethys' Festival* (the festival of the Goddess of the Sea) celebrated Anna Progenitrix by exhibiting the two other surviving royal children whom she had delivered to the world.

The thrust of this spectacle, however, has been somewhat dulled by the misleading emphases inherent in the scripted words of a printed text. Thus, in Daniel's script, Anna's younger son, the ten-year-old Prince Charles, duke of York, simply appears as "Zephyrus," but we learn much more about Charles's presentation here from a letter written by one of the audience. He noted that *Tethys' Festival* was "double" — that there were, in effect, two masques: "In the first came in the little Duke of York between two great sea slaves, the chiefest of Neptune's servants, attended upon by twelve little ladies, all of them the daughters of earls or barons." The printed text of *Tethys' Festival* then notes that as Zephyrus and others entered, the (professional) singers performed a four-part song accompanied by twelve lutes; the last of the three verses emphasized the as-yet-invisible Anna, who would represent Tethys in the principal masque.

> Bear Tethys' message to the Ocean King,
>   Say how she joys to bring
> Delight unto his islands and his seas;
>   And tell Meliades[15]
>   The offspring of his blood,
>   How she applauds his good.

One of the great "sea-slaves," a Triton, then made a speech to the king and prince "expressing the concept of the masque" as the other Triton, we gather from the observer's letter, "bore a sword worth 20,000 crowns [£5,000] at least," which "was put into the Duke of York's hands." Ten-year-old Charles brought the sword to where Henry was seated and "presented the same unto the Prince his brother [as] from the first of those ladies which were to follow in the next masque." This gift, the court was thus told, was from his mother.

Such consistent emphasis on the queen is complemented by the masque script itself, which indicates Anna's other gifts:

> From hence she sends her dear lov'd Zephyrus
> To breathe out her affection and her zeal
> To you great monarch of Oceanus [James]
> And to present this trident as the seal
> And ensign of her love and of your right.
> And therewithal she wills him [Zephyrus], greet the
>   Lord
> And Prince of th'Isles (the hope and the delight
> Of all the northern nations) with this sword
> That she unto Astraea sacred found,
> And not to be unsheath'd but on just ground.
> Herewith, says she, deliver him from me
> This scarf, the zone of Love and Amity,
> T'ingird the same; wherein he may survey
> Infigur'd all the spacious Emperie
> That he is born unto another day.

Henry was thus to temper the sword of the goddess of justice, Astraea, with love, wielding a dually conceived power seen as emanating from both parents, but by means of symbolic objects unmistakably originating with the queen.

After this presentation of gifts, the young Zephyrus returned to his earlier position on the stage, and the same observer (but not the printed text of Daniel's masque) notes that now, around Prince Charles, "The little ladies performed their dance to the amazement of all the beholders, considering the tenderness of their years and the many intricate changes of the dance which was so disposed that which way soever the changes went the little Duke was still found to be in the midst of those little dancers."[16] It was only after these prior shows calling attention to *both* her sons—especially, for the moment, Charles—that the queen and her ladies began the main spectacle. "These light skirmishers having done their *devoir*," wrote the ambassador, "in came the Princesses."

Henry was said to have had an especial interest in the Royal Navy and consequently was associated by many contemporary writers with the sea and with Neptune-like figures, and so it is not surprising that the imaging of *Tethys' Festival* represented Anna's elaboration upon this concept. The female figure Tethys, as depicted earlier in Daniel's *Vision of the Twelve Goddesses*, was the sea goddess who embraced Albion. Accordingly, the device of this "festival" of Tethys was to present all the other dancers, too, as goddesses of bodies of water.[17] Further, the masque opened with a scene depicting the harbor at Milford Haven with boats nodding on the "water." In a central position in front of this naval scene, and dominating it, sat Anna as Tethys on a sumptuous throne. This throne was "raised six steps and all covered with such an artificial stuff as seemed richer by candle than any cloth of gold. The rests for her arms were two cherubim of gold; over her head was a great scallop of silver from which hung the folds of this rich drapery. Above the scallop, and round about the sides was a resplendent frieze of jewel glasses or lights which showed like diamonds, rubies, sapphires, emeralds, and such like."

Reposing at Anna's feet was the goddess of the Thames, the fourteen-year-old Princess Elizabeth. Then, on each side of these two royal figures were structured two elaborate niches each encasing three ladies, there thus being twelve masquers in addition to the two royal women, for Anna and Elizabeth were most likely not dancing.

Proceeding through its five customary parts, which included the takings-out of male nobles, the masque, however, offered an unusual ending by emphasizing again for the courtly audience the concept of royal progeny and perhaps thus the consanguinity of mother and children. For when the masquers retired, a Triton held off the onlookers from making their usual after-masque advance on the refreshments and on the now-unmasked noble dancers. Instead, the god Mercury "most artificially and in an exquisite posture" descended to summon Prince Charles "and six young noblemen" to "attend him and bring back the queen and her ladies in their own form." An artificial grove now appeared containing the queen and her ladies, who were conducted up to the king by Charles and the small noblemen "in a very stately manner." Significantly, children had begun the masque, and they ended it, reuniting the king with the queen.

If this staging made a point about Anna as genitrix and queen, a second one was made in the choice of dancers, emphasizing the exclusivity and solemnity of this occasion. Not only had Lady Arbella Stuart, the king's closest female relative, been invited, to be one of the dancers,[18] but as Samuel

Daniel wrote in his commentary, there was also a special principle of selection for the participants in this spectacle, one that reversed, in effect, the tendency of the Jonsonian masque to use, increasingly, professional dancers and entertainers. Going against custom, *Tethys' Festival*, except for the singers and musicians, allowed no professional participants at all: everyone who appeared in the masque was apparently a courtier. According to Daniel, "In all these shows this is to be noted that there were none of inferior sort mixed amongst these great personages of state and honor, as usually there have been; but all was performed by themselves with a due reservation of their dignity. And for those two that did personate the Tritons, they were gentlemen known, of good worth and respect." But the poet himself can hardly have been the arbiter in such matters.

The important conclusion to be drawn from this event, then, is that *Tethys' Festival* was so much a function of Anna's relationship to the Prince of Wales that its very existence as a masque can only be explained by this relationship. There was no precedent or custom requiring a queen mother to present a masque during the time of the installation of a Prince of Wales, and, indeed, it is highly illustrative of the special bond between Anna and Henry that in 1616, when Charles, owing to Henry's early death, was himself to be installed as Prince of Wales, the queen did not attend the ceremony.

The 1610–11 Christmas season following Henry's June installation as Prince of Wales is, of course, best known for the performance of Jonson's *Oberon*, which has effectively eclipsed an equally important masque (also scripted by Jonson) prepared for the same festivities. This second masque, *Love Freed from Ignorance and Folly*, represents Anna's return to her own Christmas masquing. Indeed, if considered in light of Anna's—not Jonson's—connection to Henry, *Oberon* and *Love Freed* actually suggest an arrangement between Anna and her son jointly to present masques in this (and probably subsequent) Christmas seasons. This important new mode of royal entertainment—with one masque featuring the queen, and the other the prince—has been obscured by a critical tradition that assumes the primacy of *Oberon*, an assumption that originated, ironically, with Ben Jonson himself.

In their printed versions *Oberon* and *Love Freed* convey quite different impressions. Neither masque was printed before both appeared in the Jonson Folio of 1616, but the manner in which *Oberon* is reproduced makes it seem the weightier of the two. This is because Ben Jonson rather heavily annotated the first several pages of *Oberon*, documenting his iconological references. His text of *Love Freed*, the queen's masque of that same 1610–

11 season, is, however, sparing of learned commentary printed at the foot of beginning pages and also of most stage directions. In fact, it is difficult immediately to grasp that the queen and her ladies danced at all in this masque—as they indeed did—when one refers only to the bare, unannotated script![19] But the circumstances informing the publication of these masques are telling. It appears that Prince Henry had expressed an interest in the sources for the symbolism of one of Anna's earlier masques, *The Masque of Queens* (see the epistle introducing the 1609 quarto), and as a result, Jonson had laboriously annotated that printed text. He may have intended the same scholarship for *Oberon*, as witnessed by the first several pages, but when Henry's death extinguished his relevance to the court, the poet presumably lost interest not only in immediately publishing a quarto of the masque that had been danced by a figure mistakenly thought to be England's future king but even in completing the annotations for this stale matter. After 1612 there was a new heir apparent. Nevertheless, the contrast between what Jonson does offer in the way of apparatus for *Oberon* and the dearth of even minimal directions for the queen's *Love Freed* has resulted in an imbalance in critical assessments of the two pieces.

The rationale for considering *Love Freed* on very much an equal footing with *Oberon*, however, and for emphasizing Anna's continued relevance in these matters may, I think, be demonstrated by reference to England's relationship with France at this time. In the previous spring of 1610, the assassination of Henri IV of France had shaken the courts of western Europe and inevitably delayed a treaty that England had been fashioning with this monarch. Henri's successor, Louis XIII, was much too young to succeed to this fractious throne, and his mother, Marie de Medici, had succeeded in seizing the Regency until he came of age. The problem for England was that even though the English king was apparently quite anxious to conclude the planned treaty during the current year, the French queen regent and her own advisers seem not to have been in any special hurry to sign. After strenuous overtures from England, however, Laverdin, one of the marshals of France, was finally to be sent from France as ambassador-extraordinary to be the signatory of this treaty during this Christmas season of 1610–11. As a consequence, as one might expect, certain revelry at the English court was being planned for his expected arrival—not a precisely predictable event at this time of year, considering that the ship carrying the Venetian ambassador from Calais to Dover in 1603 had been blown back across the Channel to France, causing him to take horse to a more southern French port and set sail for Southampton. Laverdin was thus not expected until after the New

Year, at which time his presence at the English court would be accorded special deference and celebrated with much ceremony. Indeed, according to the Venetian ambassador Marc'Antonio Correr, James wanted Anna to "give another masque of ladies; it will precede the Prince's masque." Correr also pointed out that "the masques which the Queen and Prince are preparing are particularly directed to honor this [French] mission which has been sent on purpose at this Christmastide so as to admit of still greater favor being shown to the Marshal."

Given these circumstances, the social equivalence between *Oberon* and *Love Freed*—or even the primacy of the latter masque—is affirmed by how the English court handled what proved to be a long delay in Laverdin's arrival. Anna's masque had been planned for the end of December and Prince Henry's *Oberon* for 1 January 1611. Then Marie de Medici delayed Laverdin's visit so that he would not arrive in England in time for Christmas or even for the Twelfth Night festivities of early January, so the masques were apparently deployed as follows. The Prince of Wales's *Oberon* was to be presented on New Year's Day, with the ambassadors of Spain and Venice in attendance. Anna's *Love Freed*, however, was scheduled for Twelfth Night, usually the most festive holiday date at court, when it was thought that Laverdin would have arrived.[20] It seems clear from these arrangements that it was the queen's, not Henry's, masque that was meant to garnish an extremely delicate diplomatic occasion. Indeed, so crucial does Anna's masquing seem to have been to this occasion that when Laverdin's arrival was again put off until 16 January, the queen was still delaying the presentation of her usual Twelfth Night spectacle. In the end, the French ambassador-extraordinary did not have his first audience with King James until Sunday, 20 January—and Anna's masque was still unperformed. At this point, it may well have been Anna herself who set her own new date, 3 February, an appropriate enough choice, since this was the day after Candlemas, a time that in James's reign often saw plays at court. But in a reversal perhaps even fashioned by the waiting queen, this late date forced Laverdin to put off his return to France, because he apparently felt now he must attend *Love Freed* to avoid insulting the queen (*SPV*, 12:113).

Given this general context, some particular circumstances of the earlier masque of this season—Prince Henry's *Oberon*—serve to reemphasize the importance of the queen not to one but to *both* masquing occasions. I am particularly interested in the plans that the Prince of Wales, perhaps not strongly interested in masquing at all, nonetheless seems to have made for the takings out.[21] Thus, at that point in *Oberon* when members among the courtly auditors were to be invited to dance for the "common measures" (Part 3), "the prince [predictably] . . . took the queen to dance, the Earl of Southampton the princess, and each of the rest his lady. They danced an English [slow] dance resembling a pavanne."[22] When these measures ended, "the queen returned to her place." Next in order would come the faster dances of Part 4, the corrantoes and galliards, for which lesser or younger courtiers were usually taken out by the dancers. But Henry again took out his mother: "When the queen returned to her place the prince took her for a coranta [corranto] which was continued by others, and then the gallarda [galliards] began which was something to see and admire."

This set of galliards ending, the pace of the remaining dances in Part 4 (which could last indefinitely) quickened. Now the prince "took the queen a third time for *los branles de Poitou*, followed by eleven others of the masque."[23] This was extremely unusual attention, as our previous view of masquing at court may suggest, for not only was the queen being taken out still another time by the same dancer, but all the other dancers, rather than each taking out a particular lady, seem to have themselves been programmed to take out the queen in succession. But prior to the completion of this agenda, James presumably wanted the dancing to stop, for "as it was about midnight and the King somewhat tired he sent word that they should make an end." So the masqueraders performed the *sorti*.

If Prince Henry had wished to avoid young, single noblewomen, for reasons Polonius might have approved, there were married countesses who had danced in various of Anna's masques — the countess of Bedford, the sister of Henry's best friend, or the countess of Montgomery, or the countess of Derby — with whom he could easily have danced. But he did not choose to partner such noblewomen, and it seems clear that in the end Henry and Ben Jonson each had his own (different) plan for this masque. Jonson's major homage was to the king, and one of his figures, Silenus, addressed in *Oberon* the following lines to James:

> 'Tis he that stays the time from turning old,
> And keeps the age up in a head of gold.
> That in his own true circle still doth run,
> And holds his course as certain as the sun.
> He makes it ever day, and ever spring
> Where he doth shine, and quickens every thing
> Like a new nature; so that true to call
> Him, by his title is to say: he's all.[24]

But Henry brought an independent discourse, and in the unscripted dancing, which was the most important part of *Oberon*, it was not the fictional
Silenus but the real Prince of Wales who paid homage — with his eleven fellow dancers — to Queen Anna, publicly emphasizing, it would seem, what
the heir apparent deemed (or pronounced) the queen's significance to be.

Thus the impression conveyed in different ways, first by *Tethys' Festival* and then by the double masquings of the following Christmas season
of 1610–11, is that as Henry was accumulating influence, not only was Anna
paying public deference to him, but he himself seems to have been making a
point of recognizing the royalty of his queen mother. Further, the prospect
of dual Christmas masques in the future would certainly have reinforced
the joint status of the two royal figures, as opposed to the queen alone as
cynosure. Holiday plans for the following year, 1611–12, do in fact suggest
such a design, but international circumstances intervened to thwart this
symmetry. Anna and her ladies were indeed rehearsing a masque for this
Christmas when the wife of Philip III of Spain died. The decorum of the
situation seems to have inhibited another queen consort persisting in revels
so soon afterwards, for Anna was said to have canceled her masque for this
reason.[25] The intentions of Prince Henry were otherwise, but his plans for
his own masque in this season have been obscured in a scholarly confusion
of texts. Yet it seems clear that deference to the death of the Spanish queen
consort did not apply to him nor did it even inhibit the presentation of a
number of Christmas plays at court.[26] Indeed, the lack of inhibition in this
respect leads to the surmise that Anna's cancellation may, in the end, have
been a private gesture — possibly a unilateral show of respect to draw attention to the importance of queens consort. As for the prince, however,
the same Revels Account that lists the performance of Shakespeare's *Tempest* at court in 1611 also indicates for January 1612 [n.s.]: "Twelfe Night The
Princes Mask performed by Gentlemen of his High[ness]."[27]

It is a long conceptual leap from the image of Anna of Denmark sharing
Christmas spectacles with the Prince of Wales and celebrating the French
treaty in her lavish masque of 3 February 1611, to the moment three years
later when, on another 3 February, the queen, now in her own new palace,
Denmark House, sponsored *Hymen's Triumph*. A pastoral commissioned
for the wedding of her only Scottish lady of the Bed Chamber and performed only by young women, *Triumph* saw Anna not as dancer but as
audience, now isolated both by Henry's death and by the ascendancy of
Somerset. But the role and relevance of this last entertainment to be as-

sociated with the queen reemphasize the purpose of all the spectacles that Anna marshaled at court. For the events intervening between 1611 and 1614 suggest, again, that any entertainment associated with Anna of Denmark was seldom deployed to feed her frivolity but — on the contrary — to assert her pride of position at court.

After 1610, the pace of the slow-but-steady course by which Anna seems to have pursued an increase in her own influence through Prince Henry, began to accelerate with the rapid succession of deaths in James's political circle. Beginning as early as 1611, the attrition of James's strongest and most experienced advisers proceeded so speedily that by June 1614 George Home, earl of Dunbar, Robert Cecil, earl of Salisbury, and finally Henry Howard, earl of Northampton, all of them central to James's original attainment of the English crown, were dead. James was thus deprived of reliably delegated supervision over large areas of Crown activity, especially by Cecil and Northampton, and his "heavyweight" political circle was virtually emptied. As factional competition arose around this vacuum, one finds a noticeable tendency in the queen consort and the Prince of Wales to act together politically. But the vacuum also provided new impetus to the meteoric career of James's new favorite, Robert Carr, at a time when Anna might not yet have fully consolidated a significant power base with Henry. Carr's relationship to James is thus directly relevant to any assessment of Anna's developing status and influence.

Carr's rise, of course, was a function of his suitability to a long-standing mode of behavior on James's part. The earl of Pembroke's younger brother, Philip Herbert, may, in fact, serve as an early paradigm (although one generally neglected by literary scholars) for the later careers of such favorites as Carr and George Villiers — the future earls of Somerset and Buckingham. Between 1603 and 1605 James had greatly favored Philip, who became a gentleman of the Bed Chamber and one of James's hunting companions. Philip's prospects even enabled him to marry Susan de Vere (the earl of Oxford's daughter, the countess of Derby's sister, and Robert Cecil's niece) in an opulent court wedding during the Christmas season of 1604–5. Several months later, Herbert was in one day created both a baron and then earl of Montgomery. Obviously anticipating — especially in the rapidity of ascent — the court careers of Somerset and Buckingham, the status of the newly made earl of Montgomery nonetheless differed drastically from that of these other favorites. I would suggest that Herbert's failure to exercise meaningful power can be accounted for by the enormous influence of Robert Cecil and the rest of the older men in James's political circle. In 1604–5, these men still engrossed the king's political trust and were thereby crucial to the making of policy. As a result, Montgomery, and a fellow member of the Bed Chamber, James Hay, gained prestigious matches, were allowed glamorous court weddings, and received earldoms (Hay, much later than Montgomery, as earl of Carlisle in 1622), but they achieved little in the way of significant office. Instead, they remained merely members of the king's Bed Chamber, spending most of their time with the king at his hunting lodges in Royston or Newmarket. This was the kind of situation, indeed, still obtaining in 1618 when Antonio Foscarini, writing a general report on England before his departure, described this grouping.

There are eight or ten [gentlemen] who sleep habitually in his very chamber, who can enter when they please, no matter how private his majesty may be, and who have the greatest influence with him. These have mostly been aggrandized by him. He generally prefers one to all the others and raises him to the highest dignities. He then bestows his affection upon another and does the like, but does not entirely deprive the first of his favor, though he restricts it. He acted thus with the Earl of Montgomery, Lord Hay, and many others in England and Scotland who all remain in favor. (*SPV* 15:388)

Robert Carr was more fortunate than Montgomery and Hay, both of whom "peaked" too soon, because Carr's opportunity for special favor came after Cecil's death on 22 June 1612. However, it is relevant to the queen's situation that well before this time—as far back as 30 December 1607 when Henry was only thirteen—Carr had himself been a gentleman of the Bed Chamber.[28] Several years passed before he received further identifiable advancement, although his finances were improved on 10 January 1609 when he was awarded the confiscated estates of Sir Walter Ralegh, Henry being at that time a year away from his installation as Prince of Wales at age fifteen. It was, then, approximately half a year after Henry's installation that the first death among James's advisers occurred. The earl of Dunbar, an old enemy of Anna's, and now helping James rule Scotland, died 28 January 1611, leaving vacant not only his place on the English Privy Council but also his stall in St. George's Chapel at Windsor as Knight of the Garter. Three months later Robert Carr was newly inducted into the Order of the Garter to fill this stall, having a month previously, on Lady Day, also been raised to the peerage as Viscount Rochester with precedence over all barons (*SPV*, 12:135). This latter event, in fact, was the occasion on which courtiers began to talk noticeably about Carr's growing influence.[29]

Thus, even as Robert Carr—now "Rochester"—advanced steadily through the period of Cecil's declining health prior to his death in June and was sworn to the Privy Council in that same month,[30] the kind of remark previously associated with Anna only in her Scottish period begins to arise in English court correspondence. "The Queen," wrote John Chamberlain, "is perfectly reconciled unto him [Rochester] and he hath done her good offices."[31] What had estranged Anna from the favorite in the first place is never stated, but it seems, from this remark, at least, that with the death of Dunbar and the waning of Cecil the Queen's own activities and attitudes were again being noted by male commentators at court—this time not in Scotland but in England.

The competition generated by the passing of Cecil and Dunbar intensified in the aftermath of Carr's promotions. The struggle seems even to have involved the Prince of Wales, whose hand can be detected as early as January 1612 when Rochester received another benefit from the Crown— but this time he was compelled to share it. Awarded the reversion of Sir John Roper's office as chief clerk of the Court of Common Pleas, Rochester was required to hold it jointly with John Harington.[32]

Henry, as Arthur Wilson was later to observe in his contemporary account, "being a high-born spirit, and meeting a young competitor in his father's affections that was a mushroom of yesterday, thought the venom would grow too near him, and therefore he gave no countenance, but opposition to it." Certainly, as Wilson observed, the prince could not have been patient with the notion of a mere favorite such as Rochester pursuing a course parallel to his own as unofficial deputy ruler of England. And Anna seems to have been a natural ally of Henry in such a situation, if only because she presumably feared Rochester's impingement on the growth of her son's prerogatives and on her own increased freedom to maneuver. As Wilson put it, "The Earl of Somerset, new made Lord Chamberlain, succeeding his father-in-law the earl of Suffolk, and the Lord Treasurer [Northampton], successor to Salisbury, were not very acceptable to the Queen, [she] having the same spirit and animosity against Somerset that her son had." And thus, Wilson wrote, Anna "became head of a great faction against him."[33] Accordingly, a month after the death of Cecil, the Scottish Thomas Lord Erskine (Viscount Fenton and later first earl of Kellie), captain of James's guard, wrote Mar in Scotland: "Rochester is exceeding great with his Majesty, and if I should say truly, greater than any that ever I did see; carries it handsomely and begins to have a great deal of more temper; yet can he not find the right way to please either the Queen or the Prince, but they are both in the conceit of his court not well satisfied with him.[34]

That this league of queen and prince was opposed to the interests of

Rochester is clear from remarks made about another office-seeking courtier, Sir Henry Wotton, ambassador to Venice, whom both Anna and Henry seem to have been generally supporting. Chamberlain noted (17 June 1612): "The Queen and the Prince are earnest in Sir Henry Wotton's behalf, and the Lord of Rochester is not willing after his late reconciliation to oppose himself, or stand in the breech, against such assailants."[35] But, of course, whatever open confrontation may have been looming between Anna and Henry against the king's new favorite in the summer of 1612 fell apart in the catastrophic autumn when Henry, becoming ill in October, quickly deteriorated and died on 6 November.

The emotional impact on the queen must have been severe. Aside from the initial prostration and self-seclusion that, following Henry's death, could admittedly have resulted partially from royal posturing, contemporary comments imply a lingering and deeply felt grief. Four months later, the Venetian ambassador Foscarini informed the doge: "I have had audience of the Queen, to whom I did not offer condolences for the death of the Prince. I was advised to act thus, and so have other ambassadors, because she cannot bear to have it mentioned; nor does she ever recall it without abundant tears and sighs" (*SPV*, 12:521). And in November 1616, three years after Henry's death, this grief seems still to have been very much in evidence. At that time Charles was being installed as Prince of Wales, and John Chamberlain wrote Dudley Carleton: "The Queen would not be present at the creation, lest she should renew her grief by the memory of the last prince who runs still so much in some men's mind."[36] Certainly there was no second *Tethys' Festival*.

Aside from whatever emotional reaction the queen may have experienced—obviously we can never know—the crucial political result of Henry's sudden death for Anna's position was the complete dissipation of any emerging court influence keyed on the growing prestige of an heir apparent.[37] Rochester seemingly now had no impediment, growing ever stronger, but this advancement, though well known, has not been correlated with the responses to it by Queen Anna and her own circle of allies and friends. Yet Lord Fenton's observation, in June 1613, made to the earl of Mar in Scotland, may well remind us of comments that sprang from Scottish matters recounted in Chapter 2: "Our present state is at this time in two factions, the Howards one, to whom his Majesty inclines most; the other, Southampton and Pembroke with some of the Lower House."[38]

Fully to understand Anna's own relationship to this polarity—her sometimes overt, sometimes covert role in this factionalism—it is useful to recall how Anna's group was kin to the Southampton/Pembroke faction. Because Anna's Lord Chamberlain was Sir Philip Sidney's younger brother and Pembroke's uncle, and because her first lady of the Bed Chamber, the countess of Bedford, and her husband were friends of and related to many of the members of the Essex group, the queen cannot have considered supporting any other side but that including Pembroke and Montgomery, who was married to one of her ladies. For example, though this has not before been noted, Rochester began encountering resistance from members of Anna's circle. In the following September, it was not Rochester but the earl of Pembroke, a friend of the court of Queen Anna, nephew to *her* Lord Chamberlain, who was sworn to Dunbar's old place on the Privy Council.[39]

In connection with the foregoing, Rochester's relationship with Sir Thomas Overbury requires brief review here because Queen Anna's behavior toward this intimate of the new favorite is an apt illustration of her political involvements at this time. Overbury, a close (English) friend of Robert Carr, had through Carr's influence secured a knighthood and a place in the king's Bed Chamber. By 1611, when Carr had become Viscount Rochester, Overbury was sufficiently close to him to be the individual whom one approached for access to the new favorite. The knight seems, however, to have lacked the discretion to navigate through waters dominated by such sharks as the earls of Northampton and Suffolk, who favored Rochester but had little use for the tactless Warwickshire man who remained Rochester's confidant. Indeed, Overbury's lack of appropriate political skills seem to have become an increasing handicap when Rochester fell in love with the young countess of Essex (née Frances Howard), daughter of the earl of Suffolk and married to the third earl of Essex, the young son of the famous rebel. The course of what may have been a sexual liaison was marked by Frances's visits to Dr. Simon Forman (physician-confidant of a number of well-known women, including the countess of Hertford and Aemilia Lanyer) for love potions and perhaps, later, for other concoctions. Waiving any detailed account of a complex and not-well-understood situation, we may note that when Rochester and Lady Essex seem to have withdrawn from each other momentarily while Lady Essex's relatives put in train an annulment proceeding that would enable her to separate from Essex and marry Rochester, Overbury, in his anxiety to stay connected with the favorite, unwisely made himself obnoxious to King James, and to Rochester's powerful future in-laws. As the favorite of Rochester, the king's favorite who himself had the enmity of Prince Henry and Queen Anna anyhow, Overbury was unwise enough to reject King James's offer of a posting to the continent which would remove him from the scene. Because of this, and for reasons noted below, Overbury was sent to the Tower. Then came this sequence of events. On the morning of 15 September Overbury was found dead in his chambers there after having vomited for several days. On 3 November 1613 Rochester was created earl of Somerset, and on 26 December, Lady Essex's marriage having been annulled, she, as Lady Frances Howard, married the new earl of Rochester.

Rumors of foul play involving Rochester and his wife with Overbury had, however, been circulating since his death. Indeed, almost two years later, in September 1615, and as James was in the process of replacing Rochester with a new favorite, George Villiers, the Governor of the Tower of London sent a letter to the king informing him that one of the warders in had, in the days before Overbury was found dead, been bringing the prisoner poisoned food and medicine. Subsequent investigation implicated the earl of Somerset as well as his new wife, Frances Howard, in the instigation of these multiple poisoning efforts through various intermediaries including those of a "wise woman." The consequence was that both the earl and his countess were imprisoned in the Tower, tried by their peers, and found guilty in 1617.

All these events may serve as the context for Queen Anna's illustrative behavior in the year's before Rochester's fall toward him and thus toward Overbury himself. In 1611, for example, Overbury was suffering from the king's but especially from Anna's hostility. Thus when, on 13 November 1611, Overbury, after a consequent expulsion, was described as being restored to the king's court "by much suit," John Chamberlain added, in this letter to Dudley Carleton, "And there is hope in time to the Queen's favor."[40] The presumed cause for Anna's hostility to Overbury was that she heard him laughing about her when he was on the grounds outside her palace. A letter written by Overbury indicated that he, at least, knew that his problem was with the queen: "As your lordship was a judge of mine innocence before, so would I now crave that favor, that your lordship would vouchsafe to be a witness of the submission both of myself and cause to the Queen's mercy: which I desire you rather because, as I understand, her Majesty is not fully satisfied of the integrity of my intent that way: and to that purpose, if your lordship will grant me access and audience, I shall hold it as a great favor."[41]

Overbury, however, like the earl of Mar in Scotland ten years earlier (see Chapter 2), seems never to have been able to placate an offended Anna. A year after this point, Anna's Lord Chamberlain, writing to his wife, observed that "Sir Thomas Overbury hath leave to come to the court, but neither into the Queen's sight nor of her side." This was five months before Overbury would be committed to the Tower, an incident in which, as Sir Henry Wotton commented in a letter to Sir Edmund Bacon, Overbury's relationship with the queen was still a factor: "It is conceived that the King hath a good while been much distasted with the said gentleman, even in his own nature, for too stiff a carriage of his fortune; besides that scandalous offense of the Queen at Greenwich which was never but a palliated cure."[42]

However, the near-sensational and main event expressing the power struggle between Rochester and the members of the old Essex group, and of Anna's role in it, was the divorce and wedding through which the new earl of Rochester became formally allied to the Howards. Though recently treated elsewhere,[43] such discussion should be supplemented by noting that these transactions of Rochester raised for him an important problem that he may have underestimated. The divorce of his would-be bride, Frances Howard, was canceling a marriage with the young third earl of Essex that had been designed to bind up old wounds and hostilities between the same two groups of nobles—at least this had been Cecil's intent in pushing for that wedding. Now not only must this ceremonial union be unraveled, but the mode of unraveling—the legal justification for early seventeenth-century marital separation—must be effected through a kind of sexual insult.

That is, if Rochester was to become formally allied to the Howards through Frances, daughter of James's Lord Chamberlain, the earl of Suffolk, the grounds for annulment were a pronouncement that the young Essex was impotent and that, as a consequence, the young countess of Essex was a virgin intact. These grounds, supported by Frances's relatives, would inevitably be viewed by Essex's friends as dishonoring the manhood of the young avatar of their beloved second earl of Essex. Thus, although contemporary remarks suggest that both Frances and her husband were equally intent on divorce and may have colluded in the impotence story, which was their only means to an annulment, the emphasis on Essex's impotence, outside of legal contexts, was conceivably a way to cause great offense. Northampton, for example, an important and powerful Howard, had termed Essex "my lord the gelding."[44] In this connection, Fenton, again writing the earl of Mar in Scotland, May 1613, observed:

This same day was there in the Commission Court before the Archbishop a nullity of the marriage betwixt my Lord of Essex and his lady, for he did confess in presence of the Chamberlain [Frances's father], Worcester, and Knolleys, that he could do no thing to her. But since the matter has been intended, it is thought that Southampton and Pembroke have made him go back again, but the matter is in *prorsus* what is done this day. Which is the first I do not yet know, but it is thought for certain that it will be a nullity.[45]

Southampton and Pembroke presumably were sensitive to the social consequences of Essex's admission.[46]

By positioning himself as stallion to Essex's "gelding," however, Rochester was not only alienating a circle. He was also alienating himself further from the queen because of the connection with the Howards and Northampton who, as Frances Howard's great-uncle, was inevitably involved in these matters.[47] In fact, a letter Northampton had written to Anna's old enemy, the earl of Mar, as far back as 1 January 1608, eloquently bears witness to the queen's attitude. Alluding to an ancient Scottish custom of posting the particulars of a sick man's ailment on his front door so that any passers-by might leave off medicines they knew had cured this same sickness in the past, Northampton adapted the motif into significant metaphor:

> If your lordship [Mar] therefore will vouchsafe as well out of your love as of your skill to impart to me the composition of that recipe which drew you after long exile to the favor of the Queen, I shall hold it a very great obligation. For notwithstanding my long labor to gather the best simples and to procure the best ingredients that are to be gotten by the highest compass of my skills, yet my pains are lost, my hopes are spent, expectation is in the wane, indignation at the full, and my conclusion is uncomfortable if not desperate. . . . The disease is like the small pox, for it will run in a blood, and at this instance there is not one of my name, old or young, *priusquam fecissent aliquid boni aut mali* that can escape the whip of this severe chastisement. But God that turneth princes' hearts like mighty rivers can, when it seems good to his providence, redress these wrongs; and in the mean time I will endure with as great patience as it pleaseth the Queen my mistress to make proof of my obedience with austerity.[48]

Such factionalization of the court — and especially Anna's involvement in it — must inform our understanding of those circumstances in which she sponsored *Hymen's Triumph* during the Christmas season of 1613–14. For it was in this very next Christmas season after Henry's death that the "nullity" or annulment between Frances Essex and her husband was approved, while the man who had displaced him, Lord Rochester, was created earl of Somerset in a ceremony that James must have taken some pains to configure as a symbolic reunion of the court. For the ceremony involved six earls: three from James's political circle — Worcester, Northampton, Nottingham — and three deeply and intricately allied with the "Essex group" — Montgomery,

Pembroke, and Southampton. And the *chef d'oeuvre* of the court revels was the wedding of Frances to the new earl of Somerset — a ceremony that must have seemed avatar of his changed status. To this end, as John Chamberlain had put it earlier, "The marriage was thought should be celebrated at Audley-End," the earl of Suffolk's great house in Essex, but "the Queen being won and having promised to be present, it is put off till Christmas and then to be performed at Whitehall." Thus James allowed the elaborate court wedding as the central holiday event, the bride being led in by her great-uncle, the earl of Northampton.[49]

To celebrate this occasion, a masque was written by Thomas Campion (*The Lords' Masque*) and, at the king's expense, presented on St. Stephen's Day. In traditional fashion it was danced by men — male relatives or friends of the bridegroom. But Somerset's own male relations were less well placed than his new relatives-by-marriage, so that most of the dancers were kin of Frances Howard, the group then being filled out with important members of the king's own entourage. Dancing were all of Frances's brothers: the Lords Walden, and Thomas, Henry, and Charles Howard. Also dancing were the young earl of Salisbury (Robert Cecil's son), married to the bride's sister, Catherine Howard, as well as the duke of Lennox, and the Lords Scrope, North, and Hay. The requisite number was made up by members of the other faction: the earls of Pembroke, Dorset, and Montgomery. It is noteworthy, however, that the earl of Rutland (for whom Shakespeare and Burbage had executed an impressa for the tilting of Accession Day in the previous spring) refused an invitation to participate. His older brother had ridden with the "impotent" young Essex's father in the uprising of 1601.[50]

Such a spectacular event at Christmas might also be perceived by some courtiers as a replacement of Anna's own masquing and thus, by inference, as the usurpation by Somerset of Anna's signature event. This is perhaps why Anna seems to have herself effected such a vigorously symbolic displacement of locale during this same season, a displacement that had the effect of distancing the "idea" of her from the king's celebrations, even if she did appropriately preside with James over the Somerset-Howard court wedding itself. But it so happened that Anna's Scottish lady of the Bed Chamber (as we have seen, a highly exclusive group of two, the only other member being the English countess of Bedford) was also getting married during this season. This was Lady Jean Drummond, daughter of Patrick, third Lord Drummond (and kinswoman of William Drummond of Hawthornden); according to one account, she had once been "preceptress to the royal children."[51]

Lady Drummond was contracted to marry the Scottish Robert Ker, Lord Roxborough, and Anna seems to have taken this opportunity to present a marriage celebration as a way of foregrounding the opening of her own newly refurbished palace during this same Christmas holiday season. After four years of reconstruction, Somerset House on the strand had finally been converted to Anna's own royal palace and, unsurprisingly, renamed Denmark House. The remodeling had been extensive, involving the construction of a new court, a new gallery, and new private lodgings, as well as the rebuilding of existing private accommodations. By 1613, in fact, the refurbishment had already cost £34,500, making it one of the most expensive enterprises of James's reign. Thus Anna apparently decided to combine a formal introduction of her new palace in the city with a sponsorship of Lady Drummond's marriage, the whole offering a Christmas counterceremonial to the wedding of the new favorite whom Anna and Henry had consistently opposed. To this effect Anna spent £3,000 on the wedding, and although the ambience of this marriage could scarcely have rivalled in glamour and prestige that generated by the earl of Somerset and his bride, especially after the spectacular annulment of her former marriage, the queen nevertheless seems to have produced an impressively competitive occasion.

Planned for Twelfth Night, Anna's own usual masquing time in the days before Henry's death, the wedding celebration ultimately centered around Candlemas, being held on 3 February 1614, the day following. It included a pastoral, and I think it is quite significant that Anna once again commanded a script from Samuel Daniel, the poet whom she had chosen to write her first court masque and later the masque celebrating Henry's installation, *Tethys' Festival*. And even though there are indications that Daniel did not originally write *Hymen's Triumph* specifically for this wedding, when it became clear by November 1613 that both Lady Drummond and the earl of Somerset were to be wedded, Anna obviously decided to employ the pastoral for her counter-celebration. Why she did so is best suggested by John Pitcher, whose views are informed by his many recent studies of the poet.

One of the things for which Daniel was admired by the Jacobean literati, especially perhaps by the Scots, was his deep knowledge of Italian neoclassical writers, and his ease and skill in their vein. *Hymen's Triumph*, even if it failed to please a certain kind of English taste . . . must have seemed to many of Daniel's contemporaries at court to be an admirable fusion of pure language and neoclassical gracefulness, particularly Tasso's *Aminta* and Guarini's *Il Pastor Fido*. It was this quality which would have appealed most to Queen Anne herself, who ever since she had arrived in England in 1603 had been acquiring a taste for all things Italian—books, music, gardens, and architecture. There are indications that the new buildings at Somerset House were designed to complement and to preserve the English neoclassicism of the original house, even if they were not inspired by Palladio (this was still a year before the appointment of Inigo Jones as Surveyor of the Works).[52]

But the content itself of *Hymen's Triumph* may have been deemed equally appropriate to Anna's purposes. For if the Somerset nuptials had been made possible by the fractious "nullity" decision based on the supposed impotence of a husband, *Hymen's Triumph* seems to pick up on some of these resonances. The god of marriage, Hymen, is said in the published prologue to be "opposed by Avarice, Envy, and Jealousy, the disturbers of quiet marriage." These Vices plan to undermine all the marriages that Hymen makes, dissolving the "strongest knots of kindest faithfulness."[53] Beyond such touches, the pastoral might be even more informative of Anna's purposes were it known what persons enacted it. But though there is no way of finding out who the performers were, John Chamberlain's usual misogynist tone does convey some relevant indications. Observing that the queen meant to celebrate the wedding with "a masque of maids, if they may be found," Chamberlain not only suggests that Anna's closely held circle of countesses, all of them married, would not participate, but that in contrast to *The Lords' Masque*, and in the tradition of the queen's own past spectacles, the participants would nevertheless be women. If this is indeed so, then it is not without interest here that this *Arcadia*-like story of pastoral passions, transvestite disguisings, and lovers' quarrels calls for at least eight "male" parts, including Clarindo, described by Daniel as "Silvia disguised, the beloved of Thyrsis," who is loved, in turn, by "Cloris, a Nymph" (*Hymen's Triumph*, 2). If Anna's masques in general had broken the male sway over Elizabethan court masquing by exclusively featuring noblewomen, *Hymen's Triumph* maintained what we might today think of as Anna's feminist stance by a continued insistence on participants of the same gender as that of their cynosure, the queen. This is clear from a contemporary description by the Savoyard ambassador Giovanni Battista Gabaleone, who at the same time suggests the calculated splendor of the occasion. The events took place in

a little courtyard which the queen had wonderfully transformed with wooden boards and covered with cloth with many lights and degrees where all the lords and ladies took their seats. The King sat under a great baldachino; on his right hand sat the Queen and on the left the prince [Charles, age thirteen], close to the King. On a stool a little further forward on the other side sat the French ambassador, close to the Queen. The earls and barons sat on a great bench. . . . In front of this there were other benches where all the countesses sat, then the French ambassadress, then the baronesses.

The Savoyard continues by describing *Hymen's Triumph*, but one remark suggests that the whole was much more elaborate than reported by Daniel's text, also featuring some masquing by male nobles (of which nothing further can be determined): "In this same room was performed a pastoral which, for its gestures and its rich costumes struck me as most beautiful. It had *intermedii* . . . of two most graceful masques performed by young men in very good order." [54]

The celebration at Denmark House continued through the following week, Queen Anna feasting all the nobles who had waited at the marriage, giving them thanks and her hand to kiss. These nobles prominently included (Somerset's enemies) the earls of Pembroke, Southampton, and Worcester — "for she would not be served by any of the King's servants." [55] Thus Anna contrived once again, as in Scotland, to stage a public spectacle that served as counterstatement at a time when a political adversary held strong sway at James's court.

Finally, it must be noted that Anna's removal of her distinctive celebrations from the king's domain at Whitehall and Hampton Court to her own physically separate court at Denmark House, even if meant merely as metaphor, did profoundly alter the mode of the Jacobean court masque. During the remainder of James's reign, that spectacle hitherto associated (when not part of a wedding celebration) exclusively with Anna of Denmark and noblewomen would no longer be a feature of the court Christmas. [56] Although Anna herself was certainly never absent from Christmas celebrations that required the attendance of the royal couple as such, her cessation from masquing seems to have left a void — one that was quickly filled with masques of a different kind. Indeed, it is just this phenomenon which bears best witness to Anna's lasting and transformative influence on the court masque: It was as if the masque, once Anna's exclusive ideational vehicle, was now, perhaps even with Anna's passive assent open for appropriation. For despite her own loss of interest, this prevailing masquing mode as a part of the annual Christmas revelry, a mode established with such effort by Queen Anna, did not now disappear from court. On the contrary, the ultimate compliment to Anna's political instincts is that her newly invented masque was appropriated by James for his own political purposes. [57]

Indeed, one final masque affords yet another turn to the perspective glass through which I have tried to view Anna's importance to the high culture of the early Jacobean court. This masque of 1616 not only emphasizes the profound changes in these annual Christmas court spectacles effected by Anna's loss of interest in them after 1612. It also serves as reminder of how persistent was the "relevance," if not the "influence," of the queen consort as one of the Stuart court's wiliest "courtiers" before her health failed her. Ben Jonson's *Golden Age Restored* is said to have celebrated the ascendancy of Buckingham, an even newer favorite, over the earl of Somerset in 1616, but again I would urge that the political situation adumbrated by this court spectacle can be fully contextualized only after Anna's own intervening activities have been taken into account.

To this end, I return briefly to the time of Rochester's wedding to Frances Howard, which together with his elevation to earl had taken place by the end of January 1614—the same year that saw the introduction to the court of George Villiers, future earl of Buckingham. That Anna herself was central to this situation has often been obscured for literary history by the compressed accounts of Buckingham's "beginnings," but I think it is quite clear that these events were actually made possible by persons of Anna's court working with their friends, the members of the Pembroke-Southampton faction.

One gathers from the appropriate sources that in the several months following the Somerset wedding, what appears to have been Anna's continuing aversion to Somerset and his circle did not moderate. Indeed, her enmity toward the chief Howard, Northampton, seems actually to have precipitated a move by her brother, King Christian IV of Denmark. Less than six months after the Somerset wedding, the Danish king materialized in England, unheralded, on 22 July 1614, at Denmark House in London. Some apparently believed that he had come so quickly in response to letters from his sister regarding the new court situation and the rising influence of Northampton. But Northampton himself had died suddenly in late June 1614.[58] "In my last letter," said a long-standing intimate of James, Viscount Fenton, to another such intimate, the earl of Mar, "I wrote that the King of Denmark was drawing hither for some purpose," but that "after his coming he did not think it fit to meddle in them."[59] This ambiguity John Chamberlain tried to pierce as he observed in his letter to Carleton that "there is no other cause of his coming yet discovered than extraordinary kindness [strong sense of kinship?], though there be many discourses not improbable; some whisper that if the earl of Northampton had lived, he [Denmark] would have complained of some hard and unreverent usage and speeches of his touching the Queen his sister." [60]

Continuing to contextualize Jonson's *Golden Age Restored* as this masque of men paradoxically relates to Anna's activities, we note John Chamberlain continuing to outline his sense of the factions at court in this summer of 1614, reporting that Northampton had written Somerset requesting that neither the earl of Pembroke nor Pembroke's uncle, Robert Sidney (Viscount Lisle), "have any of his offices." It was, in fact, James's lord chamberlain, the earl of Suffolk (now Somerset's father-in-law), who assumed Northampton's old position of Lord Treasurer, Somerset himself attaining Suffolk's former post of Lord Chamberlain. Anna apparently resisted this move, according to Chamberlain, who remarked that, as regarded this grand office, "the Queen doth pretend [claim] a promise for the Earl of Pembroke." [61] But the circle of political power was now obvious, and not surprisingly, we find the earl of Somerset and two Howards, the earl of Suffolk, with the countess of Nottingham (wife of Charles Howard, the Lord Admiral) gathered together in Stratford-Bowe at that time as gossips at a christening attended by King James. [62] Anna's viewpoint at this juncture is described by Arthur Wilson, whose sense of the general situation offers useful insights.

The Earl of Somerset . . . and the Lord Treasurer . . . were not very acceptable to the Queen, [she] having the same spirit and animosity against Somerset that her son had. But whether from an apprehension that the king's love and company were alienated from her by this masculine conversation and intimacy or whether the man's insolence thus high mounted had carried him too near the beams of majesty (his creature Overbury being, a little before his commitment, condemned for presumptuous walking with his hat on in her palace garden, she being in the window) or whether, from that natural inclination that makes every one oppose pride in others though it be more active in themselves and see it not, or from the rumor of Prince Henry's death, covertly imputed to Somerset, I know not. But she became head of a great faction against him. [63]

We may be less concerned here with Wilson's personal analyses than with what he presents as a statement of fact: Anna's mode of resistance — so reminiscent, again, of her Scottish era. Thus we note that less than three weeks after Northampton died (July 1614) there was a gathering in which Anna seems to have been implicated. In London, members of the old Essex group (now Anna's faction?) met at Baynard's Castle, the city dwelling of the earl of Pembroke, to consider how to remove Somerset from his position. These persons, according to William Sanderson, were the countess of Bedford and the earls of Pembroke, Montgomery, and Hertford. It was here, presumably, that plans were laid to try to advance some new favorite who might supplant Somerset. The credibility of specific narratives after the fact must always be open to challenge, but the larger truth of the situation may reside in Sanderson's assumption that persons such as the countess of Bedford and the earl of Pembroke *must* have been determined to destroy Somerset. Here is the account (certainly that which underlies all references by historians to this situation), furnished by Sanderson:

There was a great but private entertainment at supper at Baynard's Castle by the family of Herberts, Hertford, and Bedford, and some others. By the way, in Fleet Street, hung out Somerset's picture at a painter's stall, which, one of the lords envying, bad his footman fling dirt in the face, which he did, and gave me occasion thereby to ask my companion upon what score this was done. He told me that this meeting would discover. And truly I waited near and opportune, and so was acquainted with the design to bring in Villiers.[64]

The countess of Bedford, Queen Anna's chief lady, was thus meeting with Pembroke, whom Anna had unsuccessfully supported for the Lord Chamberlainship, and with his brother, both nephews of Anna's own Lord Chamberlain, Robert Sidney. It is safe to say that if the royal person whom these earls and the countess now had in common had been a man, tradition might well have noted significance in this conspiratorial association. As it is, the complex of narratives available here strongly suggest Somerset's subsequent troubles as the result of just the kind of activity in which Anna of Denmark had been fully engaged in Scotland. There, we recall, she undermined the power of Chancellor Maitland, a far shrewder person than Somerset, again through the adroit use of disaffected nobility (see Chapter 2).

The plan of the anti-Somerset faction was to introduce James to a new potential protégé not in league with the Howards. It is thus significant that the king first met George Villiers, the candidate of this disaffected faction, only a month after the gathering described by Sanderson. The introduction of Villiers apparently occurred at the great house of Sir Anthony Mildmay, Apthorp, on 3 August 1614.[65] By 2 September (the earliest contemporary reckoning I have found), Villiers was described as a "new favorite" by Fenton writing the earl of Mar. Fenton observed, "All things are absolutely done by one man [Somerset] and he more absolute than ever he was. Neither his father-in-law [the earl of Suffolk], with whom he keeps good quarter now, nor any man dare touch him." But of equal significance is an earlier remark in this same letter: "I think your lordship has heard before this time of a youth, his name is Villiers, a Northamptonshire man. He begins to be in favor with his Majesty."

It is not surprising, then, that by 24 November Somerset appeared alert to the problem of this Villiers, for at this time the "fortune of Villiers the new favorite" seemed "to be at a stand." When it was expected that Villiers "should be made of the Bed Chamber, one Carr a bastard kinsman of the Lord Chamberlain [Somerset] is stepped in and admitted to the place."[66] Nevertheless, by 1 December, Villiers was apparently in such good standing with James that by 27 March 1615 Fenton was writing Mar, "The young man Villiers is and will be a courtier, in my conceit, [whether] who will it or who will not." But what is most significant for our general point here is that in this context Fenton adduced Anna of Denmark who, he wrote, was "the cause that some eat their meat in better order than othewise they would do, though it be not so well as it should be."[67]

Further to the point of *The Golden Age Restored*, a month following Fenton's above remark, Villiers was knighted and sworn to the bedchamber. And, again, at the center of this crucial event, according to the often-mentioned account of George Abbott, the archbishop of Canterbury, was Anna of Denmark, of whose support in this matter the archbishop suggests he and his fellow intriguants were highly confident. The archbishop wrote:

Upon importunity Queen Anne condescended, and so pressed it with the King that he assented; which was so stricken while the iron was hot that in the Queen's Bed Chamber the King knighted him with the rapier which the Prince did wear. And when the King gave order to swear him of the Bed Chamber, Somerset importuned the King with a message that he might be only sworn a Groom. But myself and others that were at the door sent to her Majesty that she would perfect her work and cause him to be sworn a Gentleman of the Bed Chamber.[68]

Other narrative traditions may, against logic, dismiss this account of the archbishop regarding the source of such events, yet even those who invoke the authority of Anthony Weldon must reckon with Weldon's own observations in this particular case. His unreliable and biased account of the Jacobean reign, although it scandalized Sanderson and Goodman as inaccurate and salacious, did make one point not disputed by Goodman at all. "We had a noble queen," wrote Weldon, "that did awe Somerset."[69]

The Spanish ambassador, Conde de Gondomar, casts further light on Anna's role here. Writing in October 1615, just before Somerset's fall, he remarked of the earl of Somerset's opponents at court: "The support given to them by the Queen (to whom Somerset did not pay sufficient respect,

nor has he known how to protect himself against her, nor shown any disposition to do so) have brought him to such a condition that in the very
chamber of the King, where he is Lord High Chamberlain, there are persons who will neither speak to him nor take off their hats to him."[70] It was
also remarked in the autumn of 1615 that when new disputes were spoken
of in the Privy Council they were said to involve the Treasurer (Suffolk) and
Somerset on one side and almost all the Privy Council on the other side —
and "to the latter side the Queen also inclines."[71]

Most tellingly, when the charges stemming from the Overbury Plot
put Somerset in the Tower by 1 November 1615, he was nonetheless able to
strengthen his position by gaining extremely important support from the
king. Indeed, only Queen Anna seems to have been able to thwart Somerset's attempts to protect himself.[72] According to Pietro Contarini's report
to the doge of Venice (28 October 1615, by English dating), Somerset had
reputedly appropriated a considerable quantity of the Crown jewels, and
he was to be accused of this theft. So, in order "to secure himself on this
question and upon every other charge he [Somerset] begged his Majesty for
an absolute pardon even so far as the crime of high treason." This written
request was granted by King James who affixed his signature. But when the
document was sent to the Lord Chancellor to receive the Great Seal, and
that official refused to affix it, both the Lord Chancellor and Somerset were
summoned to James's presence in front of the entire Privy Council. Both
men "spoke on their knees," to present their positions. The Lord Chancellor
gave his reasons against affixing the Great Seal of England to such an all-
encompassing pardon for the earl of Somerset, concluding that if he were
indeed to comply with the king's request, "that his majesty should grant
him [the Lord Chancellor] a special pardon for having done so, otherwise
it was against the laws of the realm, and at the convocation of Parliament
he would lose his head."

Continuing this astounding interchange, Somerset, responding that
the Lord Chancellor was not objective but a personal enemy, continued to
urge his petition for full pardon. In the end, attesting both to Somerset's
continued influence and to James's insistence on his own authority, "while
the rest of the Lords of the Council who were present were hanging on the
King's lips," James told the lord chancellor and the Privy Council of England that it was not in the power of any of them to divert him from his
purpose. "It rested with Somerset alone if he should not prove unworthy."
The king "then commanded the Chancellor to affix the seal without making
any reply" simply because James desired it.

Presumably the Lord Chancellor acquiesced, but it is important to note that this did not end the matter. At some point soon after this episode, decisive and speedy action on the queen's part seems actually to have reversed the king's dictum. For Contarini's account to the doge concludes simply: "When this came to the Queen's knowledge she immediately left her palace for the king's, and contrived to induce him to suspend the order to put the seal to the pardon and it has never been affixed." [73]

As many as three years after these events, other ambassadorial corroboration of Anna's interventions here surfaced. In 1618 the Venetian ambassador in England wrote his doge, presenting a verbal description of Anna and remarking, "Since the fall of her enemy, the Earl of Somerset, Mr. Villiers has risen, supported by her and dependant upon her." [74] It is, finally, quite interesting that the earl of Somerset, in fact, would not gain a pardon at any point during the remainder of Anna's life, finally being granted one by James six years after Anna's death, in 1625. [75]

Somerset, of course, soon ceased to be a problem as 1615 wore on, while Villiers, still with Anna's support, grew in grace, her purposes apparently compatible with his for the moment. Further, those lords with connections to Anna's circle also prospered now, as illustrated by a series of appointments in the summer following *The Golden Age Restored* (1616). In June, the earl of Arundel, a Howard who was nonetheless friendly with Pembroke and Southampton (and with a wife now in Anna's close circle) was made a member of the Privy Council. [76] In July, the queen also furthered her own Vice-Chamberlain. Going to Theobalds on a Monday to take her leave of the king, who was about to depart on a progress, Anna brought a warrant to swear Sir George Carew to the Privy Council "this day or tomorrow," an appointment for which Anna had "long labored." [77] Then, on 24 August the queen met James at Woodstock where George Villiers would soon be inducted into the peerage. Clearly the aim was to make him something more than a baron but something less than an earl, since after he was first created Baron of Whaddon, on 27 August, he was then created Viscount Villiers. The "Queen and the Prince were present, and all the company seemed jolly and well-apaide." The only countess present was Lucy Bedford. [78]

Such was the immediate future *after* Ben Jonson's masque *The Golden Age Restored* was performed on Twelfth Night in 1616. In the several months *preceding* this grand Christmas spectacle, the sinking Somerset had become increasingly implicated in the Overbury Plot so that, by December 1615, he had been stripped of his offices, and his place as Lord Chamberlain had been given to the earl of Pembroke. By early January, George Villiers had become earl of Buckingham, and on the day before the presentation of Jonson's masque, he had also been appointed to the earl of Worcester's old office, the mastership of the Horse. Thus, if indeed the masque was then called *The Golden Age Restored*, the title later affixed to its first printing in Jonson's 1616 First Folio, it was appropriately named. As Butler and Lindley have pointed out, the masque seems to point to the fall of Somerset and the rise of George Villiers.[79] It alludes to a court atmosphere created by the murder of Overbury, presumably plotted by the king's now-disgraced chief minister, whose current situation made it safe to condemn him. Of course, one can hardly imagine that the masque's tone of stern disapproval — reflecting a court context rife with the sensitivities of competing nobles — unilaterally originated with the citizen artisan Ben Jonson. Rather, it is more plausible to view Jonson either as sensing what the givers of the masque — including the almost all-powerful new favorite — wished, or as being informed as to what political directions would, in fact, be acceptable. To this effect, as early as the second and third of the seven stanzas of the opening speech, the masque interlocutor intoned:

Jove can endure no longer,
Your great ones should your less invade,
Or that your weak, though bad, be made
A prey unto the stronger.

And therefore means to set
Astraea in her seat again;
And let down in his golden chain
The age of better metal.

This abolition of evil great ones and the return of Justice, by "Jove" of course, connects to the subject of this chapter — the continued relevance of the queen consort to some of these spectacles — because the first theatrical event of the masque seems strikingly apposite to her. The courtly audience watched "Pallas in her chariot descending" to initiate the setting right of things, and it hardly seems coincidental that the figure of Pallas Athene, or Minerva, the goddess of wisdom, had come to be deeply associated with Anna of Denmark. In her first masque of Christmas 1603 (*The Vision of the Twelve Goddesses*), Anna had declined to impersonate a conventionally appropriate queenly symbol, Juno, queen of all the gods, for as Daniel had informed the readers of the quarto, it was "Pallas, which was the person her

Majesty chose to represent." Elsewhere in that same masque, Iris had re-inforced the identification when she invoked a (classically inaccurate) my-thology according to which all the other goddesses (including Juno) were "by the motion of the all-directing *Pallas*, the glorious patronesse of this mighty monarchy, descending in the majesty of their invisible essence." In 1611, some years after this but before *Golden Age*, John Florio, dedicating his Italian dictionary, *Queen Anna's New World of Words*, addressed Anna as "most absolute Minerva," while after *Golden Age*, the masque *Cupid's Banishment*, performed at Greenwich on 4 May 1617, presented "Occasion" in an epilogue to the queen, addressing her as "Bright Pallas and royal mistress of our muse."[80] Thus it seems to me significant that at this crucial time in court history, when Somerset, considered an enemy by the queen consort, had fallen, the figure of Pallas Athene emerged in *The Golden Age Restored* as the chief spokesperson of the masque.

Pallas Athene it is who here announces that Jove means to restore Astraea, the goddess of Justice, to her seat, to begin a new time,[81] and it is Athene who bids Astraea to come down from heaven with the Golden Age. Then, even more significantly, when the figures Golden Age and Astraea, arriving on stage, ask Pallas how they are to be expected to rule without a train to sustain their state, the goddess of wisdom replies: "Leave that to Jove," but then adds: "Therein you are no little part of his Minerva's care." Thus closely associating Jove/James with Minerva/Anna, Pallas then summons poets. Masquers costumed to represent those regarded as the great figures of Albion's literature — Chaucer, Gower, Lydgate, and Spenser among them — are bidden by Pallas to "Wait upon the age that shall your names new nourish / Since virtue pressed shall grow, and buried arts shall flourish."

Pallas Athene/Anna has thus banished ambitious rebellion by the Somerset forces against Jove/James. What will follow is a new golden age adorned with figures of high culture who, featuring Villiers, one of these "poets" dancing in the masque, will also presumably include Pembroke, the new Lord Chamberlain (Jonson's patron, and a member of Anna's faction), the Maecenas-like nephew of Sir Philip Sidney, and the son of the countess of Pembroke.

Celebrating "a new age" by picturing the rise of the arts under the aegis of Pallas, *The Golden Age Restored* could not have failed to present to its courtly audience the "idea" of Anna of Denmark. If so, this "idea" would hardly have been received as an overtly political statement. Rather, it was as if the idea of Anna-as-Pallas, attended, in a sense, by the king's new favorite, ushered in, harmlessly and in accordance with customary notions of the "female," the idea of . . . poetry. There was, of course, a potent irony in this innocent façade. Reputedly insulted by Overbury, Somerset's friend, reputedly instrumental in the rise of Villiers and the suppression of Somerset's pardon, the queen, watching this celebration with James and Prince Charles, could choose to project her persona as center of a luminous circle renowned for illustrious patronage of the arts. The circle included the countesses of Bedford, Derby, and Arundel; Anna's Lord Chamberlain was Sir Robert Sidney, Lord L'Isle, brother of Sir Philip Sidney; her grooms of the chamber were John Florio and Samuel Daniel, well-known men of letters; and two of her closest allies were Pembroke and Arundel, themselves famous patrons. The king's masque of *The Golden Age Restored* was thus a spectacle of which Anna of Denmark was in many ways the author. In this sense, then, it was fitting that it was the figure of Pallas who spoke the final lines of this presentation, calling on the represented poets to join a new Golden Age as both she and Villiers "ascended," each in a distinctive way.[82]

By the following Christmas season of 1616–17, George Villiers would be created earl of Buckingham and become important as a harbinger of a shift in the focus of court culture. A courtier who seems to have well understood the symbolic significance of masquing, the ascendant Buckingham — largely surrounded by nobles and friends from the queen' circle — soon held center stage in a newly evolving sphere of influence. Conversely, in this same year, Anna, now forty-two, (even though the same age at which Penelope Rich continued to dance in masques) began to be seriously harassed by "pleurisy," or congestive heart failure, which would kill her in early 1619. That this end might be regarded as premature even for an aristocratic woman who had undergone seven childbirths in the early modern period can be inferred from the comparative longevity of Anna's mother, Queen Sophia of Denmark, who outlived her daughter and King James, dying in 1631 at the age of seventy-three. Thus the time of Buckingham's ascendancy coincides with Anna's physical fading, which may deflect our sense of her continued potential as England's most significant "courtier."

This study of Anna as queen consort has not been configured as a formal "biography" — as a comprehensive survey of the social, political, and personal events of a queen's whole life — but as an assessment of Anna's high cultural significance to the early Jacobean court. Thus it seems appropriate to allude to some events in her last three years that seem to echo her relevance to English court culture in the years of her health from 1603 until, let us say, after the time of Somerset's downfall. The several small but representative episodes may lend credence not only to Anna's sophistication but also to that insistence with which she asserted her royal will, qualities which always made the queen consort a force to be reckoned with in the high cultural dynamics of the Stuart court.

Early in 1617, for example, we find the queen's activities converging with those of Lady Anne Clifford — but not for literary reasons. This patron of Samuel Daniel, dedicatee of Emilia Lanyer, and sole heiress of the third earl of Cumberland, had in 1609 married Richard Sackville Lord Buckhurst who, several days after their marriage and following the death of his father, had assumed the earldom of Dorset. Seven years later, in 1616, Dorset, now in financial difficulties, wanted his countess to raise cash by selling off some of the property she had inherited from her father. Despite the anger of her husband, who seems even to have enlisted James on his side in what was obviously becoming a challenge to patriarchal values, the countess refused. Visiting London in January 1617 she was housed at the queen's court while she and her husband awaited their appointment to discuss the matter with the king. Clifford wrote in her diary:

Upon the 18th being Saturday I went presently after dinner to the Queen to the Drawing Chamber where my Lady Derby told the Queen how my business stood, and that I was to go to the King; so she promised me she would do all the good in it she could. When I had stayed but a little while there, I was sent for out [*sic*], my Lord and I going through my Lord Buckingham's chamber who brought us into the King being in the drawing chamber. He put out all that were there and my lord and I kneeled by his chair side when he persuaded us both to peace and to put the matter wholly in his hands, which my lord consented to; but I beseeched His Majesty to pardon me for that I would never part with Westmorland while I lived, upon any condition whatsoever. Sometimes he used fair means and persuasions, and sometimes foul means, but I was resolved before, so as nothing would move me.

The next day, Clifford, still at court, was approached by several of Queen Anna's ladies, who advised her to soften this position: "My Lord Arundel had much talk with me about the business and persuaded me to yield to the King in all things. . . . After dinner she [Lady Ruthven] and I went up to the drawing chamber where my Lord Duke, my Lady Montgomery, my Lady Burleigh, persuaded me to refer these businesses to the King."[83] Clifford frequently used footnotes in her diaries, and here she added a particularly interesting one: "The Queen gave me a warning not to trust my matters absolutely to the King lest he should deceive me." Indeed, this support seems to have made a strong impression on Clifford, for in 1676, she would observe: "The 19th day [of January] I remembered how this day was 59 years [ago] and then Sunday in the afternoon in the withdrawing chamber of Queen Anne the Dane in the court at Whitehall did that Queen admonish me to persist in my denial of trusting my cause concerning my lands of inheritance to her husband King James's award, which admonition of hers and other of my friends did much confirm me in my purpose, so as the next day I gave the King an absolute denial accordingly which by God's providence tended much to the good of me and mine."[84] Indeed, by March 1617, John Chamberlain indicated Clifford's victory in the matter.[85]

Also in January 1617, the queen was self-assertive on a somewhat larger scale, confounding, in fact, some courtiers' predictions. James was planning to depart on 15 March for his Scottish progress. Alluding to it, John Chamberlain characteristically scoffed at Anna. He observed that it was "suspected that she dreams and aims at a regency during the King's absence in Scotland."[86] Yet Giovanni Batista Lionello, Venetian ambassador to England, informed the doge on 19 January that a six-person council was to be established in England during the king's absence, this being the group "that rules the realm." The council comprised Queen Anna, the archbishop of Canterbury (with whom Anna had cooperated in the forwarding of Buckingham), Prince Charles, the earl of Worcester, the lord chancellor (who had refused to seal Somerset's pardon), and the lord treasurer (the one remaining Howard — the earl of Suffolk). Indeed, about a month after James left for Scotland, Lionello observed (27 April) that "the Council meets frequently, at Greenwich where the Queen generally lives," and that "Prince Charles was going there tomorrow to stay some weeks" (*SPV*, 14:412, 495). The council, in fact, was active until James's return in the fall, suggesting John Chamberlain's limitations as an index of Anna's influence.

Two final interventions by Anna occurred even during the time when John Chamberlain notes that her dropsy was increasingly debilitating her.[87] These instances are especially revealing because they involve Prince Charles, suggesting that Anna, as with her late son Henry, intended to make her influence felt in matters pertaining to an heir apparent who might, after all, have considerable influence on her life if James predeceased her. Indeed, there is much to indicate that Anna by no means ignored Prince Charles, even during Henry's lifetime, as we learn from the account of Robert Carey, whom King Charles I at his coronation in 1625 would create earl of Monmouth. Carey, the tenth and youngest son of the first Lord Hunsdon and married to Elizabeth née Trevannion, was the unauthorized rider who had first brought James the news of Queen Elizabeth's death.[88] For his reward,

Carey, at his own request, had been appointed a gentleman of the (Scottish) Bed Chamber, but, he tells us, he was nudged aside when James formed his English Bed Chamber. Queen Anna, however, made his wife a lady of her own Privy Chamber and Mistress of her Sweet Coffers. Shortly afterward, Charles entered the lives of these Careys.

An extremely weak child who at the age of four could not even walk, Charles had been brought down to England after the royal family was established there. Because he was only the second son, and especially because of his health, there seemed to be no great rush by English courtiers to vie for the governorship of his household for fear that the sickly prince might die in their care. So apparently it was Anna who selected Elizabeth Carey (as she had chosen the supervisors for Henry) to oversee the upbringing of Charles, who was then still young enough not to require male governorship.[89] As a consequence, Elizabeth's husband, Robert, was given the governorship of the little prince's household, with power to appoint all other members to it, a situation much like that in which Lord and Lady Harington, the countess of Bedford's parents, provided a household for Princess Elizabeth.

From all accounts, Charles thrived under Elizabeth Carey's regime. According to her husband, she resisted any interference, even from King James himself, who, in addition to other unwelcome suggestions, apparently had wanted to have iron bands put around Charles's ankles to strengthen them and to cut the string under his tongue to facilitate his speech. In 1610, at the age of eleven, having been spared from these fatherly plans and against the odds, Prince Charles was quite healthy and robust. But eleven was also the age when the boy Charles was to be removed from the care of women. Over the objections of Prince Henry, Carey remarked, Carey himself was appointed Chief Gentleman of Charles's Bed Chamber and given the Mastership of the Robes.

Two years later, after Henry suddenly died and Charles became the heir apparent, attention to this younger prince increased dramatically. In 1616, when Charles came of age at sixteen and was about to be created Prince of Wales and begin his own household, Somerset was fading and Buckingham was rising. Competition for places around the new prince was, of course, intense. Indeed, Charles seems to have been directed by others to tell Robert Carey that after the installation Carey would not be able to convert his present position into that of permanent Lord Chamberlain of the new Prince of Wales's new court. His enemies, Carey wrote, had persuaded the king "how unfit it was that any man should hold both places . . . insomuch as they brought the King to their opinion" and James "was wrought on" to slate someone else as Charles's new Lord Chamberlain. The noble nominated for this position was the Scottish Robert Ker of Cessford, earl of Roxborough. Ker was the husband of Lady Drummond, whose marriage had been celebrated by *Hymen's Triumph* two years before at the queen's new palace, Denmark House, as a countermove to the Somerset marriage of the same season.

As Carey himself put it, this plan for Roxborough "was concluded but kept so secret as none knew of it but the King, the Prince, my good friend, and Roxburgh." (Carey continuously referred, with seeming sarcasm, to this "good friend" who may well have been Somerset if much of this intrigue transpired before autumn 1615.) But in late October 1616 about ten days before the installation of Charles as Prince of Wales, "it was whispered," wrote Carey, that Roxborough should be Chamberlain and Carey "got the true knowledge of all their proceedings, and how the king and Prince were brought in by a wile to give the place from me." In despair, Carey continued, he asked for an audience with Queen Anna. Obtaining it, he then "told her all I knew, and how secretly it had been plotted and wrought," and now he "humbly besought her Majesty to interpose" for him. When Anna had heard all this, Carey went on, she

could not believe that Roxburgh, or his friend [Somerset?], durst, or would, seek so eminent a place under her son without her knowledge and consent. But when by Roxburgh's wife [Lady Drummond] she was assured of it, she sent for me again, and told me it was true [what] I had said, but bade me trouble myself no further: her wrong was more than mine, and she would right both herself and me. Presently [immediately] she made known both to Roxburgh and his friend in what disdain she took it that they durst undertake such a business without acquainting her, and vowed they should buy the neglect of her at a dear rate. She kept her word, for Roxburgh was presently sent into Scotland in her high disgrace, and never after saw her; my other friend felt her heavy hand [for] a long time after. And at the Prince's creation, which was the Michaelmas following, I was sworn the Prince's Chamberlain and continued of his Bed Chamber.

And thus, Carey concludes rather disingenuously, "did God raise up the Queen to take my part, and by her means the storm that was so strongly plotted against me was brought to nought."[90] Indeed, John Chamberlain wrote on 21 December 1616, the installation of Charles having taken place on 4 November, "The lord of Roxborough is not so well pleased with being made Earl of Roxborough as discontented to be put by the place of Lord Chamberlain to the Prince which he pretends [claims] was promised him and made sure account of." At the same time, "his lady is likewise parting from the Queen," who had become, Chamberlain observed, "nothing so gracious as heretofore." Lady Drummond, who was Anna's only other lady of the most exclusive Bed Chamber, was, in fact, dismissed by in October 1617, replaced by Lady Grey of Ruthven.[91] So in the end, the new Prince of Wales's lord chamberlain inevitably emerged as a noble with strong ties to Queen Anna, and his enemies were banished to Scotland.

An almost identical situation occurred in 1617 when an English noble made the mistake of misperceiving the nature of Anna's pride in her position. Thomas Erskine, Lord Fenton (later first earl of Kellie), the cousin of the earl of Mar (and his frequent correspondent), was a boyhood friend of King James and the man, it was said, who had physically intervened to save James's life during the attack by the Gowries.[92] At the accession of James he had been given Sir Walter Ralegh's Elizabethan post of Captain of the Guard (the officer who protected the monarch's life),[93] but now, in 1617, Fenton was making it known that he would relinquish the post to a suitable financial bidder if the bidder had approval from appropriate quarters. Anxious for this position was the second earl of Salisbury (the son and heir of the deceased Robert Cecil). Salisbury had apparently discussed the matter with the now-powerful earl of Buckingham, who, in turn, seems to have approved his ambitions. Thus on 8 March 1617 John Chamberlain understood that Salisbury was competing with another noble for the captaincy of the guard and that "Salisbury having the Earl of Buckingham's favor is like to prevail"—he had made Fenton an offer of six thousand "Jacobus pieces."[94]

At some point, however, for the second time in six months, Queen Anna heard news she did not like, and she spoke to Fenton, indicating her displeasure with his plans for change. Although one might think that the captaincy of James's own guard would not be a prime concern for Anna, the fact remained that Salisbury, a dancer in Somerset's wedding masque and his brother-in-law, was a man for whose in-laws Anna obviously had little use. In April, Buckingham responded to what was obviously a letter of alarm from Salisbury.

For any promise my Lord Fenton has made to the Queen it can be no more than I told you before. But I have so much assurance in his Majesty's promise that I know there is no cause of doubt. . . . If it please God to continue the favor of his Majesty to me, I am confident all shall be done to your contentment, and therefore I would not have you trouble yourself any further with any doubts of the success [outcome], but to carry yourself toward the Queen with all respect, that you give no advantage against yourself.[95]

Several days later, however, Salisbury wrote Lord Gerard, one of the Queen's court, seeking a private conference with Anna and complaining to Gerard that he had requested an audience of her already.

> Her answer was that I might come when I would, and if she came not abroad the first time, that I might attend her leisure, expressing much violence against me in this business, saying that she loved her children as much as any loved theirs, and that she would be very careful who should be admitted into those places of trust, adding withal that she would never give way that I should be Captain of the Guard as long as she lived. This puts Henry Riche in a great deal of hope that either he shall have the place himself or at least that the Queen's power with my Lord Fenton will make him keep it still.[96]

Salisbury went on to assure Gerard that the earl of Buckingham would "never have brought my name thus upon the stage . . . but that his Lordship was very well assured that I should be fully satisfied to my content."

But this letter apparently produced no results, because Salisbury subsequently wrote two drafts of a missive to Buckingham that express his continued indignation and surprise—a mood probably shared by a number of previous courtiers, Scottish and English, who had not taken the will of the queen consort sufficiently into their calculations. After repeating Anna's comments, Salisbury remarks: "I protest I am a little troubled to have such rubs in this business considering that I have his Majesty's allowance [and] your lordship's favor." His second draft expands on this:

> Besides she hath earnestly [?] with my Lord Fenton to keep his place, and it is here said that he will keep it because he sees he cannot part with it but that either Rich or myself must be unsatisfied. But my lord at the first I could never have imagined that I should have found this opposition considering that his Majesty was pleased to give his allowance to my desire and that I had your Lordship's furtherance.

Yet, by the middle of January 1618, Salisbury was writing a face-saving letter in which he renounced all claim to the coveted position. In fact, it was Sir Henry Rich who became the new Captain of the Guard of King James,[97] a position achieved not through Buckingham at all but through a perhaps wilier courtier, Anna of Denmark.

In late November 1617 Antonio Foscarini, who had been the Venetian emissary in England for five years, provided what may be the last available description of the queen consort. At this time he was being succeeded in his post by Gregorio Barbarigo, and both emissaries had visited Anna. Several days later, Foscarini returned with his secretary, Rizzardo, to make his own formal farewell. Some of his report is worth quoting here. It describes a woman who had been seriously ill throughout October with congestive heart failure. Foscarini's report to the Venetian Senate serves as a cameo, a brief visual and auditory impression that tends to confirm the presence in Anna of Denmark of qualities that might easily encourage us to see her as influential in matters having to do with the high cultural aspects of the early Stuart court. As translated and abbreviated by the editor of the volume of the English state papers having to do with Venice in 1618, Foscarini's report tells us:

I found Her Majesty standing in the gallery at Greenwich alone, waiting for me. After I had made the usual obeisance and drawn near, Her Majesty turned towards the canopy, placed her hand on my arm as a mark of favor, moved towards the canopy and sitting down, made me at the same time cover myself and do the like. She was most richly and extraordinarily arrayed, wearing jewels of inestimable price, and she kept me for an hour and more, most graciously, discussing various topics, nor, as an additional compliment, did she choose any one else to remain in the gallery save the Mistress of the Robes and the Secretary Rizzardo. . . . She asked me about the well-being of Your Excellencies; whether I had any tidings of the election of the new doge and on whom I thought the election would fall. She added assurances of her especial affection for the republic to which, she said, she was immensely obliged, not merely for the love borne towards herself and her consort, but also for the partiality extended to her brother, the King of Denmark, for which she charged me to thank your lordships, requesting me to back her letters with language of my own. She expressed herself in very affectionate terms and enquired of me in what she could aid and further the welfare and consequence of your Excellencies. . . . When I deemed it time, which was after a long and pleasing discourse evidently agreeable to Her Majesty, I took leave, whereupon the Secretary Rizzardo, who was at the end of the gallery, drawing near, the Queen got up from under the canopy and, leaning on me, moved to the center of the platform where he kissed her hand, adding a few but appropriate words which were reciprocated by her in a complimentary strain, showing that she remembered his name and that of his family and that his conduct at the court had pleased her. . . . Two days later she sent me the letters addressed to your Serenity [the doge], and as a mark of extraordinary favor her secretary presented me in her Majesty's name with a large and handsome diamond in a ring. (*SPV* 14:96–97)

Finally, in calling attention to the unusual absence of the queen consort from traditional literary discussions of the Jacobean court, I have not attempted to challenge the extent of King James's political power or that of his favorites. Rather, I have suggested that the high culture associated with this early Stuart court is not attributable to the influence of James alone. Instead, I have claimed for Anna of Denmark a place that, while by no means positioning her as one of the powerful political figures of James's English reign, would disestablish the continuing myth of her marginality—and thus of her irrelevance to the culture of the royal court. I have pursued two related ideas. It has been necessary, first, to challenge traditional descriptions of Anna of Denmark's "frivolity" and "idleness"—the notion of her general irrelevance and impotence. Accordingly, I have been concerned with contemporary commentary arguing in Anna an extremely strong will, a persistence in self-assertion, and a relentless enmity against those who challenged what she took to be her prerogatives as queen consort. However, if such a redrawing of Anna's image makes more credible her potential influence in the sphere in which she moved, then the second matter that required development was how to reconcile this strong-minded queen consort with the entertainments she chose for self-display—with masques, building commissions, and dancing. These presumably "idle" pastimes would seem to bring us full circle to the traditional critical disparagements of Anna's person and intellect.

I have sought to address this seeming contradiction by challenging a traditional equation. Was Anna, because of her association with Jacobean court masquing, necessarily frivolous? In claiming that this was not the case, I have repositioned her masquings within a larger milieu that Anna herself invented, that is, the sphere of influence comprising Anna's own court. This court, which included an inner circle of countesses of considerable reputation, provided a centralized focus of "place" for the consolidation of arts patronage around Anna herself. Inevitably, Anna's circle, selected in accordance with the queen's aesthetic *and* political values, came to be identified with a political stance as well: anti-Howard. And in the same context, if an efflorescence of the arts is to be attributed to Henry Prince of Wales, then, as I have suggested, such activity was not independently generated, but must also be reevaluated within the joint aesthetic/political agendas of the queen consort and the heir apparent. It was, after all, Anna and her circle who molded Henry's English experience—an experience that would have taken an entirely different shape without Anna's violent Scottish intervention.

No individual removed from us by over three hundred years can ever be properly or accurately assessed by means of particular documents whose capricious survival constitutes them as "representative" of a milieu. Thus, if my subject has focused on Anna's recorded responses to her experiences and on the social patterns she originated at court, it is because I have sought to interpret what is known about Anna's life as it bears on a revisionist description of a particular court dynamic. In the end, my aim has been to alter the puzzlingly patriarchal skew in narratives that have implied that James I of England was the sole royal presence at the Jacobean court and thus — inevitably — the font of all high culture that might be associated with it. It is, in fact, important to note that the court position I have here proposed for Anna is neither anachronistic nor unusual for early modern Europe of this time. Indeed, Anna's stormy Scottish sojourn may well have been more typical of the continental case than was her English reign.

But students of early modern English artistic productions will in the end regard Anna's English sojourn as of greater interest. Certainly, Anna's circle is crucial to our understanding of the artistic milieu in which not only Ben Jonson but also Shakespeare and many of his talented contemporaries flourished. In fact, several persons from this distinguished group can almost directly be associated with William Shakespeare himself. These were the earl of Southampton to whom Shakespeare dedicated his first two long poems; the countess of Bedford at whose father's house we find the only recorded performance of *Titus Andronicus*; the earl of Rutland for whom Shakespeare and Richard Burbage executed an impresa in 1613; and the earl of Pembroke whose support of both Shakespeare and his works, when Shakespeare was alive, is alluded to by Hemings and Condell in their dedication to the First Folio. But Anna's circle also included patrons of many other writers and artists, such as Sir Philip Sidney's brother and nephew and the siblings and son of the earl of Essex. And as the circle expanded, these relationships (by blood and marriage) became increasingly complex: the countess of Montgomery, for example, an inspiration for Lady Mary Wroth, was the daughter of Sir Philip Sidney's brother, Robert, and one of the nieces of Robert Cecil; and the earl of Arundel, well-known collector of paintings and nephew of Northampton, was married to one of the countesses closest to Anna. That Anna's allies may collectively have been sufficiently influential to affect the political careers of Somerset and Buckingham is, in one sense, beside the point. My argument is that a queen with the judgment and skill to create a court around an illustrious and accomplished group of noblewomen was extremely likely to have promulgated these women (together with their relatives and friends) as a group, to have protected and defended their prerogatives — in short, to have created them as a coherent and highly visible social entity.

To conclude, my implicit assumption throughout this study is that feminist investigations of the early modern period, even as they have widened our understanding of the position of women in Tudor and Stuart England, have paradoxically neglected Queen Anna. In focusing on women who produced poetry, prose, painting, and music, such scholarship has rightfully concerned itself with unearthing lives and works buried under a plethora of texts preoccupied with the patriarchal imperative. These efforts have in turn generated the rich rewriting of the early modern history of English literature, drama, and the fine arts. But few would claim that early modern women, when offered advantages rivaling those granted men or even when deprived of these advantages, inevitably discovered or revealed their potentialities through the practices of art alone. Such women, like their male counterparts, may have found alternative modes of expression in religion, science, commerce, and politics. Thus we need not rediscover the early modern queen, Anna of Denmark, as poet, musician, painter, or even dancer, to urge her relevance. It seems enough to identify Anna as a woman who sought and found her self-validation in behavior available only to someone in the privileged position of queen consort. Because her pursuit of royal status also led her to create for the arts in the early Stuart court a rich and hospitable climate—a climate, ironically, which historians have subsequently credited to her husband—her actions render Anna an appropriate subject for the history of early modern artistic production. Accordingly, future discussions of poets such as William Shakespeare, John Donne, Mary Wroth, and even Ben Jonson, as well as of the English translators of such figures as Montaigne and Cervantes, might well consider that while much of their work was accomplished during the reign of King James, it is likely to have flourished because of the rich milieu created by Anna of Denmark.

APPENDIX: ANNA OF DENMARK AND CATHOLICISM

Although this study of Anna of Denmark has not been conceived as a conventionally historical biography of the kind that (rightfully) seeks to account for and to register every extant documentary record in which she might figure, the question of Anna's religious affiliation has raised inquiry often enough to warrant attention here. A study seeking to follow Anna's relationship to and effect upon the quality of her courtly environment must, at the very least, accept the responsibility of determining whether, in the end, this question of religion was relevant, even within the restricted parameters delineated by this book. The question is more nuanced than simply, "Was Queen Anna a Catholic?" Large assumptions may hide within the Trojan horse of a question for whose entertainment and obeisance one may break down conceptual walls. As Wittgenstein reminded us long ago, although there are many questions that may be put to a chess piece, determining the assumptions buried in such questions imparts a certain rigor to the procedure. We may ask, "Is the queen in chess supposed to be short or tall?" An answer would presumably be configured in terms of the rules of the conceptual game through which we intend to conduct the figurine.

This is as much as to suggest that any discussion of Anna of Denmark and Catholicism must, at the outset, clarify the purpose of the exercise itself. If, for example, one does state that Queen Anna was a Catholic, what then? By the same token, if one were to state the opposite — that Queen Anna was definitely not a Catholic — what kind of significance should be teased out of that statement? Given the uncertainties of divining motivation in historical figures according to one or another theory of psychodynamics, adding "Catholic" to this particular cloud of unknowing, early modern Catholicism in Europe itself being a multifaceted proposition, complicates more than it simplifies.

Obvious scenarios do come to mind, of course, if we take religious labels as indications of purpose in historical individuals — scenarios with which, however, one assumes an informed student of the period might be less than comfortable. Thus, as one paradigm might decline the matter, if Anna was indeed a Catholic, then one could assume that, like Mary Tudor, she wished for England's change of religious orientation away from Protestantism, plotted Spanish marriages for her offspring in order to strengthen Spain's military ability forcibly to return England to that Catholicism, and accordingly worked to place English Catholic nobles in positions of power for these ends. All such goals might plausibly be attributed to the pope, whose word, the paradigm would conclude, Anna, as a Catholic, was bound to follow if she could. If we hesitate before this extreme, however, then any affirmative answer to the question of Anna's Catholicism must bring with it some kind of reduction in our scope of concomitant speculation. We might, for example, conjecture the effect of her (Catholic) religion on Anna's everyday behavior, choice of friends, and spiritual ontology. In effect, averring that Anna was a Catholic brings with it some assumption regarding the historical relevance of this situation. Accordingly, this appendix can only be concerned with speculations that, in the end, merely tug at the fringes of larger questions. Thus the effort to determine whether Anna's religious affiliations bear on the concerns of our foregoing study becomes, as it were, an investigation in itself, for which our space here forbids all but the broadest of speculations.

The most convincing documentation of Anna's formal relationship to the Catholic Church comes from A. W. Ward, author of the copious entry on the queen in the *Dictionary of National Biography* (1885), which still stands as the most substantial historical essay on Anna now available in such a format.[1] Thus it is worth our close attention that, having in this *DNB* article observed that Anna's "coquettings with Rome" came to an end rather early on and that "their history on the whole forms the most curious chapter in her life, though different historians have put very different interpretations upon it," Ward later changed his outlook, responding positively to the argument advanced by Wilhelm Plenkers, whose study of Anna's potential Catholicism was published in Danish in 1888.[2] Plenkers adduced the account of the Scottish Jesuit, Father Robert Abercromby, who reached Scotland in 1588 after fourteen years in Poland (thus shortly before Anna arrived there as James's bride). Abercromby wrote that he himself, in 1600, had instructed her in Catholicism, remaining in Scotland until she crossed the border as England's new queen consort in 1603. Abercromby then described himself as present at her English court until he left England (before 1608) to avoid the increasing severity being visited upon Jesuits there. In Braunsberg he wrote his account, a copy of which was sent by the German Jesuit Gretsen living in Ingolstadt to John Stuart, prior of the Benedictines in Ratisbone.

Accepting the documentation for this 1600 conversion of Anna to Catholicism, Ward nevertheless expressed dubiety, in his words, as to "whether she *died* a Catholic."[3] For Ward the issue revolved around whether, on her deathbed, the queen had rejected the Catholic concept of the intercession of saints to effect her salvation. Nevertheless, if Abercromby's account is accurate—there seems no good reason to doubt it for the time in question—we must advert to the question posed earlier. How is this information to be used to cast light not on the queen's personal psychobiography (unknowable at best) but on her recorded activities as queen consort, first in Scotland and then in England? Lest we adopt a sense of the inevitability of resultant "Catholic" behavior according to the paradigm suggested above—Anna's involvement in some kind of political activity directed toward effecting papal and Spanish dominance of the English political process—it may be useful to contextualize Anna's historical situation. As the daughter and sister of Danish kings such contextualizing can offer possible paradigms other than that according to which a Danish royal figure converted to Catholicism would necessarily become the secret spiritual servant of Rome and secret political servant of Spain.

The religious situation in Denmark during Anna's childhood seems, as in England, to have been a complex amalgam of personal belief and social politics. Frederick I of Denmark, himself from Lutheran Schleswig, had openly repudiated papal authority in 1526 and encouraged the introduction of Lutheranism into Denmark. Four years later, the Confessio Hafniensis (the Copenhagen Confession), delineating the faith and beliefs of Danish Lutherans, appeared almost simultaneously with the German Augsburg Confession. When Christian III, Frederick's son, succeeded him to the throne in 1533, he proclaimed new evangelical church ordinances and in 1539 declared the king to be supreme in all ecclesiastical matters.[4] Further, Christian III's Bible of 1550, the first Danish translation of the Bible in its entirety, was the significant monument of Danish Lutheranism which, with the Confessio Hafniensis, emphasized dependence on a biblical Christianity, polemical, popular, and untheological in form.[5]

Anna's father, Frederick II, who came to the throne in 1559, had his eldest son, Christian IV, educated by the Lutheran pastor Hans Mikkelsen, whose assigned texts included Erasmus's *Institutio Principis Christiani.*

Further, the regency government that took over Christian's education after Frederick II died, Christian being eleven, continued to raise him not only as a Lutheran but in the royalist culture and ideology that placed the king firmly as the head of the state.

International circumstances, however, led both Christian and his father before him to evince a certain tolerance for Catholics (if not for the Catholic Church itself) because of the complex set of interrelationships obtaining on the Continent at this time. As Lockhart reminds us, Denmark, while Baltic in orientation, was politically and geographically a continental state. The élite culture of Copenhagen was in essence German, offering greater cultural opportunities than even the largest university towns of the impoverished north German principalities. Thus Denmark—as it existed in the sixteenth century—inevitably had dealings with the Habsburgs. Christian III in 1544 had concluded a very successful treaty with Emperor Charles V, father of Spain's Philip II, and this Treaty of Speier kept the German Protestant Holy Roman Empire, in which the Danish monarchy was inevitably intertwined through familial relationships, from any confessional struggles with Spain. In 1604, however, when the Norwegian Jesuit Nicolai Laurentius Norvegus became active in Norway, and when it became clear that a growing number of affluent Danish as well as Norwegian families were sending their sons to Jesuit schools, Christian IV did initiate anti-Catholic legislation.[6]

Continuing to pursue Anna's early ideological environment, it is therefore important for us to maintain the distinction urged by historians of early modern Europe between political Calvinism and that tissue of de facto ententes whereby the northern (Scandinavian) states coexisted with the Spanish hegemony. As is well known, part of the Netherlands, which had been a Spanish possession, turned to Calvinism, initiating rebellion and civil war that in the sixteenth century made the Low Countries a battleground for Catholic and Protestant forces. Lockhart has observed that as a Lutheran and as an aristocrat, Christian distrusted the Calvinist "merchant republic," and as a supporter of monarchy, he disliked the Dutch as rebels: in 1611 he even refused to receive a mission from the States-General because he recognized Philip III of Spain as their rightful ruler.[7]

Thus when Anna came to Scotland, the chances were that her background would have inclined her to a series of different kinds of responses in terms of "religion." The Scottish Reformation had not been *imposed* by the weak monarchy of the Scottish kings before James VI; it had been generated from below. John Knox had landed in Scotland in 1559, now a Calvinist, and Scotland, at least in theory, had become a fully Calvinistic nation by 1561. But because of Knox's, and later Melville's, efforts to create a distinction between church and state, Kirk and King, James VI, as is well known, was hardly in the business of exiling all Catholics. Indeed, the Gowrie conspiracy against James involved nobles of strongly Protestant views, while the insistence by many followers of Calvin on the equality of church and state would not have been a stance to which the Danish kings would have been sympathetic. Not only did they cultivate the idea of "Princely Power" but they were conflicted regarding the general implications for monarchy of the rebellion in the Netherlands.

Scottish Calvinism with its insistence on the separation of church and state might well have repelled Anna if she shared in any way her Danish brother's upbringing. On the other hand, her early cultivation of the Catholic countess of Huntly (see Chapter 2 above) need not have resulted from religious principles: the countess was the sister of James's second cousin Lodovic Stuart, duke of Lennox, himself converted to Protestantism and very close to James. Indeed, the Protestant Lennox seems to have been one of the few nobles about James whom Anna trusted. As for other activity in Scotland, it is well worth noting that Anna's falling-out with James about the Gowries—she refused to stop seeing the Ruthven sisters—was an adherence to a family with strong Protestant views. Finally, the religious persuasions of those nobles riding with Anna to try to seize Henry from the earl of Mar in 1603 seems to have been a mixture: two nobles were Catholic, two were Protestant.[8]

The same religio-political confusions attended on James's and Anna's way with the upbringing of Prince Charles. The strongly Protestant earl of Mar was appointed Prince Henry's governor. Alexander Seton, Lord Fyvie (later earl of Dunfermline and chancellor of Scotland) was Prince Charles's governor from birth (20 November 1600), and Charles remained at Dunfermline in Fyvie's general charge from 1600 until 1603, not making the journey to England until 1604 because of what were considered dangerous physical debilities. It is interesting, therefore, that the Venetian ambassador, Scaramelli, remarked in a letter to the doge, that "Seaton," the "governor of his Majestie's second son," though "very deep in the King's confidence," was "thought to be a Catholic at heart, for he was maintained at the University of Rome by Pope Gregory XIII at a cost of ten ducats a month, and took his doctor's degree at Bologna."[9]

Anna again puzzles, if we are now to think of her as a doctrinaire Catholic. After delivering Charles to England in the summer of 1604, Fyvie returned to his many other duties in Scotland. At that time, Carey, Charles's new English governor reported, "The Queen (by approbation of the Scotch Lord Chancellor [Fyvie]) made choice of my wife, to have the care and keeping of the Duke." Indeed, Lord Fyvie's guardianship of Charles was formally discharged on 12 February 1605, and Charles was raised by Lord and Lady Carey.[10] Jean Drummond, Anna's only Scottish lady of the bedchamber, had been Charles's first governess, from his birth until he was three.[11] The Careys were Protestants.

Anna's further activities with her children in England, from her first days, are also difficult to ascribe to the urgings of a militant Catholicism. In her selection of nobles who strategically surrounded Prince Henry and Princess Elizabeth, she chose the decidedly Protestant father and mother of the countess of Bedford, Lord and Lady Harington, as the governors of Princess Elizabeth, while Prince Henry's closest friend was the younger brother of the Queen's lady of the bedchamber, Lady Bedford, related to the decidedly Protestant Sidneys. Also noted above (Chapter 3) is the fact that, against opposition from King James and from Robert Cecil, the queen chose as her own lord chamberlain the brother of Sir Philip Sidney, Robert, thus placing an emphatic signature on the generally Protestant message her court seemed to be sending. This court of ladies was made up of countesses associated not only with the Sidney and Harington families but also with the earldoms of Derby and Pembroke, all of whom were also emphatically Protestant, the dowager countess of Pembroke almost being an English icon in this respect. In other words, if Anna was a Catholic in 1600, her new religious affiliation does not seem to have done Catholic nobles any great good. Even at levels much lower than the nobility, she seems, for instance, to have preferred (the Protestant) Samuel Daniel as her writer of masques to (the Catholic) Ben Jonson, whom many literary historians associate with King James.

To move to questions of dynastic designs as these might have been motivated by Catholic politics — if Queen Anna indeed practiced them — the matter is somewhat more complex. Whom did Anna wish her children to marry? By marrying Anna, James VI of Scotland had already made the most logical alliance with a powerful Oldenburg state that controlled most of Scandinavia and the waters around it. The king of Denmark was James's firmly Protestant (if Lutheran) brother-in-law. What remained was the vague Protestant entity of the Holy Roman Empire with its tangled alliances stretching from Christian Hungary to the duchies of Germany face-to-face with Ottoman imperialism, while the Low Countries had no settled, native royalty because they were not kingdoms. Henri IV of France had converted to Catholicism to attain the French crown, but he was assassinated in 1610 and his widow, Marie de Medici, was operating as regent during the minority of Louis XIII. Thus, if one were to think of crowns for one's princely children, there remained the Catholic city-states of Italy, the unsettled legacy of France, and the undoubted (Catholic) power of the Spanish empire.

One diplomatic step, interestingly opposed by Anna, was using Princess Elizabeth, inserting her into the vexed Palatinate situation by marrying her to the Elector Frederick V, titular head of the Evangelical Union — the association of Protestant German states formed after the diet of Regensburg in 1608 — and thus leader of the radical Protestant princes in northern Europe. Obviously Frederick fell victim to these confusions, but we note that despite popular English Protestant ferment for war to recover his crown, James never did approve an expedition to restore Elizabeth's deposed husband. As for the princes, before Henry's death, Anna was said to be in favor of marrying him to one of the Spanish infantas. Henri IV of France had four daughters, all Catholic, so the choice of royal brides could hardly be a religious one.

In Spain Philip III and Margaret of Austria, whom he married in 1599, had produced eight children, but only three seem to have survived, two of them daughters. One daughter, Anne, married Louis XIII and became queen of France; another daughter, Maria, was the Infanta James hoped for Charles, but she married Ferdinand III and became empress of the Holy Roman Empire. Thus, in Spain, there were two Infantas and a complex political situation dominated by the women in the family of Philip III in which Margaret of the Cross persuaded Philip not to marry Maria to Prince Charles.[12] In other words, it was difficult to be rigidly Protestant when arranging a marriage for a future king of England. Prince Charles eventually married a Catholic daughter of Henri IV. After Anna's death in 1619, the royal — if not the popular — inclination was indeed toward a peace-making alliance with Spain. The phenomenon of the Spanish ambassador Gondomar as well as the Quixotic journey of Charles and Buckingham to Spain were events one might well attribute — in theory — to a Catholic Anna (had she not now been dead), rather than a Protestant King James.[13]

It is useful, although, again, not definitive, finally, in turning to the question of the significance of "Anna and Catholicism" to turn to other kinds of indications — to the commentaries of ambassadors who visited England throughout James's reign and whose duty it was to send reports back to their masters on a number of subjects including, of course, the inclining of king or queen consort to this or that European court and its confessional orientation. Here, individual quotations can be misleading because emissaries seem not to have been unanimous. Commentary on the subject may be found in the missives of the ambassadors from the doge of Venice (Catholic), from Henri IV (Protestant/Catholic), and from Savoy and Florence. Most consistently useful here are the full reports sent from time to time by departing Venetian ambassadors who had been in residence for a number of years and often presented the doge with a "state of England" report.

On 18 May 1603 Scaramelli, Venetian ambassador to England, sizing up the new reign, wrote the doge the following assessment from, of course, his own Catholic (but anti-Spanish) viewpoint (18 May 1603): "The Queen, whose father was a Martinist [Lutheran] and who has always been a Lutheran herself, became a Catholic, owing to three Scottish Jesuits, one of whom came from Rome, the others from Spain. Although in public she went to the heretical [Anglican] church with her husband, yet in private she observed the Catholic rite. With the King's consent the mass was sometimes secretly celebrated for her. . . . She has obtained leave to bring up her only daughter, a girl of eight, as a Catholic." [14] Because Scaramelli was inaccurate about Princess Elizabeth's future, considering who her governor was, even while accurate about the Scottish situation, we may accept his later remarks with mingled confidence as he writes several months later (13 July 1603): "The Queen is most obedient to her husband, and goes with him to the heretical [Anglican] services, but all the same she endeavors to place in office as many Catholic nobles as possible, and, as the King is extremely attached to her, she succeeds in all she attempts" (*SPV*, 10:68). More accurately, he notes the events of the coronation as he writes (3 August 1603) that although Anna was asked to take the Sacrament on Coronation Day after the Protestant rite, and even after the archbishop of Canterbury tried to persuade her, "Her Majesty, after very quietly saying 'no' once or twice, declined to make any further answer" (*SPV*, 10:81).

At this time, the French embassage was making its own assessments. At the accession, Beaumont had been ambassador, although Sully would make a trip as ambassador-extraordinary in 1603. Unfortunately, Sully's *Memoirs* appeared long after the fact and may have been colored by retrospect. He notes, for what it is worth, receiving letters from Beaumont in 1603. Apparently, upon her arrival in England Anna had "so entirely neglected or forgot the Spanish politics, as gave reason to believe she had, in reality, only pretended to be attached to them." Indeed, "some ladies, in whom this princess reposed the greatest confidence, positively assured Beaumont she was not so perfect a Spaniard as was believed."[15]

In 1607, Molino wrote his long "State of England" report, as it were, to the doge. He remarked about Anna's Catholicism in a context worth quoting:

> The Queen is very gracious, moderately good looking. She is a Lutheran. The King tried to make her a Protestant; others a Catholic; to this she was and is much inclined, hence the rumour that she is one. She likes enjoyment and is very fond of dancing and of fetes. She is intelligent and prudent; and knows the disorders of the government, in which she has no part, though many hold that as the King is most devoted to her she might play as large a role as she wished. But she is young and averse to trouble; she sees that those who govern desire to be left alone and so she professes indifference. All she ever does is beg a favour for some one. She is full of kindness for those who support her, but on the other hand she is terrible, proud, unendurable to those she dislikes. (*SPV*, 10:513)

On the political front, John Chamberlain observed her attitude toward the Netherlands State General in 1607. The Guild of the Merchant Taylors gave a feast to the commissioners of their profitable trading partner on 20 July. The queen not only refused to attend but also refused the commissioners access to her.[16] This is comprehensible in light of King Christian's attitude toward the state as an illegal one in rebellion against its true monarch, Philip III of Spain.

In July 1615, the wife of the ambassador from the archduke of Austria wrote the queen asking her to intercede for the release of ten Catholic priests being held at Wisbeach Castle,[17] but she was unsuccessful. Yet the letter suggests Anna's reputation. In May 1618 she confided to the Venetian ambassador her opposition to a Spanish match for Prince Charles, and King Christian attempted to dissuade James in this matter (*SPV*, 15:206). In 1596 Anna was friendly with the reputed Catholic Alexander Seton, who was Lady Jane Drummond's brother-in-law and chairman of the "Octavians" who had worked with Anna in Scotland and been named to administer the Crown finances.

In 1617, Scaramelli, Venetian emissary, wrote the doge suggesting the line Anna was capable of drawing between politics and religion, rather recalling the principle of "adelsvaelden" of her Danish brother. Scaramelli observed what had happened to Sir John Digby, James's ambassador to Spain, who tried to negotiate Charles's marriage to the Infanta:

When Sir Digby some months ago fell out of favour with the Queen it was thought that her Majesty would lose all inclination towards the Spanish party, and signs of this became apparent at once. This is thought to be of some moment in its bearings upon the Prince's marriage, although her Majesty has never meddled in affairs of State. The results are now appearing more markedly as the Queen has effected almost a revolution in her court, those dependent on Digby or friendly to his party being removed. Among other matters, it has appeared like an outrage to see Mrs. Drummond also deprived of her favor, who came with her from Scotland and has always been her first lady. She has been obliged to leave the Court and England and possibly to give up the pension which she received from the Catholic ambassador, and to retire to Scotland her native country. (*SPV*, 14:6)

This is a good example of the difficulties inherent is assessing the implications and thus the meaning of "Anna's Catholicism." Anna's anger at Lady Drummond derived from discovering that she was secretly attempting to establish her husband, Lord Roxburgh, with the help of Somerset, as the new lord chamberlain for Charles as he was to be installed as Prince of Wales. It was for this reason that Lady Drummond was sent to Scotland, as Carey (whom Anna supported as Charles's lord chamberlain) tells us (see above, pp. 154–56). Thus one assumes that Digby, who had simply been following James's wishes in the Spanish negotiations, was found by Anna to be part of the circle trying to gain control of Charles's court. This occurrence was in late October 1616. James had then departed on his Scottish progress, leaving a governing council that included Anna.

In 1618, the next Venetian ambassador remarks: "She is very anxious for him [Charles] to marry in Spain, and does her utmost to that end; she hates a French marriage and opposes it openly, speaking unreservedly against the legitimacy of the Most Christian King and his brother and sisters. All this leads her to desire the marriage of her son to any one rather than to France, and this is well known by the most Christian King and his ministers." He adds, "In France he [Charles] was offered the second Princess, a great beauty of about his own age [eighteen]. This alliance was favored by the King's own sentiments and backed by the Duke of Lennox and others of French sympathies. When the principal points had been arranged and everything seemed settled, and it was laid before the [Privy] Council as such, the Spaniards upset all by the offer of their second princess [infanta] and bribed a large part of the Council to offer such strong opposition that the affair was broken off" (*SPV* 14: 393). These accounts put Anna on the opposite side of the question of the Spanish match, but the more fundamental point is that factors other than religion must have been determinant in choosing between French and Spanish princesses, since all the candidates were Catholic. The influence of Anna's supposed Catholicism on her own position seems, then, unknowable. One might just as readily assume that Anna shared James's concern with making some sort of alliance with Spain through a royal marriage, peace having formally been effected by the treaty of 1604. Conversely, it would be easy enough to have claimed—if Anna had been alive during the quixotic journey of Charles and Buckingham to the Spanish court—that her Catholicism played a part in this intrigue. Thus all that can reasonably be concluded, I think, is that Anna's Catholicism was not as strong an influence on her political decisions as proved to be the case with her daughter-in-law, Henrietta Maria.

A remark by Piero Contarini in 1618, included in another lengthy ambassadorial report to the doge, is an appropriate summary: "Some consider her a Catholic because she would never go to the English church, but really her religion is not known" (*SPV* 15:420).

As a coda, finally, Anna's relationship to the archbishop of Canterbury is not without interest. She worked closely with him to overthrow Somerset, a situation the archbishop himself recalled in his memoirs. Thus one can only speculate on the report of Anna's death, again by the Venetian ambassador. The archbishop of Canterbury, wrote the emissary, reported that the queen abjured the intercession of saints as necessary to salvation and thus, presumably, she died an Anglican. But, then, we are all familiar with the modern "press release." In Anna's day, too, there was much to be said for promulgating an official version of England's queen dying "respectably." Indeed, the archbishop may have felt that by this story he could, in some way, repay his benefactress.

NOTES

CHAPTER 1. QUEEN ANNA AS CONSORT

1. The queen's first name, for obvious reasons, seldom appears in the correspondence of others to whom she was simply "the queen," but at least three instances indicate that she considered the Danish "Anna" her name. She so signs it
in a holograph letter (1603) to James ("so kissing your hands/ I rest/ yours/ Anna
R[egina]"). Similarly, her oath of office, when she was invested as queen of Scotland, began in a Scottish account of 1590: "The Quenis Majesties Aithe: 'I Anna, be
the grace of God, Queine of Scotland.' " See *Papers Relative to the Marriage of King
James the Sixth of Scotland* (Edinburgh, 1828), v, xviii. A doggerel poem by John
Burel of the same year, describing the "form and manner" of the queen's Scottish
coronation, has one stanza beginning: "Anna, our well-beloved Queen": see *Scottish Poems of the Sixteenth Century*, ed. Sir John Graham Dalyell (Edinburgh, 1801)
468. John Dowland's *Lachrimae* (London, 1604) is dedicated to "the most sacred
and gracious princess Anna Queen of England," while John Florio, a gentlemen of
the Queen's Privy Chamber and her Italian teacher, offered his second rendering
of his well-known Italian dictionary, *Queen Anna's New World of Words* (London,
1611), to "the Imperial Majesty of the highest-born Princess, Anna of Denmark."

2. The events that dominate most biographies of James include the poisoning death of Thomas Overbury, the marriage of Robert Carr and Frances Howard,
the fall of Carr, the rise of Buckingham, the escape, recapture, and despairing death
of Arabella Stuart, the maneuverings for a Spanish marriage of Prince Charles, and
the playhouse phenomenon of *A Game at Chesse*. G. P. V. Akrigg's enormously
useful biographical study, *Jacobean Pageant* (Cambridge: Harvard University Press,
1962), may nonetheless be cited as a representative influence on many literary scholars. Akrigg emphasizes the political intrigues generated by the succession at court
of James's favorite, and he focuses especially on the rise of court factionalism after
1614.

3. S. N. Eisenstadt, "The Causes of Disintegration and Fall of Empires:
Sociological and Historical Analyses," *Diogenes* 34 (1961): 82–107, so distinguishes
between "state" and "empire."

4. See *London's Love to Prince Henry* (London, 1610) — STC 13159, and Dudley Carleton's letter (2 June 1610) to Sir Thomas Edmondes in Sir Ralph Winwood,
Memorials of Affairs of State (London, 1725), 3: 179.

5. For these distinctions see François Chabod, " 'Y-a-t-il un état de la Renaissance?" in *Actes du Colloque sur la Renaissance* (Paris: Lib. Philosophique J.
Vrin, 1958), 57–74; Eisenstadt, "Causes of Disintegration" and Fernand Braudel, *The*

Mediterranean, 2 vols., trans. Sian Reynolds (New York: Harper and Row, 1973), 2:681–701. See also John Guy, *Tudor England* (Oxford: Oxford University Press, 1988), ch. 13: "The Making of the Tudor State," 352–78.

6. For traditional (negative) attitudes toward Anna of Denmark, see Agnes Strickland, *Lives of the Queens of England* (London: George Bell and Sons, 1842–88), 4:62–65; Frances Yates, *John Florio* (Cambridge: University Press, 1934), 248–49; Maurice Lee Jr., *John Maitland of Thirlestane* (Princeton: Princeton University Press, 1959), 204, 286–88; David Harris Willson, *James VI and I* (New York: Oxford University Press, 1956), ch. 6 (whose last sentence is: "Alas! The King had married a stupid wife"). Akrigg. In a book-length biography, Anna has been given quite a silly character, perhaps unintentionally, by E. C. Williams, *Anne of Denmark* (London: Longman, 1971). More useful material is still the essay in the *Dictionary of National Biography* by Adolphus William Ward, and some of the documentation to be found in Strickland, but they both betray the shapes of their narratives via such descriptive terms and passages as "frivolous" (Ward) and "like most weak women" (Strickland, 66). I have argued against this view elsewhere. See "The Court of the First Stuart Queen," in *The Mental World of the Jacobean Court*, ed. Linda Levy Peck (Cambridge: University Press, 1991), 191–208, and "Theatre as Text: The Case of Queen Anna and the Jacobean Court Masque," *Elizabethan Theatre* 14 (1996): 175–93.

7. As opposed to the "treason" that a disobedient wife figuratively showed to her husband, as Lena Cowen Orlin has pointed out in *Private Matters and Public Culture in Post-Reformation England* (Ithaca, N.Y.: Cornell University Press, 1994), 125–30.

8. For example, in 1626, when Buckingham sided with the new King Charles in his argument with Henrietta Maria (the youngest of the French king's three daughters) over her rights, the Venetian ambassador in England wrote the doge that "the French [around Henrietta Maria] here oppose his plans as much as possible and consequently live under constant threat of expulsion and being sent back to France as the cause of the disturbances." In the end, though, Charles "will not dismiss them out of the respect he owes" the French king, thus attesting to the forces a queen consort could marshal if pressed. See *Calendar of State Papers . . . of Venice*, ed. R. Brown et al. (London: Historical Manuscripts Commission, 1864-), 19:497–98 (hereafter cited as *SPV*).

9. See Henry Kamen, *Philip of Spain* (New Haven: Yale University Press, 1997), 248, 297.

10. See Magdalena S. Sánchez, *The Empress, the Queen, and the Nun* (Baltimore: Johns Hopkins University Press, 1998), esp. 45–54.

11. See Frederic J. Baumgartner, *France in the Sixteenth Century* (New York: St. Martin's Press, 1995), 234–37; Robin Briggs, *Early Modern France, 1560–1715* (New York: Oxford University Press, 1977), 86–89.

12. See Paul Douglas Lockhart, *Denmark in the Thirty Years' War, 1618–1648* (Selinsgrove, Pa.: Susquehanna University Press, 1996), 27–31.

13. See Lockhart, *Denmark*, 46 and n. 39; 53 and n. 47.

14. See Roy Strong, *Henry, Prince of Wales, and England's Lost Renaissance* (London: Thames and Hudson, 1986), 16, 25. Strong does not specify his evidence for his statements about Queen Anna.

15. See David Mathew, *James I* (London: Eyre and Spottiswoode, 1967), 277–78. Cf. Maurice Lee, Jr., *Great Britain's Solomon* (Urbana: University of Illinois Press, 1990), 142.

16. See Linda Levy Peck, *Court Patronage and Corruption in Early Stuart England* (Boston: Unwin Hyman, 1990), 68–70. My essay in *The Mental World of the Jacobean Court*, ed. Peck, 191–208, takes a different viewpoint.

17. I shall be arguing in these instances along lines delineated by Susan Frye and Carole Levin in their views of Elizabeth I's close attention to the importance of maintaining control over such representational situations. See Susan Frye, *Elizabeth I: The Competition for Representation* (Oxford: University Press, 1993), esp. 86–90; Carole Levin, *"The Heart and Stomach of a King": Elizabeth I and the Politics of Sex and Power* (Philadelphia: University of Pennsylvania Press, 1994), esp. ch. 2. More recently, Levin has discussed Queen Elizabeth's sense of the importance of such representation from a different viewpoint. See " 'We Princes, I Tell You, Are Set on Stages': Elizabeth I and Dramatic Self-Representation," in *Readings in Renaissance Women's Drama: Criticism, History, and Performance, 1594–1998*, ed. S. P. Cerasano and Marion Wynne-Davies (London: Routledge, 1998).

18. Mathew's summary judgment of Anna seems especially condescending. A woman with few intimates, but especially fond of dogs, "we can see her best standing on the short turf holding her Italian greyhounds by a crimson lead" (*James I*, 278).

CHAPTER 2. ANNA IN SCOTLAND

1. Uraniborg held sixteen stone furnaces for distilling. On the upper floors were a library and a museum, and on the second floor, a large sitting-room adjoining four apartments. The towers contained observatories and the whole was supplied with running water powered by a pressure pump from a well eighty feet deep. See Joakim A. Skovgaard, *A King's Architecture* (London: Hugh Evelyn, 1973), 15–16.

2. Further, on one of Sophia's frequent visits to Hven, Brahe interested her in the work of his friend, the historian Anders Sorensen Vedel (Velleius). At Brahe's urging, Sophia encouraged Vedel to gather and publish all the old Danish ballads he happened to have in his personal collection, a collection which today represents an important source of early Danish folk literature. See J. L. E. Dreyer, *Tycho Brahe* (Edinburgh: Adam and Charles Black, 1890), 200n. 1.

3. In 1589, when Anna was betrothed to James VI, the ages of the siblings were as follows: Elizabeth, 16; Anna, 15; Christian, 12; Ulric, 11; Augusta, 9; Hedevig, 8; and Hans, 6.

4. For the comment to Burleigh, see Sir Henry Ellis, ed., *Original Letters Illustrative of English History*, 2d series (London, 1827), 3:149: the letter of Daniel Rogers to Lord Burleigh in 1588. It is also quoted by Adolphus William Ward in *DNB*, 1:431. Scottish commentators several times remarked on Sophia's strong personality—see *Calendar of State Papers Relating to Scotland and Mary Queen of Scots*, 13 vols. (Edinburgh, 1898–1969), 10:297, 371 (hereafter cited as *CSPS*). Citations

from calendared papers are, of course, assumed to be abstracts rather than verbatim transcripts of originals.

5. For these matters see Ellis, *Original Letters*, 3:149, and Paul Douglas Lockhart, *Denmark in the Thirty Years' War, 1618–1648* (Selinsgrove, Pa.: Susquehanna University Press, 1996), 116, 166–67, 309n. 92.

6. The formal wedding was planned for November 1589, but Anna's crossing was so delayed by storms that James sailed to Norway, where he married her on 23 November. See David Moysie, *Memoirs of the Affairs of Scotland* (Edinburgh: Bannatyne Club, 1830), 79–81. Queen Sophia invited the couple to Copenhagen, and James visited Hven to meet Tycho Brahe, being impressed enough by his experience at Uraniborg to write three poems about Brahe. For the texts see James I, *New Poems*, ed. Allan F. Westcott (New York: Columbia University Press, 1911), 26–27, and James VI, *Poems*, ed. James Craigie (Edinburgh: Scottish Text Society, 1958), 2:100–101. For a description of Anna's coronation, see David Calderwood, *The History of the Kirk of Scotland* ed. Thomas Thomson (Edinburgh: Woodrow Society, 1844), 5:95–98. For the only account of Anna's marriage in the past forty years, see David Harris Willson, *James VI and I* (New York: Oxford University Press, 1956), ch. 6. For a Danish account of the wedding see David Stevenson, *Scotland's Last Royal Wedding* (Edinburgh: John Donald, 1997), 79–122; Michael Lynch, "Court Ceremony and Ritual," in *The Reign of James VI*, ed. Julian Goodare and Michael Lynch (East Linton, Scotland: Tuckwell Press, 2000), 71–92.

7. In the nine years from the birth of her first son to Anna's accession as queen of England, she bore five children (two of whom did not survive beyond the age of two) and became pregnant with another.

8. See Jennifer M. Brown, "Scottish Politics, 1567–1625," in *The Reign of James VI and I*, ed. Alan G. R. Smith (London: Macmillan, 1973), 22–40, and Keith M. Brown, *Bloodfeud in Scotland, 1573–1625* (Edinburgh: John Donald, 1986), 107–44.

9. For these matters, *CSPS*, 10:437; Moysie, *Memoirs of the Affairs of Scotland*, 102, and *Complete Peerage*, ed. H. A. Doubleday et al. (London: St. Catherine's Press, 1910–59), 6:680.

10. The queen's inclining to Lady Huntly is referred to in *CSPS* 11:93, 171, 181, 296, 321, 368, 370; 13:1, 398–99. In 1600 she would be one of the gossips at Prince Charles's baptism (*CSPS*, 13:2.758). In 1596 and again in 1597, Sir William Bowes, the English agent, would express concern that the countess would influence Anna in an action—see *CSPS*, 12:383, 467 (487?); *CSPS* 13:162, 730. Cecil wrote that Huntly was "a great practiser, and great with the Queen" (*CSPS*, 13:436. Another lady to whom Anna was inclined was the countess of Erroll, daughter of the earl of Morton (*CSPS*, 13:162). Indeed, this letter (2 February 1598) to Lord Scrope in Berwick-on-Tweed noted this countess was "so far beloved as plurality of her Majesty's kisses do well witness."

11. Stuart, arriving from France in 1579, had become an important influence upon the thirteen-year-old James, who had created him first duke of Lennox. But the earl of Gowrie, after kidnaping James in 1582, had forced Lennox into exile. Dead in France by 1583, Lennox left four children whom James fostered throughout their lives. The two daughters were married to his childhood friends, the earls of

Mar and Huntly. Anna's friend, Henrietta, countess of Huntly, was thus very closely bound to James as well. She was formally a Protestant, owing to her father's careful recantation, but her husband was one of the group of powerful Catholic earls that included Erroll, Crawford, Maxwell, and Claude. For these matters, see Maurice Lee, Jr., *John Maitland of Thirlstane* (Princeton: Princeton University Press, 1959), 38–41; *CSPS*, 10:437; Moysie, *Memoirs of the Affairs of Scotland*, 102, and *Peerage*, 6:680. Huntly had received his education at the Valois court, and his wife, Henrietta, had also been raised in France, to which she would return in her widowhood and where she would die.

12. See *CSPS*, 10:450, 507, and for other such activity this year see *CSPS*, 10:543–44. In those early days Anna also twice sided with Maitland in persuading James to readmit nobles forbidden the court, such as Sir Walter Scott, laird of Buccleuch, in December 1591—see *CSPS*, 10:602–10.

13. See *CSPS*, 11:150. To this group around Anna should be added Sir Thomas Lyon of Auldbar, master of Glamis—see Lee, *Maitland*, 253–54.

14. *Manuscripts of the Earl of Salisbury Preserved at Hatfield House*, 23 vols., ed. M. S. Giuseppi (London: HMC, 1883–1976), 4:178; *CSPS*, 10:722. For Anna's later pressure on the chancellor, see *CSPS*, 10:788, 803, 824.

15. Apparently, Anna wished to go visit the earl of Atholl, who was not getting on well with James at the time. After first agreeing to her trip, the king later sent an order forbidding it. Thus constricted, the queen, according to a report to Burleigh in England from his Scottish agent, many times "falleth into tears, wishing herself either with her mother in Denmark, or else that she might see or speak with her majesty [Queen Elizabeth]" (*CSPS* 10:722).

16. See *Manuscripts of the Earl of Mar and Kellie . . . at Alloa House*, ed. Henry Paton (London: HMC, 1904), 40. All Scottish quotations, except when specified, have been silently Anglicized.

17. Lockhart, *Denmark in the Thirty Years' War*, 59–60.

18. Elizabeth, Anna's sister, married Duke Heinrich Julius of Brunswick-Wolfenbüttel, one of the most active, militant, and respected princes of the Löwe Saxon Circle (an area embracing northwestern Germany from Göttingen to the west to Rostock). See Lockhart, *Denmark in the Thirty Years' War*, map, 280.

19. For a parallel account of the 1595 troubles, see *The Original Letters of Sir John Colville*, ed. Thomas Thomson (Edinburgh: Bannatyne Club, 1858), 163–77; Calderwood, *History of the Kirk*, 5:365–66. Walter Scott of Buccleuch and Robert Kerr of Cessford were said to be in greatest favor with the queen on 3 March 1595, and they may have incited her to go after her son (*CSPS*, 11:543, 554). According to George Nicolson, servant to the English ambassador in Scotland, Sir Robert Bowes, the Queen's Council in 1593 consisted of "[James] Elphinstone [of Innernochtie], John Lindsay [of Balcares], Thomas Hamilton [of Drumcairne], Pluscardin [Alexander Seton Lord Urquhart]," *CSPS*, 12:90. All these were to be members of the Octavians, created in 1596 to fill the vacancy created by Maitland's death. Significantly Anna's four councillors became the core of this group after the queen presented James with a bag of gold, saying that she was giving him money that her councillors had saved for her in their administration of her finances. Asked who these were, she named the above and James appointed them as a council to administer his own

funds. The other Octavians appointed by James were Walter Steward Lord Blantyre, Sir Peter Young of Easter Seaton, Lord Menuir, Lord Balmerino, and Sir Alexander Seton.

20. Bothwell, who had been trying to assassinate James, had finally been banished from Scotland in 1595, but he had not yet departed the islands—see Maurice Lee, Jr., *Great Britain's Solomon* (Urbana: University of Illinois Press, 1990), 76 and n. 32. Because Bothwell was still in England, James may have suggested his proximity as a convincing reason for keeping the infant Henry under heavy guard.

21. See *CSPS*, 11:602, 626–27. For Aston, see Neil Cuddy, "The Revival of the Entourage: The Bedchamber of James I, 1603–1625," in Starkey, 188–89. On 20 June Roger Aston sent a lengthy analysis of the situation to Robert Bowes (*CSPS*, 11:617–18).

22. Maitland's switch back to the queen suggests the factional utility each held for the other, but for a sympathetic appraisal of Maitland's role here, see Lee, *Great Britain's Solomon*, 286–88. The anonymous *Historie and Life of King James the Sext* (Edinburgh: Bannatyne Club, 1825) wrote that involved here in August 1595 were "the Queen, Lord Chancellor [Maitland], Lord Treasurer [master of Glamis], the Lord [Alexander Sixth earl] Home, Sir Robert Kerr of Cessford, Sir Walter Scott of Branxholme [and Buccleuch]," and "all the border men from Dumfreys to Berwick" (348). Another source (*CSPS*, 11:660) adds the specific names of Thomas Hamilton of Drumcairne, Lord Fleming, and Livingston.

23. For these instructions, see *Mar and Kellie*, 43–44.

24. See Lee, *Great Britain's Solomon*, 47 and n. 51.

25. She intervened, for instance, to try to resolve Mar's feud with Livingston. See Brown, *Bloodfeud in Scotland*, 130–32.

26. Thomas Lake wrote Robert Sidney on 1 October: "The King's displeasure against the Chancellor is so great that he has absented himself from the court. The parties that should have been doers in that attempt are all our borderers, as Hume and Cessford." See *Manuscripts of the Lord de L'Isle and Dudley Preserved at Penshurst Place*, 6 vols., ed. C. L. Kingsford and William A. Shaw (London: HMC, 1936), 4:168.

27. She joined the court consensus in persuading King James to allow the husband of her friend the countess of Huntly to return from his European exile. Huntly had been banished in March 1595 at the instigation of the anti-Catholic Kirk in punishment for his murder of the earl of Moray (*CSPS*, 10:633–36; 11:561).

28. See *CSPS*, 13:133, 264. On 10 July 1596 Burghley had also written Robert Cecil about Anna's evilly disposed counselors. See *CSPS*, 12:266.

29. Sir Roger Aston, for one, Sir George Home, and the earl of Mar all suggested to the king Anna's complicity in the assassination plot. But in this famously tangled ambiguity, we also note the duke of Lennox, Anna's usual ally, observing that if there was a plot, he himself did not know "whether the practice proceeded from Gowry or the King." See *CSPS*, 13:2 721–37. Anna's life was made even more difficult at this time because of the death of her second child, Margaret, at the age of two years and eight months (born 24 December 1598). In 1606 Anna again lost a child over a year after birth. For Margaret's death, see *CSPS*, 13:691.

30. See *The Border Papers*, 2 vols., ed. Joseph Bain (Edinburgh: HMTO, 1896), 2:698.

31. See *CSPS*, 13:721. Lord Willoughby, the general in charge of England's northern borders, wrote Cecil that Anna's brother, the king of Denmark, had received an account of the Gowries' death from King James translated into "Dutch" (German was one of the languages of the Danish sovereignty). Christian "never vouchsafed to read it but gave it to [the] Queen mother there [Sophia]." Willoughby also noted that the king of Denmark might be going to Scotland in the summer, all of which suggests the degree of polarization between Anna and James occasioned by this situation. See *Border Papers*, 2:713.

32. In England, however, rumor was still current. For example, Sir Henry Neville wrote Ralph Winwood on 15 November 1600 that "out of Scotland we hear there is no good agreement but rather an open diffidence between the King of Scots and his wife, and many are of opinion that the discovery of some affection between her and Earl Gowry's brother (who was killed with him) was the truest cause and motive of all that tragedy." See Sir Ralph Winwood, *Memorials of Affairs of State*, 3 vols., ed. Edmond Sawyer (London, 1725), 1:275. See also *Border Papers*, 2:698.

33. See *CSPS*, 13:719, 727, 737, 789; Moysie, *Memoirs of the Affairs of Scotland*, 141–43.

34. At this time Thomas Douglas described the queen and "her faction" as being aligned against Mar, Sir George Home, and Thomas Erskine (*CSPS*, 13:762). In May she was said to be making plans against the King's Bed Chamber (*CSPS*, 13:779), and, a little later, to be aligned not only against Erskine and Home, but also against the comptroller, Sir David Murray (829). Members of Anna's group at this time included Patrick, master of Gray, and David Lindsay, the earl of Crawford's brother, as well as Alexander Lindsay Lord Spynie (see *CSPS*, 13:829, 849–50).

35. See *CSPS*, 13:795. The ruling group referred to included the earl of Mar, Sir Thomas Erskine, and Sir George Home (*CSPS*, 13:762), all of whom would accompany James to England.

36. Anna's frequent pregnancies suggest either James's great concern to have as many children as possible or a relationship between these two persons that is not borne out by conventional biographies of James as barely heterosexual.

37. See Agnes Strickland, *Lives of the Queens of England* (London: George Bell and Sons, 1842–88), 4:55, who has also commented on this event.

38. *CSPS*, 13:1095–96; see also Strickland, *Lives of the Queen of England*, 55.

39. That previous summer, significantly, there had been more rumors about the prince moving from Mar's custody to the queen's—see *CSPS*, 13:1007–8, 1003, 1013—and friction about this with Mar: 13:1026, 1028–29. For the queen's scheduled departure date for England, see *Salisbury MSS*, 15:53. Significantly, in April 1603, King James also entrusted the education of Prince Charles to a Scottish noble, Alexander Seton, Lord Fyvie, through a decree of the Scottish Privy Council. See Walter W. Seton, "The Early Years of Henry Frederick, Prince of Wales, and Charles, Duke of Albany, 1593–1605," *Scottish Historical Review* 13 (1916): 366–79.

40. See Calderwood, *History of the Kirk*, 6:230–31. These were presumably James Marquis of Hamilton, James Cunningham, seventh earl of Glencairne, John,

master of Orkney, Alexander Livingston, earl of Linlithgow, and Alexander, fourth Lord Elphinstone. For another list of the participants see *Register of the Privy Council of Scotland* 1st series, ed. David Masson (Edinburgh, 1877–), 6:571–72 (hereafter cited as *PCS*). As for their religious persuasions, Hamilton and Glencairne were thought to be Protestants but not politically active; Linlithgow and Elphinstone were thought to be Catholics, the latter also deemed a "gret actor." See *Letters and State Papers during the Reign of King James VI . . . from the MS Collections of Sir James Balfour of Denmyln*, ed. Adam Anderson (Edinburgh: Abbotsford Club, 1838), 333–53.

    41. See Sir William A. Craigie, *A Dictionary of the Scottish Tongue* (Chicago: University of Chicago Press, 1931–), 1:406, 5:231.

    42. *Balfour Letters*, 48–57.

    43. For the Venetian ambassador's account, see *Calendar of State Papers . . . Venice*, ed. Horatio F. Brown (London: HMTO, 1900), 10:40, (subsequently cited as *SPV*) and see 10:42 for a parallel account by the Venetian ambassador in France. For Calderwood, *History of the Kirk*, see 6:231. Anna had suffered a similar episode in 1595, during one of her earlier battles for Henry, being then, apparently, seriously ill and again close to giving birth. James had appointed a jury of matrons and Dame Margaret Stuart, Lady Ochiltree (nurse to the queen and her children from 1590 to 1603) to investigate Anna's claim of illness. They pronounced it genuine. See Seton, "Early Years," 377.

    44. Calderwood, *History of the Kirk*, 6:231.

    45. *Balfour Letters*, 49–50.

    46. Craigie, *Dictionary of the Scottish Tongue*, 2:269, 277: *elest*.

    47. *Balfour Letters*.

    48. See *Mar and Kellie*, 50. The next day, members of the official group of English noblemen designated by the Privy Council to escort the new queen from the Scottish border at Berwick south knew that something was wrong. Lord Norris, one of the group, stopped his journey north at Doncaster, wrote Cecil on 15 May, "I meet diverse reports here in Yorkshire that the Queen will not begin her journey shortly . . . for here they say she will not set forward this month." To this the earl of Lincoln, in Northallerton, added that he was told by the earl of Orkney and others "of her Majesty's unfitness to remove for a long time." William Lord Compton wrote from Newcastle of "finding that the news that came daily from the north was somewhat uncertain, and humorously [variously] delivered by such Scots as I met." The earl of Cumberland, somewhere south of Newcastle, also wrote Cecil: "I pray you if there be any more certain word come since I saw you what day the Queen comes for Berwick send me word by this bearer." See *Salisbury MSS*, 15:90, 112, 117.

    49. *Mar and Kellie*, 50–51.

    50. The king at this time was also quite concerned about the nobles who had accompanied Anna to Stirling. See James Symple's letter to Cecil in this month: "The King told me that the Earl of Linlithgow should be certified by me that he was too bold in that he attempted to join himself as surety with the rest of the noblemen for the Prince's delivery to the Queen without his Majesty's warrant; and if

he should deal with rigor with them all, they should lose their heads. I pray you destroy this part of the paper and you shall hear more" (*Salisbury MSS*, 15:116).

51. Calderwood, *History of the Kirk*, 6:230.

52. See *PCS*, 6:571 and n. 1.

53. Yet, significantly, James, aware that Prince Henry would be proceeding from Stirling to Edinburgh to Berwick through border territory that harbored inimical elements, intended to assure himself that Mar would remain in the vicinity of the royal party, for this same letter adds a proviso to the disclaimer — "the said Earl [of Mar] resting always in his person bound and obliged by virtue of the foresaid act, upon his honor and fidelity, to continue his careful and vigilant attendance upon the person of the Prince, his preservation and safe convoy in company of the Queen, his dearest mother, till he present him in safety to his Majesty. At the which time his Highness promises in his princely word to see him [Mar] gratified with a condign remembrance to him and his in a perpetual record of his said service." See *Mar and Kellie*, 51-52. For the Privy Council entry see *PCS*, 6:571.

54. For Alexander Lord Fyvie, see Seton, "Early Years," 378.

55. *Balfour Letters*, 53-54.

56. Calderwood, *History of the Kirk*, 6:231. Calderwood had named five lords: Hamilton, Glencairne, Linlithgow, Elphinstone, and the master of Orkney.

57. *Balfour Letters*, 53-55.

58. Calderwood, *History of the Kirk*, 6:232.

59. Calderwood, *History of the Kirk*, 6:230. Evidence of Henry's own attachments at this time may be found in the recollection of one of the men brought up with the young prince published long after Henry's, Anna's, and James's deaths. Recalling the old countess of Mar as a lady "who kept all such as were about [the prince] in awe," he also remembers the prince from those Scottish days "before his coming to England, the Earl [of Mar] delivering him in presence of the Council to the charge of other lords appointed to wait on him in his journey, he suddenly embracing the said Earl, burst forth into tears, albeit he was known to weep as little as any child whatsoever." W. H., *The True Picture and Relation of Prince Henry* (Leiden, 1634), sig. A3.

60. See *Mar and Kellie*, 43-44; E. C. Wilson, *Prince Henry and English Literature* (Ithaca, N.Y.: Cornell University Press, 1946), 5n. 8. For James's long-range plans for Henry, see *SPV*, 10:40.

61. See Roy Strong, *Henry Prince of Wales and England's Lost Renaissance* (London: Thames and Hudson, 1986), 16, 25.

62. All of them, except Erskine, were sworn to the English Privy Council by 4 May 1603. See *Acts of the Privy Council of England* [1542-1604], 35 vols., ed. J. R. Dasent (London, 1890-1907), 32:496-97 (hereafter cited as *PCE*). Erskine replaced Sir Walter Ralegh as captain of the Yeomen of the Guard (James's personal protectors). Several months after his accession, James also awarded Lennox and Mar the Order of the Garter. Sir George Home became Baron Home of Berwick (and earl of Dunbar in Scotland), returning to Scotland in 1606 as James's regent. Balmerino and Hamilton also returned. See Maurice Lee, Jr., *Government by Pen* (Urbana: University of Illinois Press, 1980), 56n. 2 and ch. 3.

63. Maximilian de Bethune, duke of Sully, *Memoirs* (Edinburgh, 1805), 3:115–16. Sully was Henri IV's most important minister — see, for example, Robin Briggs, *Early Modern France, 1560–1715* (Oxford: Oxford University Press, 1977), 82–84 — but Sully is the only source I know for the story about Anna's miscarried child. Sully actually came to England, however, *after* Anna had arrived in London.

CHAPTER 3. QUEEN ANNA'S ENGLISH COURT

1. For a recent analysis of this process, see Carole Levin, *"The Heart and Stomach of a King": Elizabeth I and the Politics of Sex and Power* (Philadelphia: University of Pennsylvania Press, 1994), esp. chs. 2–5.

2. See Pam Wright, "A Change of Direction: The Ramifications of a Female Household, 1558–1603," in Starkey, 147–72.

3. For these matters see John Stow, *Annals [as Continued by Edmond Howes]* (London, 1615), sig. 3Z5 (p. 826) and *Manuscripts of the Earl of Salisbury Preserved at Hatfield House*, 23 vols., ed. M. S. Giuseppi (London: HMC, 1883–1976), 15:52. Dating throughout this book is *English* New Style (the new year begins 1 January rather than 25 March ("Lady Day"), but English 1 January = Continental 11 January).

4. The following were the officers of the queen's household, appointed, for the most part, in July 1603: Sir Robert Cecil, Lord High Steward; Sir Robert Sidney, Lord High Chamberlain and Surveyor General; Sir George Carew, Vice Chamberlain and Receiver; Sir Thomas Mounson, Chancellor; the earl of Southampton, Master of the Game; Thomas Somerset, Master of the Horse; William Fowler, Secretary and Master of Requests. See Edmund Lodge, *Illustrations of British History* (London: J. Chidley, 1838), 3:65. For discussion of the place of queenship in political theory, see Constance Jordan, "Woman's Rule in Sixteenth-Century British Political Thought," *Renaissance Quarterly*, 40 (1987): 421–51, and of Elizabeth's especially, Levin, *"Heart and Stomach,"* ch. 6: "Elizabeth as King and Queen." For Cecil's relationship to Anna's court, see Pauline Croft, "Robert Cecil and the Early Jacobean Court," in *The Mental World of the Jacobean Court*, ed. Linda Levy Peck (Cambridge: Cambridge University Press, 1991), 134–47.

5. This was more than a month after her death, because the English Privy Council wanted to ensure an appropriate period of mourning and because the nobility had to be gathered from all over England for the funeral procession itself (*Salisbury MSS*, 15:56).

6. See *Salisbury MSS*, 15:52–53. For the date of Anna's actual departure from Edinburgh after the troubles described in Chapter 2, see David Calderwood, *History of the Kirk of Scotland* (Edinburgh: Woodrow Society, 1845), 6:232.

7. See Sir Henry Ellis, ed., *Original Letters Illustrative of English History*, 1st series (London, 1824), 3:70; John Nichols, *The Progresses... of James the First*, 4 vols. (London, 1828), 1:190; *SPV*, 10:27.

8. For example, consider only the "two ladies" in the group. They were named by John Stow as "Lady [Anne] Herbert" and "Lady [Audrey] Walsingham." Lady Herbert probably was not Mary Herbert, the countess of Pembroke's daughter. A more logical candidate is the Lady Anne Herbert whose mother, Lady Eliza-

beth Russell (the widow of Sir Thomas Hoby and then of John Lord Russell), was Robert Cecil's aunt. Anne, a maid of honor with Queen Elizabeth, married the earl of Worcester's son, Henry Somerset, traditionally styled "Lord Herbert," in 1601, with Queen Elizabeth in attendance at the wedding. Now twenty-eight, Lady Anne Herbert might logically have been chosen by her mother-in-law, wife of the Master of the Horse. "Lady Walsingham" was Audrey Shelton Walsingham, married to a knight, Sir Thomas Walsingham, who worked for and reported to Cecil. As keeper of the queen's wardrobe under Queen Elizabeth — see *Calendar of State Papers: Domestic Series, of the Reigns of Edward VI, Mary, Elizabeth I, and James I (1547–1625)*, 12 vols., ed. Robert Lemon and M. A. E. Green (London: HMC, 1856–72), 12:427 (hereafter cited as *SPD*) — she must have been chosen for her trustworthiness. She went now toward Scotland with her husband, sending a packet of letters to Cecil from Berwick after their arrival at the border town.

9. A member of the Privy Council, the earl had been Elizabeth's special envoy to Edinburgh to bear England's congratulations on the occasion of James's marriage to Anna. See E. C. Williams, *Anne of Denmark* (London: Longman, 1971), 243. In 1602 he was also prestigious enough to increase to three the number of acting companies allowed in London, when his troupe began playing at the Boar's Head. See E. K. Chambers, *The Elizabethan Stage* (Oxford: Clarendon Press, 1923), 2:225–26.

10. There is an allusion by the earl to his wife's "service" to the queen (*Salisbury MSS*, 12:43). The countess was also included among the ladies awarded prizes by Sir Thomas Egerton and his wife at the Harefield entertainment of Queen Elizabeth the previous summer: see *The Egerton Papers*, ed. J. P. Collier (London: Camden Society, 1840), 353 (the forgeries in this Collier edition being on 340–42). The countess's age is not known, but she had been married to Worcester since 1571 and if, as was true of many of her peers, she had married as young as fifteen, she was at least forty-seven in 1603. See *Peerage*, 12:2.856.

11. See *Peerage*, 7:240, for one date of remarriage — 1601 — but she was already remarried by 23 August 1600: *L'Isle MSS*, 2:479. Kildare married Frances Howard in 1590 but died in 1597 fighting in Ireland in the wars against Tyrone: see *Peerage*, 7:240. After her remarriage to Cobham, who was of lower degree, Lady Kildare retained her former title, as was customary (e.g., the dowager countess of Derby married to Sir Thomas Egerton also retaining her title).

12. Her apparent knowledge of Queen Elizabeth's private activities (or the perception that Kildare had this knowledge) and her presence at the Harefield entertainment with the countess of Worcester also suggests her inclusion among Elizabeth's circle of ladies (Levin, "*Heart and Stomach*," 167–68; *Salisbury MSS*, 13:84). Kildare's influence would be attested to by what happened after her husband, Lord Cobham, was attainted for treason against the new king in 1603 and put in the Tower for life. Although the lands of an attainted noble were ordinarily confiscated by the Crown, on 13 May 1604 Frances was granted Cobham Hall along with Cobham's other lands for the rest of her life, the reversion of Cobham Hall only then being granted to the duke of Lennox: see *Peerage*, 3:349n. g.

13. She was married to Thomas, Lord Scrope of Bolton, warden of the West Marches and keeper of Carlisle in the north (*Peerage*, 11:549–50). He had attended

upon James when the king's progress had reached Newcastle-upon-Tyne on 12 April, and perhaps Lady Scrope was chosen as a result of her husband's presence there with the king: see *Salisbury MSS*, 15:46–47.

14. See *Peerage*, 11:549–50, and Robert Carey, *Memoirs*, ed. F. H. Mares (Oxford: Clarendon Press, 1972), 25n.; *L'Isle MSS*, 2:204, 400. Lady Scrope had enjoyed sufficient standing at court as the queen's chief lady to speak to Elizabeth in Essex's defense when the queen was enraged at him in 1599, two years before the uprising: see *L'Isle MSS*, 2:400.

15. See *L'Isle MSS*, 2:35, 475, 461. For the text of this missive, see Sylvia Freedman, *Poor Penelope* (London: Kensale Press, 1983), 132–33.

16. There she was in such need of bedding, hangings, and linen that the Privy Council had to order her husband to send them. See *Acts of the Privy Council of England, 1542–1604*, 35 vols., ed. J. R. Dasent (London, 1890–1907), 31:176 (hereafter cited as *PCE*).

17. See *SPD*, 8:32. For James's treatment of the young Essex early in 1603, see *SPV*, 10:26.

18. See John Stow, *Annals [as continued by Edmond Howes]* (London, 1615), sig. 3Z3^v [p. 823]. With the countess were two women who themselves are of some significance. They were her mother, Ann Kelway Harington, who with her husband would be entrusted with the guardianship of Princess Elizabeth and also Lady Hatton. This second noblewoman was niece of Sir Robert Cecil, her father being Cecil's older brother, Thomas Lord Burghley, son and heir to Queen Elizabeth's great servant. Elizabeth Burghley had married William Hatton, nephew and heir of Sir Christopher Hatton, Queen Elizabeth's late Lord Chancellor. Upon her husband's death in 1597, Elizabeth Hatton surprised observers by declining the optimal marriages she might then have made as a result of her dead husband's fortune and her own Cecil lineage. She married, instead, Sir Edward Coke (future Lord Chancellor of England).

19. Relevant here is Essex's own systematic cultural patronage in the appointment of personal secretaries such as Edward Reynoldes. See Paul E. J. Hammer, "The Uses of Scholarship: The Secretariat of Robert Devereux, Second Earl of Essex, c. 1585–1601," *English Historical Review* 109 (1994): 26–51, who also notes the links between this group surrounding Essex and the circle around Prince Henry (50n. 5).

20. See John Chamberlain, *Letters*, ed. N. E. McClure (Philadelphia: American Philosophical Society, 1939), 2:85.

21. "Leicester" was Lettice (or Laetitia), countess of Leicester, mother of the executed earl of Essex and of his sisters, Penelope (Devereux) Rich and Dorothy (Devereux), countess of Northumberland. Leicester was now married to Mountjoy's kinsman, Sir Christopher Blount, one of the five or six persons connected with the special performance of Shakespeare's *Richard II* before the Essex rebellion and one of the few persons executed for the conspiracy. See Barroll, "A New History for Shakespeare and His Time," *Shakespeare Quarterly* 39 (1988): 441–64.

22. For these two passages, see *L'Isle MSS*, 2:322; Chamberlain, *Letters*, 1:179.

23. For Bedford's friendship with the earl of Pembroke, see Michael Brennan, *Literary Patronage in the English Renaissance* (London: Routledge, 1988), 156. Unfortunately, when Pembroke married on 4 November 1604, his spouse, Mary Talbot,

one of the three (known) daughters of the seventh earl of Shrewsbury, though apparently willing, and positioned through her husband's closeness to the queen's group to join it at an early stage in Anna's reign, does not seem to have been able to fit in here (see Lodge, *Illustrations of British History*, 3:151–52, 161–62). This is in interesting contrast to Mary's sister, Althea, who seems to have gained quick access to the queen after she married the young earl of Arundel on 30 September 1606.

24. See *The Border Papers*, 2 vols., ed. Joseph Bain (Edinburgh: HMTO, 1896), 2:678.

25. Calderwood, *History of the Kirk*, 6:232.

26. See *Dudley Carleton to John Chamberlain: 1603–1624*, ed. Maurice Lee, Jr. (New Brunswick, N.J.: Rutgers University Press [1972]), 35; *The Diaries of Lady Anne Clifford*, ed. D. J. H. Clifford (Wolfeboro Falls, N.H., 1991), 23.

27. See *Clifford Diaries*, 23.

28. See *Clifford Diaries*, 23. The other (necessary) exception was the low-ranking Lady Walsingham, whose practical experience with Queen Elizabeth must have led her, on 26 July, to be made guardian and keeper of the queen's robes (see *SPD*, 12:427).

29. *Carleton to Chamberlain*, 35. Identification of "Lady Essex" in July 1603 is problematic because Frances Walsingham, widow of Sir Philip Sidney and then of the earl of Essex, would have by then married the (Irish) earl of Clanricard (by 12 April 1603: Chamberlain, *Letters*, 1:193). I assume that the Irish earldom could not claim the (English) precedence of the Essex name and that, consequently, the countess of Clanricard, as Essex's widow, was still known as the countess of Essex. (Clifford's "Lady Essex" was almost certainly not Laetitia, widow of the first earl of Essex and then widow of the earl of Leicester, and again widow of the conspirator Christopher Blount, unless she used her Essex rather than her Leicester name. I have not found an instance of her doing so.)

30. See Nichols, *Progresses*, 1:190.

31. Indeed, Kildare may have gained an intimacy with Anna because she showed the kind of initiative displayed by the Bedford group. As the official ladies, of whom she was one, waited in Berwick during the long delay caused by the queen's miscarriage in Scotland, Lord Compton, one of the nobles in the official escort group, wrote Cecil from Newcastle on 30 May that "my Lady Kildare would needs quit her companions at Berwick and went to Edinburgh" (*Salisbury MSS*, 15:112) where the queen was about to make her appearance after the miscarriage. Anna arrived in Berwick on 6 June, then spent the night in Newcastle-upon-Tyne on 8 June and in York on 11 June: see *Salisbury MSS*, 15:126.

32. *Clifford Diaries*, 9. The countess of Kildare was appointed Elizabeth's governess on 5 June and was with the princess on 4 July. But she and the princess were also at Combe Abbey visiting Lord and Lady Harington on 13 and 25 June. The Privy Seal order consigning Elizabeth exclusively to the Haringtons is dated 19 October 1603. For these matters see Mary Anne Everett Green, *Elizabeth Electress Palatine*, rev. S. C. Lomas (London: Methuen, 1909), 4–7.

33. *Clifford Diaries*, 24n. 4. That Penelope Rich was indeed congenial now with the queen is reemphasized in a remark several weeks later by Dudley Carleton, who had noticed that Rich was one of three ladies especially in favor with Anna.

34. *Salisbury MSS*, 15:388.

35. See Winwood, *Memorials of Affairs of State*, 2:40. Lady Hatton would dance once, as a guest, in the *Masque of Beauty* presented in the Christmas season of 1607-8. She is also recorded as having run afoul of Anna in 1616, and she was denied the court as a result: see Chamberlain, 2:14, 113.

36. Rich is mentioned in July by Anne Clifford (*Clifford Diaries*, 35).

37. See Lodge, *Illustrations of British History*, 3:88-89. Although Worcester (probably with more authority than most) described Bedford as being of the "Bed Chamber," Dudley Carleton described her as having been sworn to the "Privy Chamber." See Nichols, *Progresses*, 1:190. For a general discussion of the Privy Chamber, see Chambers, *The Elizabethan Stage*, 1:54; Wright, "A Change of Direction," for the chamber under Queen Elizabeth; and Neil Cuddy, "The Revival of the Entourage: The Bedchamber of James I, 1603-1625," in Starkey, 173-225.

38. She was either Anne Woodhouse, wife of Sir Julius Caesar, or Mary Woodhouse, wife of Sir Robert Killigrew. See R. C. Bald, *John Donne: A Life* (Oxford: University Press, 1970), 441-42, 454. A list of Anna's "servants," compiled before 18 March 1606, is calendared in *Salisbury MSS*, 24:65-67.

39. See Anne Clifford as quoted by Nichols, *Progresses*, 1:196n. 2, and John Pitcher, "Samuel Daniel, the Hertfords, and a Question of Love," *Review of English Studies* 35 (1984): 449-62.

40. Winwood, *Memorials of Affairs of State*, 2:39.

41. Lodge, *Illustrations of British History*, 3:88.

42. For the expression of Hertford's unhappiness, see A. L. Rowse, *Simon Forman* (London: Weidenfeld and Nicolson, 1974), 231. Hertford is now perhaps better known by Lennox's new English title when he was created duke of Richmond. She lived on after the duke's death in 1624 as the duchess of Richmond, dying in 1639.

43. More than forty years previously, Edward Seymour, first earl of Hertford, without Queen Elizabeth's permission, had married Lady Catherine Grey, sister to Lady Jane Grey, granddaughter of Henry VIII's sister and thus of royal blood. Elizabeth held Hertford and his new wife in the Tower from 1561 to 1567. After having borne Hertford a son there, Catherine died, and Hertford was freed from the Tower in 1582. (For a recent but slightly different discussion of this matter, see Wallace MacCaffrey, *Elizabeth I* (London: Edward Arnold, 1993), 83 and note 2. He then married Frances Howard, sister of the earl of Nottingham, who was a Maid of Honor to Queen Elizabeth (her "Franke") for many years. The Earl, however, continued his efforts to establish his child by Catherine Grey, Edward, as his legitimate male heir (and thus as someone in the royal line). For this, Hertford was briefly committed to the Tower but soon released owing to his wife's influence.

44. See the article on Beauchamp by A. F. Pollard in *Dictionary of National Biography*, ed. Leslie Stephen and Sidney Lee, 66 vols. (London: Smith, Elder, 1885-1901), 17:1250 ff., and *Peerage*, 6:505 ff., for these matters.

45. "For the elder Earl of Hertford, crippled as he is, swears that he will have himself carried to London, and there sign the proclamation [of James as king] himself and pledges his son's hand to the same. . . . And so the crown falls peacefully to his Majesty." See *SPV*, 10:3; cf. Chamberlain, *Letters*, 1:190; *Salisbury MSS*, 15:223.

46. Hertford was to be found at the great house of the countess of Pem-

broke—"He comes often to Wilton and has made known his love to Lady Anne [Herbert]"—but Lady Pembroke did not want to marry her daughter to him. See *L'Isle MSS*, 2:465.

47. It is important to distinguish among four Frances Howards adducing what dates are available. (1) Frances Howard, died 1598 [second countess of Hertford], daughter of William Lord Howard of Effingham and Margaret Gamage; (2) Frances Howard, died 1628 [countess of Kildare], daughter of Charles Howard, earl of Nottingham, and Catherine Carey; (3) Frances Howard, 1578–1639 [who, in 1601, became third countess of Hertford], daughter of Thomas Howard Viscount Bindon and Mabel Burton; (4) Frances Howard, 1593–1632 [countess of Essex and then Somerset], daughter of Thomas Howard, earl of Suffolk, and Catherine Knyvett.

48. Although there is no reference to Scottish ladies or nobility by Worcester, a lady of the Bed Chamber missing from this list and important to note is Jean Drummond, daughter of Patrick, third Lord Drummond, who had served as Anna's lady of the Bed Chamber in Scotland and come to England with Anna. Indeed, eleven years later, in 1614, the countess of Bedford would attest to Drummond's elevated status when, writing to her close friend Lady Jane Cornwallis, Bedford observed that her plans to visit Cornwallis were on hold because of Lady Drummond's illness. Bedford was expected to fill in for Drummond, who became ill when she was scheduled to serve her waiting time as lady of the Bed Chamber. Later that year Anna sponsored an elaborate wedding for Drummond, with a masque by Samuel Daniel, when she married Robert Kerr of Cessford, first Lord Roxborough. For the details of the occasion see Samuel Daniel, *Hymen's Triumph*, ed. John Pitcher (Oxford: Malone Society, 1994), introduction, and below, chap. 5. For Cornwallis, see *The Private Correspondence of Jane, Lady Cornwallis*, ed. R. N. Braybrooke (London, 1842), 30.

49. See Joan Rees, "Samuel Daniel and the Earl of Hertford," *Notes and Queries*, n.s. 5 (1958): 408; Pitcher, "Samuel Daniel." (A company of players bearing the earl of Hertford's name, having toured the provinces throughout the 1590s, made their first Christmas appearance at court in over ten years when they played there on Twelfth Night 1603, Martin Slater being the payee. See Chambers, *The Elizabethan Stage*, 2:117.)

50. As previously remarked, there was little relationship between the political status of these women and the power of their husbands or fathers, but there seem to have been several exceptions. Lady Southwell was Elizabeth née Howard, daughter of the earl of Nottingham and widow of Sir Robert Southwell, vice admiral for Norfolk and Suffolk under his father-in-law. Lady Southwell would soon remarry, but for now, her wealth and her father's name defined her status. See *Peerage*, 9:782, and Robert Kenny, *Elizabeth's Admiral* (Baltimore: Johns Hopkins University Press, 1970), 93 and note 11. The countess of Suffolk (née Catherine Knyvett) was the wife of James's new Lord Chamberlain, but the lord chamberlainship was such an important office at court that it may have been far easier to include than to exclude her. I also find it significant that after having danced in Anna's first two masques, the countess appeared in none of her subsequent spectacles. Some of Lady Suffolk's activities with Anna may be indicated by Arbella Stuart's letter to the earl of Shrews-

bury, her uncle, before the first court masque in the Christmas season: "The Queen intendenth to make a mask this Christmas to which end my Lady of Suffolk and my Lady Walsingham hath warrants to take of the late Queen's best apparel out of the Tower at their discretion" (Lodge, *Illustrations of British History*, 3:81). Both of these ladies had been influential in the former reign, since the countess's husband was acting Lord Chamberlain during Queen Elizabeth's last year while Walsingham was Keeper of Queen Elizabeth's Wardrobe.

51. See Freedman, *Poor Penelope*, 81, for Rich's patronage of Hilliard.

52. For this identification of the dowager countess as one of the queen's ladies, see French R. Fogle, "Such a Rural Queen," in *Patronage in Late Renaissance England*, ed. French R. Fogle and Louis A. Knafla (Los Angeles: Clark Memorial Library, 1983), 3–29, and Barbara K. Lewalski, "Milton's Comus and the Politics of Masquing," in *The Politics of the Stuart Court Masque*, ed. David Bevington and Peter Holbrook (Cambridge: University Press, 1998), 298.

53. See John Orrell, "Antimo Galli's Description of *The Masque of Beauty*," *HLQ* 43 (1979): 13–23. In his *Rime* (London, 1609), sig. 12^v, Galli admittedly has the correct first names for all the other women in the masque.

54. For Egerton's own patronage, see Louis A. Knafla, "The 'Country' Chancellor: The Patronage of Sir Thomas Egerton Baron Ellesmere," in *Patronage in Late Renaissance England*, 31–115.

55. See *Clifford Diaries*, 23. Fourteen years later, this countess of Derby was still in an influential position at the queen's court. Clifford, attempting to influence the king about her inheritance, in January 1617 regarded "Lady Derby, my Lady Bedford, My Lady Montgomery" as a group. See *The Diary of Anne Clifford, 1616–1619*, ed. Katherine O. Acheson (New York: Garland, 1995), 62–64. Lady Walsingham was probably Audrey Shelton Walsingham.

56. Elizabeth had two younger sisters. Bridget, born in 1584, married Francis Norris, the future earl of Berkshire. Susan, born in 1587, married the earl of Pembroke's younger brother, Philip Herbert, earl of Montgomery.

57. Elizabeth is described in the 1589 west panel of the Burghley Memorial in Westminster Abbey as fourteen years old and grieving bitterly "for the loss of her grandmother and mother, but she feels happier because her most gracious Majesty has taken her into service as a Maid of Honor"—trans. from the Latin by B. M. Ward, *The Seventeenth Earl of Oxford, 1550–1640* (London: John Murray, 1928), 262.

58. Chambers, *The Elizabethan Stage*, 2:99–102. Elizabeth's father, the earl of Oxford, was reputed to have written plays, being mentioned by Francis Meres (with Shakespeare) as a writer of comedies, but since he had not often been near her, he probably did not influence her tastes, except negatively, since he was separated from her mother. For Oxford, see E. K. Chambers, *William Shakespeare: A Study of Facts and Problems* (Oxford: Clarendon Press, 1930), 2:193–94.

59. For William, earl of Derby's other patronage, see Virgil B. Heltzel, *English Literary Patronage, 1550–1630*, unpublished typescript, Folger Shakespeare Library, under "Stanley," and Thomas Heywood, "The Earls of Derby and the Verse Writers and Poets of the Sixteenth and Seventeenth Centuries," in *Remains . . . of Lancaster and Chester* (London: Chetham Society, 1853), 29. See also *Salisbury MSS*, 13:609

and Chambers, *The Elizabethan Stage*, 2:194. The countess of Derby's mother-in-law was married now to Sir Thomas Egerton (later Baron Ellesmere), himself well known as a patron and as the person whom John Donne served as secretary.

60. For documentation of these points, see Chambers, *The Elizabethan Stage*, 2:127.

61. The countess appears to have been highly competent. For example, she assumed responsibility for the administration of the Isle of Man, part of her husband's domain. Her son referred to her as "wise" and noted that after her death her husband grew "infirm and disconsolate and willing to repose himself from the troublers of the world." See J. J. Bagley, *The Earls of Derby* (London: Sidgwick and Jackson, 1985), 68 ff., and Barry Coward, *The Stanleys* (Manchester: Chetham Society, 1983), 60–61.

62. See *Carleton to Chamberlain*, 66–67.

63. See Bald, *John Donne*, 341. John Donne, *Letters to Several Persons of Honor* (London, 1651), sigs. D4ᵛ–Eᵛ, wrote the countess in 1619. For Susan de Vere, see also Graham Parry, *The Golden Age Restor'd* (Manchester: University Press, 1981), 108–11.

64. See *L'Isle MSS*, 3:412, 421; 4:45, 276, 282.

65. See *Amadis of Gaule*, trans. Anthony Munday (London, 1619), sig. A4ᵛ. See Brennan, *Literary Patronage*, 157, for the countess of Montgomery's interest in *Amadis de Gaule*. Susan died in 1628, after which her husband married Lady Anne Clifford, who as countess of Montgomery has sometimes been confused with Susan de Vere Herbert.

66. See Florence Humphreys Morgan, "A Biography of Lucy Countess of Bedford, the Last Great Literary Patroness," Ph.D. diss., University of Southern California, January 1956, 52–157; B. H. Newdigate, *Michael Drayton and His Circle*, corrected ed. (Oxford: University Press, 1961), ch. 5; Barbara K. Lewalski, "Lucy, Countess of Bedford: Images of a Jacobean Courtier and Patroness," in *The Politics of Discourse*, ed. Kevin Sharpe and Stephen Zwicker (Los Angeles: University of California Press, 1987), 52–77.

67. See *The Private Correspondence of Jane, Lady Cornwallis*, ed. Braybrooke, 50–51.

68. For Lucy Bedford's age, see Newdigate, *Michael Drayton*, ch. 5.

69. See Newdigate, *Michael Drayton*, 64n. 1.

70. For Bacon's friendship with Rich, see the letter from her to Bacon quoted by Sylvia Freedman in *Poor Penelope*, 117.

71. See Gustav Ungerer, "An Unrecorded Elizabethan Performance of *Titus Andronicus*," *Shakespeare Survey* 14 (1970): 102–9.

72. For the complications, see Barroll, *Politics, Plague, and Shakespeare's Theater* (Ithaca, N.Y.: Cornell University Press, 1991), 126–27.

73. See Chambers, *William Shakespeare*, 2:153. There is often confusion concerning the identity of the Rutlands. Francis Manners, sixth earl of Rutland (made a Knight of the Bath at the creation of Prince Charles as duke of York in 1605 [see *Carleton to Chamberlain*, 67]) was not the son but the younger brother of the childless fifth earl of Rutland, who died 26 June 1612 (*Peerage*, 11:259–62).

74. The countess herself seems to have enjoyed a reputation as a writer, for

she was described by Ben Jonson as "nothing inferior to her father in poetry." See *Conversations with Drummond* in Jonson, *Works*, 11 vols., ed. C. H. Herford and Percy and Evelyn Simpson (Oxford: Clarendon Press, 1925–52), 1:138, *Epigram 79*. John Florio not only dedicated his first publication, his Italian dictionary—*John Florio's World of Words*—to the countess of Rutland (as well as the earls of Rutland and Southampton), but also the second book of his translation of Montaigne.

75. See Sidney Lee in *Dictionary of National Biography*, 16:1006–9; M. S. Rawson, *Penelope Rich and Her Circle* (London: Hutchinson, 1911), 276–77; Ben Jonson, *Works*, 7:114.

76. See Sir Robert Naunton, *Fragmenta Regalia*, ed. J. S. Cerovski (Washington, D.C.: Folger Books, Associated University Presses, 1985), p. 80.

77. See *DNB* 9:677–81; Brennan, *Literary Patronage*, ch. 8.

78. For commentary on Pembroke, see Webb's "Memoirs" prefixed to Inigo Jones, *Stonehenge . . . Restored*, ed. John Webb (London, 1725)—these remarks do not appear in the first, 1665, edition (Wing STC 654); Sidney Lee in *DNB*, 9:677ff.; E. K. Chambers, *Elizabethan Stage* (Oxford: Clarendon Press, 1923), 2:308; Dick Taylor, Jr., "The Earl of Montgomery and the Dedicatory Epistle of Shakespeare's First Folio," *Shakespeare Quarterly* 10 (1959): 121–23.

79. See Margaret P. Hannay, *Philip's Phoenix* (New York: Oxford University Press, 1990), 210 and 278n. 19. See also Dick Taylor, Jr., "The Third Earl of Pembroke as a Patron of Poetry," *Tulane Studies in English* 5 (1955): 41–67.

80. See also F. A. Yates, *John Florio* (Cambridge: University Press, 1934), 246. In Scotland, Anna's Secretary had been a literary figure, the poet and scholar William Fowler, who became her Secretary and Master of Requests in England. (see *n. 4* above). For his other activities, see *DNB* and William Fowler, *Works* 3 vols., ed. H. W. Meikle, James Craigie, and John Purves (Edinburgh: Scottish Text Society, 1914–40), vol. 3. See also James K. Cameron, "Some Continental Visitors to Scotland in the Late Sixteenth and Early Seventeenth Centuries," in *Scotland and Europe*, ed. T. C. Smout (Edinburgh: John Donald, 1986), 45–61. He regularly entertained intellectuals visiting Scotland, including the nephew of Tycho Brahe in 1602. See also Edward J. Cowan, "The Darker Vision of the Scottish Renaissance," in *The Renaissance and Reformation in Scotland*, ed. Ian B. Cowan and Duncan Shaw (Edinburgh: Scottish Academic Presses, 1983), 138.

81. Parry, *The Golden Age Restor'd*, 149; Roy Strong, *Henry, Prince of Wales, and England's Lost Renaissance* (London: Thames and Hudson, 1986), 88–92, 106.

82. See Oliver Millar, *The Tudor, Stuart, and Early Georgian Pictures in the Collection of H. M. the Queen* (London: Phaidon Press, 1977), and for a general description of Anna's activities in fine arts patronage, see Strong, *Henry, Prince of Wales*, 249n. 5.

83. Chamberlain, *Letters*, 2:56.

84. See Diana Poulton, *John Dowland* (Berkeley: University of California Press, 1982), 60–61. In fact, Anna seems to have been conversant enough with lute music so that, when John Dowland was dismissed from his position with King Christian of Denmark in 1606, the English queen wrote Lady Arbella Stuart, James's first cousin, asking her to allow her lutanist Thomas Cutting to go to the Danish court in Dowland's place (Poulton, 399).

85. As we shall see, the queen was close to Prince Henry and was involved in Buckingham's career. As for her relevance to Prince Charles and to the earl of Arundel, we should note that Lady Carey who, by 23 February 1605, had been chosen to bring up Prince Charles, was one of the ladies of Queen Anna's Privy (Drawing?) Chamber (see *SPD*, 12:458). Arundel's wife became a member of Anna's inner circle in 1608, while he traveled with Princess Elizabeth, along with Inigo Jones, when the princess, accompanied by the countess of Bedford's mother and father, left for the continent with her new husband, the Elector Palatine.

86. The countess of Bedford bore a child in September 1610, but it died. She may have absented herself from the June 1610 *Tethys' Festival* because of her pregnancy, since she had no children, one having been born in January 1602 but living only a month (see Morgan, "A Biography of Lucy Countess of Bedford," 47). Bedford was described as "very weak" after the 1610 birth. In October 1611, her third pregnancy ended in a miscarriage (Morgan, "Biography," 175).

87. To be sure, the disgrace into which Rich fell when she actually married Devonshire (26 December 1605) after being granted a divorce (instead of an annulment) from Lord Rich might well have kept her from dancing again.

88. Three other women who also became "regulars" were Elizabeth Guildford, Catherine Windsor, and Anne Winter, all daughters of the earl of Worcester. They appear in the last two masques after the 1608 *Masque of Beauty* for which there are lists: *The Masque of Queens* and *Tethys' Festival*.

89. See *Malone Society Collections*, vol. 6, ed. David Cook and F. P. Wilson (Oxford: University Press, 1961), appendix B.

90. See Lodge, *Illustrations of British History*, 3:11–12. The queen's lord chamberlain in Scotland had been Henry Wardlaw. See *Register of the Privy Council of Scotland*, ed. David Masson (Edinburgh, 1877–), 1st series, 6:302. For the group that would manage the queen's affairs in Scotland after 1603, see 6:556–57.

91. For Carew's correspondence with Cecil, see *The Letters of Sir Robert Cecil to Sir George Carew*, ed. John Maclean (London: Camden Society, 1864). Sir George Carew (or Carey) is sometimes confused by literary scholars with other Carews and Careys. This was the second son of George Carew, D.D., dean of Windsor and of Exeter. See *Peerage*, 12:2.798. Robert Carey was Lord Hunsdon's younger brother and the future earl of Monmouth, with a wife in the Queen's Privy Chamber. See Chapter 5.

92. See Ellis, *Original Letters*, 1st series, 3:82.

93. See the "Memorial of Thomas Nevitt to the Earl of Leicester," in *Sidneiana*, ed. Samuel Butler (London, 1837), 87–88.

94. Anna, nevertheless, would become quite supportive of Carew: see Chamberlain, *Letters*, 2:18; *SPD*, 9:373, 385. It is thus interesting that he too had an interest in letters. For his activities translating Spanish and Irish literature, see Alonso de Ercille y Zuniga, *The Historie of Araucana*, ed. Frank Pierce (Manchester: University Press, 1964), viii. Carew was also a friend of William Camden, Robert Cotton, and Thomas Bodley (see *English Historical Review*, 42: 261ff.). Through his wife, Joyce, daughter of William Clopton, he had Stratford-upon-Avon connections, being married and buried there. See *Archaelogia*, 12:401 ff. M. V. Hay, *The Life of Sir Robert Sidney* (Washington, D.C.: Folger Books, 1984), has quite a differ-

ent view of Sidney's career, assuming that King James himself appointed Sidney as the Queen's Chamberlain: see ch. 10.

95. Robert Sidney, *Poems*, ed. P. J. Croft (Oxford: Oxford University Press, 1984), 81–83.

96. He was married to Barbara Gamage, who was described by Rowland Whyte as (like Queen Sophia) very concerned for her children — "She sees them well taught, and brought up in learning and qualities fit for their birth and condition." Quoted from the L'Isle correspondence by Josephine A. Roberts, ed., *The Poems of Lady Mary Wroth* (Baton Rouge: Louisiana State University Press, 1983), 5.

97. For the godparents, see *L'Isle MSS*, 2:194, 238, and Hay, *Life of Sir Robert Sidney*, 155, 177–78.

98. See Robert Sidney, *Poems*, ed. P. J. Croft (Oxford: Clarendon Press, 1984), 52, and Poulton, *John Dowland*, 315.

99. For Penshurst activities see J. C. A. Rathmell, "Jonson, Lord L'Isle, and Penshurst," *English Literary Renaissance* 1 (1971): 251. For Sidney's poetry, see Hilton Kelliher and Katherine Duncan-Jones, "A Manuscript of Poems by Robert Sidney: Some Early Impressions," *British Library Journal* 1 (1975): 107–44; and Katherine Duncan-Jones, " 'Rosis and Lyso': Selections from the Poems of Sir Robert Sidney," *English Literary Renaissance* 9 (1979): 240–63. For Robert Sidney and music, see Sidney, *Poems*, ed. Croft, 48–54. For Sidney and the Bodleian, see Hay, *Life of Sir Robert Sidney*, 207, and Hannay, *Philip's Phoenix*, 278n. 19.

100. See Robert C. Evans, *Ben Jonson and the Poetics of Patronage* (Lewisburg, Pa.: Bucknell University Press, 1989), 226–27. My account also differs from the assessment of Jonson's relationship with Anna (and her masques) to be found in David Riggs, *Ben Jonson: A Life* (Cambridge, Mass.: Harvard University Press, 1989), 118–19.

101. Ben Jonson, in fact, seems to have received enough advance notice of Sir Robert's absence to work it elaborately into his script for the *Entertainment at Althorp*. See Ben Jonson, *Works*, 7:127, 10: 294. See also Nichols, *Progresses*, 1:282. Sir Robert's absence may have been justified by royal command. During the reign of Queen Elizabeth, Frederick, duke of Wurtemberg, had been elected to the Order of the Garter but had never been formally installed. Spencer, raised to the peerage as Baron Spencer of Wormleighton four days before James's coronation, would cross the channel to Stuttgart to confer the order in an elaborate ceremony. During the time Anna was visiting Spencer's Althorp, the 1603 Garter awards, usually held 23 April and postponed by the queen's death, were to be made at Windsor on 26 June (the traditional feast being held as usual on 2 July). Sir Robert's German mission may already have been planned and he may have been required at Windsor to witness the elaborate Garter ceremonies at the Chapel of King George so that, in less than a month, he might better be enabled to play his part with Duke Frederick. Certainly the ceremony of awarding the Garter to "strangers" was complex. See Elias Ashmole, *The Institutions, Laws, and Ceremonies of the Order of the Garter* (London, 1672), who describes Spencer's Continental trip with the Garter King at Arms, Sir William Dethick (411 ff.). See also John seventh earl of Spencer, "Lord Spencer's Garter Embassy to the Duke of Wirtemberg in 1603," *Northamptonshire Past and Present* 1 (1949): 1–11.

102. See *Clifford Diaries*, (ed. Clifford), 23–24.

103. If the speech was accurate, we recall that the only "duke" here could have been Lennox (there was now no other in England or Scotland) whose presence Anna had required if she was to go to England with Prince Henry under the supervision of any noble in James's circle.

104. For details of the Spencer wealth, see Mary E. Finch, *The Wealth of Five Northamptonshire Families, 1540–1640* (Oxford: Northamptonshire Record Society, 1956). This wealth later enabled William Spencer, Sir Robert's oldest surviving son, to marry Penelope Wriothesly, Southampton's oldest daughter, in 1615.

105. This woman is erroneously designated "Alice Spencer" in Kathy Lyn Emerson's pioneering *Wives and Daughters* (Troy, N.Y.: Whitston, 1984), 209.

106. See Thomas Milles, *The Catalogue of Honor* (London, 1610), sig. 3M3^v.

107. The only detailed account of Elizabeth Spencer Hunsdon and her husband as patrons is Ernest A. Strathman, "Lady Carey and Spencer," *ELH* 2 (1935): 33–57.

108. The best account of Lady Alice remains that of French R. Fogle, "Such a Rural Queen."

109. See Chambers, *The Elizabethan Stage*, 2:128–31. Thus two of these Spencer sisters had in common the fact that their husbands, Lord Strange and Lord Hunsdon, had been patrons of the company that after 1603 became the "King's Men."

110. See Heltzel and Heywood, note 56 above, and Knafla, "The 'Country' Chancellor."

111. See A. C. Judson, *The Life of Edmund Spenser* (Baltimore: Johns Hopkins University Press, 1945), 5 ff., an account which supplements *DNB* and *Peerage*. For Lady Alice's age, see W. B. Hunter, Jr., "The Date and Occasion of Arcades," *English Language Notes* 2 (1973): 47. Hunter obtained Lady Alice's birthdate from French R. Fogle, who was writing a life of Alice, dowager countess of Derby.

112. For a partial text of this entertainment, see John Milton, *Poetical Works*, ed. H. J. Todd (London, 1809), 6:151 ff.

113. For the text, see John Lyly, *Works*, ed. R. W. Bond (Oxford: Clarendon Press, 1902), 1:492 ff. Bond's assignment of this anonymous entertainment to Lyly is disputed by Chambers, *The Elizabethan Stage*, 4:68, who thinks the assignment is based on a forgery.

114. The earl of Nottingham presented one stag and one buck, and the earl of Sussex presented six pheasants and two bucks. See *The Egerton Papers*, 353 (the forgeries in this Collier edition are on 340–42).

115. I am not certain as to the sequence of events leading up to this occasion. Indeed, another question is who decided that the queen would visit Althorp in the first place. The dowager countess herself might have taken the initiative here.

116. See Ben Jonson, *Works*, 1: 180. As for Sir Robert Spencer, however, he seems never to have had anything to do one way or the other with Jonson (or Jonson with him) for the rest of their lives, despite the flattering reference to Spencer (now a new baron) in Jonson's printing of *The Entertainment at Althorp* in 1604 (STC 14756).

117. See, for example, Rosalind Miles, *Ben Jonson: His Craft and Art* (London: Routledge, 1990), pp. 85–87, 95–96. J. Sanders, " 'Twill Fit the Players Yet,' " citing

Lewalski, adopts a different approach to Anna's entry into masquing: see Richard Cave et al., *Ben Jonson and the Theatre* (London: Routledge, 1999), 179–90.

118. The countess of Suffolk, wife to James's new Lord Chamberlain, is another exception, but I am assuming that, as the spouse of an important Howard with the highest office at court other than Cecil's as First Secretary, the countess could hardly have been left out from the eight ladies of the Drawing Chamber.

119. See Ronald A. Rebholz, *The Life of Fulke Greville* (Oxford: Clarendon Press, 1971), 94.

120. See Joan Rees, *Samuel Daniel* (Liverpool: Liverpool University Press, 1964), 76n. 19.

121. See Yates, *John Florio*, 54.

122. See STC 6258. Ben Jonson did not deliver a similar panegyric on the king's accession until James held his first session of Parliament on 19 March 1604 (see STC 14756).

123. See Joan Rees's edition of *Twelve Goddesses* in *A Book of Masques in Honor of Allardyce Nicoll*, ed. G. E. Bentley (Cambridge: University Press, 1967), 30. In my argument for Daniel's relevance to the masque, here I differ from David Norbrook, *Poetry and Politics in the English Renaissance* (London: Routledge and Kegan Paul, 1984), ch. 7, who emphasizes Jonson's relationship to the court masque.

124. See Barroll, *Politics, Plague*, ch. 2.

125. See Barroll, *Politics, Plague*, 42–49.

126. See Chambers, *The Elizabethan Stage*, 2:49, and *Malone Society Collections*, 1:3.267. Bedford's high standing with the queen at this time is reemphasized by a letter from Dudley Carleton to Sir Thomas Parry in Ellis, *Original Letters*, 1st series, 3:82. See also Lodge, *Illustrations of British History*, 3:88–89.

127. For a statement that challenges this tradition of denigration and that also describes Daniel's articulated theoretical premises regarding masques, see Geoffrey Creigh, "Samuel Daniel's Masque 'The Vision of the Twelve Goddesses,'" *Essays and Studies* 24 (1971): 22–35.

128. In Samuel Daniel, *The Tragedy of Philotas*, ed. Laurence Michel (New Haven: Yale University Press, 1949), Michel placed the offending performance on 3 January 1605 (36 and note 1). Although almost universally accepted, this date is based on the conjecture that when Daniel's company was paid for acting at court on 3 January 1605, *Philotas* was the play presented. But *Philotas* was entered by a printer in the Stationers' Register 29 November 1604: by Christmas 1604 *Philotas* was already a commodity whose primary value lay in selling books, not in attracting audiences. All this suggests that the script was available in November 1604, and hence that the play may well have been performed earlier. See also Chambers, *The Elizabethan Stage*, 3:275.

129. See Samuel Daniel, *Complete Works*, 5 vols., ed. A. B. Grosart (London, 1885–96), 1:xxii.

130. See Lodge, *Illustrations of British History*, 3:88–89, and for Penelope Rich's indictment along with the earls of Essex, Rutland, Southampton, Bedford, and Sussex, see *SPD*, 5:546.

131. See Chambers, *The Elizabethan Stage*, 3:275–76.

132. See David M. Bergeron, "Women as Patrons of English Renaissance

Drama," in *Patronage in the Renaissance*, ed. Guy Fitch Lytle and Stephen Orgel (Princeton: Princeton University Press, 1981), 283–85. For *Cynthia's Revels*, see also W. W. Greg, *A Bibliography of English Printed Drama*, 4 vols, (London: Bibliographical Society, 1939–59), 1:#181.

133. For Jonson's lines in the *Epistle* to the countess of Rutland, see Jonson, *Works*, 8:115.

134. Winwood, *Memorials of Affairs of State*, 2:140.

135. The only two married English earls whom James seems to have trusted were the earl of Suffolk, Lord Chamberlain (whose wife Anna had been put into the Drawing Chamber with Derby, Montgomery, and Penelope Rich), and the earl of Worcester, Edward Somerset, married to Elizabeth Hastings, one of Queen Elizabeth's ladies.

136. See above, Chapter 2, n. 52.

137. Strong, *Henry, Prince of Wales*, 224.

CHAPTER 4. THE STUART MASQUE AND THE QUEENLY ARTS OF CEREMONY

1. Something of a *locus classicus* for this approach is Ben Jonson, *Works*, 11 vols., ed. C. H. Herford and Percy and Evelyn Simpson (Oxford: Clarendon Press, 1925–52), 2:265–66. For a recent and more complex view of the situation, see Stephen Orgel, "Marginal Jonson," in *The Politics of the Stuart Court Masque*, ed. David Bevington and Peter Holbrook (Cambridge: Cambridge University Press, 1998), 144–75.

2. Since Stephen Orgel's seminal works, *The Jonsonian Masque* (Cambridge: Harvard University Press, 1965), and, with Roy Strong, *The Theatre of the Stuart Court*, 2 vols. (Berkeley: University of California Press, 1973), discussion of the Stuart masque has been extensive but primarily focused on the symbolism of costume, setting, and allegorical sequence. Political contexts have also been suggested in connection with James, the nobles in his circle, and the masque authors, rather than with Queen Anna. See Jonathan Goldberg, *James I and the Politics of Literature* (Baltimore: Johns Hopkins University Press, 1983) and David Lindley, ed., *The Court Masque* (Manchester: Manchester University Press, 1984).

3. See E. K. Chambers, *The Elizabethan Stage* (Oxford: Clarendon Press, 1923), 1:168.

4. See Chambers, *The Elizabethan Stage*, 3:351, and James I, *New Poems*, ed. Allan F. Westcott (New York: Columbia University Press, 1911), lviii.

5. See Chambers, *The Elizabethan Stage*, 1:169–70. Again, the occasion is intime, the ladies, in effect, maintaining a kind of seclusion in the context of a "private" wedding.

6. Edmunds's letter is dated 17 October—see Lodge, *Illustrations of British History*, 3:122. His previous letter to his master, Shrewsbury is dated 9 October: the prince arrived on 11 October. See the journal of Cecil's assistant (246), in Howard Vallance Jones, "The Journal of Levinus Munck," *English Historical Review* 68 (1953): 234–58.

7. See *The Diaries of Lady Anne Clifford*, ed. D. J. H. Clifford (Wolfeboro Falls, N.H., 1991), 27. The above entry refers to a period in 1603 between Michaelmas (29 September) and Christmas (see 15–16) and is her last (known) before the 1616 diary commences.

8. For Beaumont's letter to Villeroi, see Chambers, *The Elizabethan Stage*, 1:171n. 2.

9. For the translation, see John Orrell, "The London Stage in the Florentine Correspondence, 1604–1618," *Theatre Research International*, n.s. 3 (1978): 157–75.

10. Certain politically significant weddings between powerful noble families also seem to have taken place at court during this season, thus becoming court events themselves, as, for example, the marriage of Frances Howard to the young earl of Essex in Christmas 1605 (see below).

11. Arbella was the king's unmarried female cousin and officially the ranking lady at court after the queen. For her remark, see *The Letters of Lady Arbella Stuart*, ed. Sara Jayne Steen (Oxford: Oxford University Press, 1994), 197.

12. Throughout this chapter such joined dates as "1603–4" denote the period of Christmas–New Year court revels, usually starting in mid-December (1603) and lasting through to Lent (1604).

13. See *Carleton to Chamberlain* 54.

14. See *SPV*, 10:106. Chambers, *The Elizabethan Stage*, 2:241, wrongly implies that Lennox was the king's first cousin. For a fuller discussion of Lennox, see Chapter 2.

15. During the previous summer, Esmé's influential brother had also secured for him the license to export six thousand tons of double beer from England for a six-year period, a lucrative possession when sold or rented to London brewers — see *SPD*, 8:33. Other honors lay in the future when Aubigny would become earl of March and then briefly succeed his brother as duke of Lennox. For his Bed Chamber status, see *Peerage*, 7:605.

16. For Pembroke see *Carleton to Chamberlain*, 35.

17. The earl of Pembroke never succeeded in gaining the Bed Chamber himself. See Chambers, *The Elizabethan Stage*, 1: 53n. 2.

18. King James thought well enough of Hay to send him to Henri IV of France with the official message of condolence for the loss of Henri's sister, the duchess de Bar (see *SPV*, 10:140). Hay became Lord Hay three years later and finally earl of Carlisle.

19. See Lodge, *Illustrations of British History*, 3:65. Another dancer was a member of the king's Bed Chamber, Sir Richard Preston, who had accompanied James from Scotland. Made a Knight of the Bath at the coronation, he would eventually be created earl of Desmond. The last dancer named, Sir Henry Goodyer, came from a family well acquainted with the countess of Bedford. Knighted by Essex in Ireland, Goodyer had at James's accession become, like Pembroke, a gentleman of the less prestigious Privy Chamber, but he was also, significantly, attached to the countess of Bedford's household. Goodyer's father was patron of the poet Michael Drayton, who noted the intimacy between the Goodyer and Harington families. For further information on Goodyer, who had been close to John Donne for sev-

eral years prior to this masque, see R. C. Bald, *John Donne: A Life* (Oxford: Oxford University Press, 1970), 153 ff.

20. Aubigny, with an interest in literature. was the recipient of the epistle prefacing Ben Jonson's *Sejanus*, and close enough to Jonson, for example, to keep him current on the prospect of a pardon after Jonson and Marston were jailed for *Eastward Ho!* See Chambers, *The Elizabethan Stage*, 3:255.

21. "On New Year's night we had a play of Robin Good-fellow and a masque brought in by a magician of China." The King's Servants were paid for playing at court on 1 January 1604 — *Malone Society Collections*, ed. David Cook and F. P. Wilson (Oxford: Oxford University Press, 1961), 6:38.

22. From other masques whose surviving texts offer detailed stage directions, two torchbearers per masque personage seem to have been the rule in these initial processions. See Daniel, *The Vision of the Twelve Goddesses* (1604); Thomas Campion, *Lord Hay's Masque* (1607); *The Lords' Masque* (1613).

23. *Carleton to Chamberlain*, 54.There were also diplomatic dimensions to this display, as may be gathered from Carleton's description of the first knight. "The first gave the King an impressa in a shield with a sonnet in a paper to express his device and presented a jewel of £40,000 value which the King is to buy of Peter van Lore, but that is more than every man knew and it made a fair show to the French ambassador's eye whose master would have been well pleased with such a masquer's present, but not at that price." Carleton's observations on *The Orient Knights* quoted below are from pp. 54–55.

24. See, for instance, G. K. Hunter, *English Drama: 1586–1642* (Oxford: Clarenden Press, 1997), 525–32.

25. Thus in one respect the masque remains a rough, rather than a fine, indication of the individual prestige of the participants because its organizer (the queen or here the duke of Lennox) had to honor nobles in multiples of four — that is to say, eight persons or, if more than eight persons, then not nine, or ten, but twelve (the number to be found in the queen's masques).

26. Thus when Beatrice in *Much Ado* speaks of the difference between courtship, wedding, and repentance as being like various kinds of dances, she observes that "the first suit is hot and hasty like a Scotch jig, and full as fantastical; the wedding mannerly modest as a measure, full of state and ancientry" (*Ado*, 2.1.74–77). The term *measure* for this masque phase was also used by Benvolio as he and Romeo planned the gentlemen's masque brought to the Capulet house. Deciding to forego any boring prologue or explanation of their costumes, Romeo proposed: "But let them measure us by what they will, / We'll measure them a measure, and be gone" (*RJ*, 1.4.9–10). The only description of an English "measure" surviving from the period, a manuscript at the Bodleian Library entitled "My Lord of Essex Measure," gives detailed directions, recounted by Mabel Dolmetsch in her study *Dances of England and France from 1450 to 1600* (London: Routledge and Kegan Paul, 1949), chapter 3. For further suggestions about dance in these situations, see the important study by Otto Gombosi, "Some Musical Aspects of the English Court Masque," *Journal of the American Musicological Society* 1.3 (1948): 3–19. Some idea of the complexity possible in these initial measures of Part 2 may be derived from the annota-

tions of Thomas Campion for Lord Hay's masque. "*The nine masquers in their green habits solemnly descended to the dancing place in such order as they were to begin their dance. . . . As soon as the chorus ended, the violins or consort of twelve began to play the second new dance.*" Then a speech, a visit to a grove with music, and then "*the motet being ended, the violins began the third new dance which was lively performed by the masquers, after which they took forth the ladies and danced the measures with them*" (222–25). In other words, Campion's Part 2 (exhibition dancing by nobles) consisted of three dances working up from slow and stately movements to a lively third dance.

27. See *SPV*, 15:114. The editor erroneously (111) refers to this masque as *The Vision of Delight*.

28. Cf. Campion, 225: "The motet being ended, the violins began the third new dance, which was lively performed by the masquers after which they took forth the ladies and danced the measures with them."

29. "Lady Southwell the elder" was not a member of Anna's court, but she was the eldest daughter of the venerable and influential earl of Nottingham, Lord Admiral. In Queen Elizabeth's close circle of ladies, she had married Sir Robert Southwell, heir of a wealthy northern family: see Robert Kenny, *Elizabeth's Admiral* (Baltimore: Johns Hopkins University Press, 1970), 93 and n. 11. She may indeed have been taken out at this time because she was Nottingham's daughter.

30. The Venetian ambassador, Antoine de la Boderie, writing about a court masque in 1609, observed that his granddaughter was honored in the dancing because Prince Charles, having been taken out by one of the ladies in the masque, returned to take out the granddaughter: "Le Duc d'Yorck ayant été pris à danser par une des Dames du ballet, il vint aussitôt chercher madite fille où elle étoit, & l'y mena." See Mary Sullivan, *Court Masques of James I* (New York: G. P. Putnam's Sons, 1913), 218.

31. Cf. Campion: "Now the masquers began their lighter dances as corrantoes, levaltos, and galliards wherein when they had spent as much time as they thought fit, Night spake thus" (226).

32. *Carleton to Chamberlain*, 54. Cf. Campion, 227: "At the end of these words the violins began the fourth new dance which was excellently discharged by the masquers. . . . After the dance followed this dialogue of two voices . . . performed with several echoes of music . . . at the end whereof the masquers, putting off their vizards and helmets, made a low honor to the King."

33. Bedford's intercession here in the matter of masques was reiterated fourteen years later when the "little ladies" of the Ladies' Hall in Deptford at Greenwich presented *Cupid's Banishment* to Queen Anna. The author of the masque, Robert White, dedicated the manuscript of his work to the countess of Bedford "in regard of the honorable furtherance and noble encouragement your Ladyship gave us in presenting our masque to her Majesty. . . . I confess a lower patronage would have served a higher work, but . . . I thought it injustice to devote the fruits which your honor first sowed to any but yourself." See *Cupid's Banishment*, ed. C. E. McGee, *Renaissance Drama*, n.s. 19 (1988): 225–64 (at 240).

34. Thus despite Anne Clifford's own generalized intimations regarding the queen that "in my youth I was much in court with her and in masques attended her,"

Anna invited Clifford only for two consecutive years (1608, 1609) to be a visitor: in *The Masque of Beauty* and *The Masque of Queens*. (For the circumstances, see Chapter 5 below.) Lady Mary Wroth was the daughter of Anna's Lord Chamberlain, Robert Sidney, and she danced as a visitor only in *The Masque of Blackness*.

35. Anna elected not to be Juno, which would have been an appropriate enough role, this goddess being queen of all the other Roman gods and goddesses and spouse of Jupiter. The queen here chose to dress as Athene, goddess of wisdom. We need not, of course, argue here for or against the suitability of this selection, but it is nonetheless important that Anna demonstrably wished to be identified with this quality. Indeed, other masques and the words of some dedications also associate Anna with Athene and thus helped to promote her English, as opposed to her Scottish, persona. See Chapter 5 below.

36. Most striking is the selection of the fortyish Penelope Rich — not a countess — to play Venus. We recall, though, that she was viewed by the teenaged Anne Clifford as one of the *younger* ladies at court (see Chapter 3).

37. See *Letters to James VI*, xxxv, facsimile 3, lxv.

38. Some notion of why the countess never danced again may be derived from an inappropriate reaction reported about her in connection with Anna's brother, the king of Denmark, in his 1606 visit to London at a reception on his ship. After returning to Denmark, Christian IV wrote Anna, complaining, according to Dudley Carleton, about "my lady of Nottingham for a letter of defiance she sent after him upon a scorn or disgrace she conceived to be offered her husband in the king's [Denmark's] ship at the last feast which touched her in honor. The matter was no more than that our king [James], asking what o'clock it was and desirous to be gone, my lord admiral [Nottingham] as willing to hasten him answered four; the king of Denmark seeking all means to stay them said it was but two and for doubt of not being understood made a sign with his two fingers [also the sign of "horns" or cuckoldom] to my lord admiral, which the good man took no worse than it seemed to be meant, but she being now with child and jealous of her credit would not so put it up, but thought to revenge herself with a railing letter, for which she is banished from both the king's and the prince's courts" (*Carleton to Chamberlain*, 90).

39. Samuel Daniel, *The Vision of the Twelve Goddesses*, ed. Joan Rees, in *A Book of Masques*, ed. G. E. Bentley (Cambridge: Cambridge University Press, 1967), 29.

40. *Carleton to Chamberlain*, 55. It would be interesting to be able to determine the gender of the Three Graces. Were lesser ladies allowed to play these figures, or were they impersonated by men? Certainly nymphs were routinely played by men, and because the Three Graces would be singing, the probability is that we are dealing with choirboys from the Children of the Chapel Royal.

41. He is alluding to the horse in a famous horse act put on by a John Banks. For the reference, see *Carleton to Chamberlain*, 54.

42. Indeed, Carleton, who had critiqued sloppy dancing in *Orient Knights*, saw this instance as "nothing inferior to" the grand entrance that had so entranced him. See *Carleton to Chamberlain*, 53, and *Vision of Twelve Goddesses*, 30.

43. For details of Monteagle's background, see David Mathew, *James I* (London: Eyre and Spottiswoode Mathew, 1967), 144–46, and for the Essex connec-

tion specifically, see *Marquess of Bath Manuscripts*, ed. G. Dyfnallt Owen (London: HMSO, 1980), 5:278. Robert Cecil, the king's most powerful English adviser, was, owing to his physical handicap, most certainly not taken out at his own request.

44. *Carleton to Chamberlain*, 56.

45. *Carleton to Chamberlain*, 56.

46. For example, Jonson's *Hymenaei* celebrated the wedding of the young earl of Essex to Frances Howard in 1606. Dancers were friends and family of the Howards and of the Essex circle—for instance, Lord Howard of Walden and Sir Thomas Howard in the former case, the countesses of Bedford and Rutland in the latter. See Chambers, *The Elizabethan Stage*, 3:378.

47. See Enid Welsford, *The Court Masque* (New York: Russell and Russell, 1927), chs. 1 and 2.

48. These are the six masques presented by the queen, in chronological order and with the inclusive dates for the relevant Christmas holiday season: *The Vision of the Twelve Goddesses* (1603–4), *The Masque of Blackness* (1604–5), *The Masque of Beauty* (1607–8), *The Masque of Queens* (1608–9), *Tethys' Festival* (June 1610), and *Love Freed from Ignorance and Folly* (1610–11). Lists of the dancers' names exist for the first five only.

49. I have dealt with this matter in greater detail in "Inventing the Stuart Masque" in *The Politics of the Stuart Court Masque*, 121–43.

50. *Salisbury MSS*, 16:388. This concern with display is also illustrated by the jewel episode in *The Orient Knights*—see n. 23 above.

51. See, for example, the works cited in Barroll, "Theatre as Text: The Case of Queen Anna and the Jacobean Court Masque," *Elizabethan Theatre* 14 (1996): 175–93.

52. The countess of Nottingham had a nostril polyp, which may have precluded her participation (Sir Ralph Winwood, *Memorials of Affairs of State* [London, 1725], 2:39), but there is no great assurance that she would have danced this year. She did not dance in Anna's remaining masques, despite her husband's status as Lord Admiral.

53. Anne Herbert, about whom little is known because she died young and unmarried, was obviously being honored by the queen through her placement amidst countesses. The daughter of the countess of Pembroke, she was the niece of Sir Philip Sidney and of Queen Anna's Lord Chamberlain and thus first cousin to Lady Mary Wroth, the sister of the earl of Pembroke, and now the sister-in-law of Susan de Vere, who was married to Anne Herbert's other brother, Philip. Lady Anne's presence then honored the Queen's Lord Chamberlain, whose daughter was also in the masque, but it also honored one of Anna's favorite ladies of the Privy Chamber, Susan de Vere. Illustrative of the temporary nature of these "extra" positions is the fact that both Effingham and Wroth appeared only on this occasion. Bevill and Herbert probably would have been treated similarly, but there is no way to confirm this because they both died before Anna's next masque.

54. See Winwood, *Memorials*, 2:44, and Jonson, *Works*, 10:448–50.

55. Winwood, *Memorials*, 2:44.

56. For a detailed description of the de Vere–Herbert wedding, see Barroll, "Defining 'Dramatic Documents,'" *Medieval and Renaissance Drama in England*,

9 (1997): 112–26. For the masque attending the wedding, see Chambers, *The Elizabethan Stage*, 3:377. This was a masque of eight noblemen that Ottaviano Lotti had described as "very lovely and well-devised. After the show the end of everything was a new and very elegant dance." Carleton described the scenery of the masque both to John Chamberlain (*Carleton to Chamberlain*, 66–67) and to Winwood (Winwood, *Memorials*, 2:43), telling the former that "their conceit [device] was a representation of Juno's temple at the lower end of the great hall which was vaulted, and within it the masquers seated with stores of lights about them, and it was no ill show. They were brought in by the Four Seasons of the year and Hymenaeus, which for songs and speeches was as good as a play. Their apparel was rather costly than comely, but their dancing full of life and variety." Those dancing were the groom's brother (the earl of Pembroke), Lord Willoughby, and a number of the Gentlemen of the king's Bed Chamber who, according to Carleton (66–67), were Sir James Hay, Sir Robert Carey, Sir John Lee, Sir Richard Preston, Sir Thomas Germain, and Sir Thomas Badger. The latter two were close enough friends of Lord Hay to be in his ambassadorial group when he went to Paris in 1616 (see *Carleton to Chamberlain*, 2:13–14), albeit described as "buffoons" by Lady Haddington. Badger and Preston both danced in *Lord Hay's Masque* (6 January 1607), suggesting the ongoing coherence of this group of gentlemen of the king's Bed Chamber of which Montgomery was a member.

57. Winwood, *Memorials*, 2:44.

58. For the Florentine ambassador, see Orrell, "The London Stage in the Florentine Correspondence," 160.

59. See Winwood, *Memorials*, 2:57, and for the various expenses attending one or both births, see the payment orders in Frederick Devon, *Issues of the Exchequer* (London, 1836). See p. 23: for 29 May 1605 — £100 to Alice Dennis for attending the queen; p. 49: for 8 March 1606 — Bestowed on the queen by the king at the christening of Lady Mary: £1,550: "a certain jewel of diamonds with pearls pendant" the whole cost being £2,530 (cf. p. 48); p. 29 for 22 January 1606 — £1,498.1.4 "for workmanship of divers things made for the childbed of the queen"; p. 35 for 17 April 1606 — £600 for "certain linen and other necessaries, as well for the use of the said Queen in her childbed as for the child's body"; p. 47 for September 1606 — £100 again to Alice Dennis; p. 55 for 7 February 1607 — £3,132.9.10 "in part of payment of the sum of £15,593.14 limited to be by him [Sir Roger Dallison] over to divers shopkeepers . . . of divers things made for the childbed of the Queen."

60. Devon, pp. 21, 35, are several of many allusions to these tombs in this edition of the Pell Records.

61. For the appointments, see Winwood, *Memorials*, 2:54, 59; *Calendar of State Papers: Domestic Series, of the Reigns of Edward VI, Mary, Elizabeth I, and James I (1547–1625)*, 12 vols., ed. Robert Lemon and M. A. E. Green (London: HMC, 1856–72), 8:203, 250 (hereafter *SPD*).

62. During the Christmas season before, there had been some expectation that "both marquises and earls" might be created on New Year's Day 1605, but then this major event was put off "until the Queen's lying down." For the ceremony see Philip Gawdy, *Letters*, ed. I. H. Jeayes (London: Roxburghe Club, 1906), 155. Two of the four men created baron on this occasion also had a relationship to the queen's

circle: her vice chamberlain, Sir George Carew, became Baron Carew of Clopton, and Thomas Arundell, a man who had offended Queen Elizabeth but was married to the earl of Southampton's sister, Mary Wriothesly, was created Baron Arundel of Wardour. See *Peerage*, 1:263 n. (f).

63. See Stow, *Annals*, sig. 4C5–4C5ᵛ [pp. 862–63].

64. See Orrell, "The London Stage in the Florentine Correspondence," 161, and Lodge, *Illustrations of British History*, 3:162. I think Lotti was conflating the queen's churching with the traditional Whitsunday celebrations, which often featured tilting and also brought Edward Alleyn with his trained bears to the palace for bear baiting.

65. See Stow, *Annals*, sigs. 4C5ᵛ [p. 863] and 4C6 [p. 864].

66. See *Carleton to Chamberlain*, 1:228: "The Queen was brought abed on Sunday morning of a daughter [22 June] and the child died on Monday night after it was christened and called Sophia" (Cf. Stow, *Annals*, sig. 4E3ᵛ [p. 883]). The warrant for the child's tomb is dated 17 March 1606/7: see *Laing Manuscripts Preserved in the University of Edinburgh* (London: HMSO, 1914), 109.

67. But her seclusion is noted by Zorzi Giustinian, who wrote that some time after 15 July the king of Denmark went with James to Greenwich where he was met at the steps by Princess Elizabeth, Princess Mary, and Prince Charles. "They all went upstairs to the Queen's apartments; she still keeps her rooms because of her recent confinement. After staying a while with the Queen the King of Denmark was conducted to his own apartments." *SPV*, 10:383. For the churching, see Stow, *Annals*, sig. 4E4 [p. 886]. After this time Anna was always described as present at the remaining ceremonies for Denmark.

68. The difference between *Hymenaei* and a queen's masque, in fact, can here be briefly indicated by the almost wholly different "cast" of noble dancers. *Hymenaei*, as a wedding masque, was traditionally given by the groom's party. The dancers here consisted of eight male and eight female masquers. The young Essex's side was represented by the countess of Bedford, the countess of Montgomery (whose husband was also a dancer in the masque), and the countess of Rutland (Sir Philip Sidney's daughter). But the other ladies were Lady Knolleys (married to Lord Knolleys), Lady Berkeley (Elizabeth Carey, Lord Hunsdon's daughter, married to the heir of Lord Berkeley), Dorothy Hastings (the earl of Huntington's daughter, married to Sir James Stuart, heir of Lord Blantyre), and Blanch Somerset (the earl of Worcester's daughter, married to Thomas Baron Arundel of Wardour). The other men were Lords Willoughby and Howard of Walden, Sir James Hay, Sir Thomas Howard (second son of the earl of Suffolk), Sir Thomas Somerset (a son of the earl of Worcester), and Sir John Ashley (future Master of the Revels). Thus the composition of the masque represented the families of the bride and groom, with friends and relatives of the Howard side prominently featured. In effect, this Jonsonian masque was probably comparable to the Vere-Herbert wedding masque of the previous Christmas of 1604–5, the script for which has not survived (suggesting that it was not executed by Ben Jonson).

69. The accounts of the lord treasurer allocate only 118 shillings "for making ready at Whitehall against the masque, barriers, and plays." See Jonson, *Works*, 10:465. Some indication of the cost of this kind of masque beyond that of the physi-

cal structures is indicated by remarks about a similar wedding masque for Lord Haddington (1608), where it was said that it would cost the dancers "about £300 a man" (Lodge, *Illustrations of British History*, 3:343) because the Crown attached some importance to the marriage that the masque celebrated. For commentary on this matter, see the remarks of the Venetian ambassador, *SPV*, 10:308. This passage is reprinted in Jonson, *Works*, 10:465.

70. The French emissary said that no ambassadors had been invited: see Chambers, *The Elizabethan Stage*, 3:241. The masquers, in the order listed by Campion, were Lord Walden; Sir Thomas Howard; Sir Henry Carey "Master of the Jewel House"; Sir Richard Preston (see n. 59) and Sir John Ashley (see n. 59) "Gentlemen of the King's Privy Chamber", Sir Thomas Jarrett "Pensioner"; Sir John Digby "one of the King's Carvers"; Sir Thomas Badger "Master of the King's Harriers" (see n. 59); "Master Goringe" (probably Sir George Goring, also close to Lord Hay: see *Carleton to Chamberlain*, 2:14). For the list, see Thomas Campion, *The Description of a Masque . . . in honor of the Lord Hay* (London, 1607), sig. B. David Lindley has demonstrated Lord Hay's closeness to Cecil and the Howards, who paid for this masque: see "Who Paid for Campion's 'Lord Hay's Masque'?" *Notes and Queries*, n.s. 27 (1979): 144–45. Significantly, Lady Mary Wroth, daughter of Anna's Lord Chamberlain, would later be accused of satirizing Hay: see Josephine A. Roberts, "An Unpublished Literary Quarrel Concerning the Suppression of Mary Wroth's 'Urania' (1621)," *Notes and Queries*, n.s. 24 (1977): 532–35.

71. See Chamberlain, *Letters*, 1:250–51.

72. Although we are to understand here that, presumably, the wearing of jewelry derived from a distinctly female emulative ostentation, we should recall the "extraordinarie braverie" in which King James himself had been described as dining several days earlier — on 4 January (Chamberlain, *Letters*, 1:250–53).

73. Giustinian wrote that at the close of the ceremony, King James observed "that he intended this function to consecrate the birth of the Great Hall which his predecessors had left him built merely in wood, but which he [like Augustus, one presumes] had converted into stone" (*SPV*, 11:86).

74. *SPV*, 11:86. Herford and the Simpsons, however, observe (Jonson, *Works*, 10:457): "The fiction that the Queen was 'authoress' of the whole was well kept up; one wonders what Ben and Inigo thought of it." The real question is what the politically sensitive ambassador considered to be of greater importance: poetry, scenery, dance, or the incredible wealth in the display and deployment of noble women for, essentially, a political purpose. If the latter, then Anna was indeed the author.

75. Significantly, there is indication that the queen valued the occasion enough to expend her own funds, for she paid for this masque herself: see *SPV*, 11:76.

76. See *Ambassades de Monsieur [A. Le Fèvre] de la Boderie en Angleterre, 1606–11*. 5 vols. (Paris, 1750), 3:14.

77. As Ben Jonson put it in the published text, the queen wanted the dancers to be the twelve daughters of Niger, as in *Blackness*, "but their beauties varied, and their time of absence excus'd, with four more added to their number" (Jonson, *Works*, 7:181). Anna incidentally omitted (and never readmitted) the lord chamberlain's wife, the countess of Suffolk, from her masquing. Because her husband was

an important member of the Howard group, which included the earl of Northampton, the countess of Suffolk may, at this early point, have become a victim of Anna's growing alienation from that faction (see Chapter 5).

78. Elizabeth [Somerset] married Sir Henry Guildford, and Katherine [Somerset] married William, Baron Petre of Writtle, in a double ceremony on 8 November 1596 at Essex House, the occasion being celebrated by Edmund Spenser's *Prothalamion*. The other two women were Anne [Somerset] married to Sir Edward Winter (11 August 1597), and Catherine [Somerset] married to Henry, sixth Lord Windsor before 14 January 1608 (*Peerage*, 12:2.799–800). Lady Petre did not dance with her three sisters in following year's *Masque of Queens*, but since she is to be found in *Tethys' Festival*, the next masque for which there is a list of the dancers, I assume her absence from the former was not because she was out of the circle.

79. Lady Hatton and Lady Anne Clifford appeared for the second and last times in this *Masque of Beauty*. Arbella Stuart, dancing in this same masque for her second visit, would make a final appearance in *Tethys' Festival*, in which Anna wanted all members of James's family represented.

80. For La Boderie's account, see Sullivan, *Court Masques of James I*, 218–19.

CHAPTER 5. MASQUING AND FACTION

1. For the appointment of Essex, see *SPV*, 10:26. In the portrait, because the prince wears the George rosette, thus having been inducted as a Knight of the Garter on 2 July 1603, the painting was probably executed during the first summer of the reign, the background suggesting Oatlands, site of the prince's first household. For the portrait with Harington, see J. W. Williamson, *The Myth of the Conqueror* (New York: AMS Press, 1978), figure 2, who notes the Essex copy on p. 45n. 6, and Roy Strong, *Henry, Prince of Wales, and England's Lost Renaissance* (London: Thames and Hudson, 1986), figure 8 (detail of Essex in the Hampton Court copy of the painting) and figure 24 (Henry with Harington) and 242n. 73. Strong does not associate the two paintings.

2. Lord Harington died during this visit. See *Complete Peerage*, ed. H. A. Doubleday et al. (London: St. Catherine's Press, 1910–59), 6:322–23.

3. Because of the outbreak of plague in the area during September, however, Prince Henry, presumably with Chaloner, traveled with Queen Anna when the royal family withdrew to the west of England.

4. Edmund Lodge, *Illustrations of British History* (London, 1838), 3:96. "Mr. Murray" was Sir David Murray, Keeper of the Privy Purse, who must have remained in Henry's vicinity, since he would be appointed Groom of the Stole when Henry organized his own court and made Murray a gentleman of the Bed Chamber. See Stow, *Annals*, sig.4G4 (p. 908).

5. In May 1609 Marc'Antonio Correr, the succeeding Venetian ambassador, would make a similar remark (*SPV*, 11:276).

6. It is important to recall that the specific wording of these quotations is from a nineteenth-century English synopsis of an Italian original as calendared in the *SPV*. As for the marriage prospects mentioned here, the countess of Bedford

had indeed been trying to effect one between her brother and Cecil's daughter, but Cecil had no interest in the match (*Manuscripts of the Earl of Salisbury Preserved at Hatfield House*, 23 vols., ed. M. S. Giuseppi (London: HMC, 1883–1976), 17:629–30. Instead, Frances Cecil married Henry Clifford, son and heir of the fourth earl of Cumberland. See Lawrence Stone, *The Crisis of the Aristocracy* (Oxford: Clarendon Press, 1965), 633, 651.

7. Salisbury seems to have grasped Harington's position as early as the previous year when he enjoined Thomas Edmonds to be sure to show deference to the youth (*SPV*, 11:215–16 and *Salisbury MSS*, 20:232–33).

8. The fact that these two nobles were allied with the group around the queen may explain why, when Henry dined in state on the evening of his investiture on 4 June 1610, Pembroke was honored by being appointed Server and Southampton as Carver. See Sir Ralph Winwood, *Memorials of Affairs of State* (London, 1725), 3:180.

9. See *SPV*, 12:79–80; Stow, *Annals*, sig. 4G4 (p. 908). The Venetian ambassador saw Prince Henry, in fact, as "delighted to rule" and as desiring the world to think him prudent and spirited. He had even been considering a conservative dress code for his courtiers as he attended to the disposition and decoration of his own houses. "Indeed the vivacity of this Prince grows apace, and every day he gives proof of wisdom and lofty thoughts in advance of his years" (*SPV*, 11:516).

10. John Harington himself died two years after the prince, and many noted his death. James Whitelocke, a judge of the court of the King's Bench, observed that young Harington was "the most complete young gentleman of his age." See Sir James Whitelocke, *Liber Famelicus*, ed. John Bruce (London: Camden Society, 1858), 70:39.

11. The expense of this barriers ceremony to the Crown was only £2,466, but this was because the noble jousters paid for their own accoutrements and warrior costumes. (A masque, according to the Privy Council, cost £4,000 — see Chapter 4.)

12. This account is from Stow *Annals*, 897. For other accounts, see E. K. Chambers, *The Elizabethan Stage* (Oxford: Clarendon Press, 1923), 3:393, and Ben Jonson, *Works*, 11 vols., ed. C. H. Herford and Percy and Evelyn Simpson (Oxford: Clarendon Press, 1925–52), 10:508–17, who cite Stow.

13. Later, as previously mentioned, Daniel would write *Hymen's Triumph* as the first entertainment offered in Anna's newly redecorated city palace, Denmark House.

14. A warrant being signed for the funds on 4 March, the masque was scheduled for 5 June in the Banqueting House at Whitehall, five days before the ceremony of Henry's installation. See John Orrell, "The London Stage in the Florentine Correspondence," *Theatre Research International* 3 (1978): 157–76, esp. 165–66, and Mary Sullivan, *Court Masques of James I* (New York: G. P. Putnam's Sons, 1913), 219–20.

15. Meliades was Henry's chosen knightly name for the tournament of the barriers in the previous Christmas. For a brief but informative discussion on the name, see Jonson, *Works*, 10:515n. 122. Interestingly, in the chivalric romance of this name, Meliadus was the name both of the son and of the lover of the Lady of the Lake who, like Tethys, was a water goddess.

16. Winwood, *Memorials*, 3:181.

17. For Henry's interests in the navy, see the informative chapter 3 of J. W. Williamson, *The Myth of the Conqueror* (New York: AMS Press, 1978): "Prince of Wales: 'He Delights to Go upon the Deep.' "

18. Of the other women, the countess of Bedford, recovering from illness, was absent, and there were several new countesses. Anne Clifford had married in 1609 and appeared here as the countess of Dorset. Elizabeth Radcliffe, daughter of the earl of Sussex, had been celebrated in Jonson's *Lord Haddington's Masque* of 1608, at the time of her marriage to Viscount Haddington, who had defended James by killing the earl of Gowrie and his brother in the attempted assassination plot.

19. *Love Freed* has been edited most recently by Norman Sanders in *A Book of Masques in Honor of Allardyce Nicoll*, ed. G. E. Bentley (Cambridge: University Press, 1967), 73–93. To give body to this masque I have included Inigo Jones's sketch for it (fig. 8). That this sketch indeed depicts *Love Freed*, a matter of some ambiguity in Bentley and in the Warburg Institute's labeling of the photograph reproduced here, is, I think, established by the prison/fortress-like structure alluded to in Jonson's written text and by the fact that the text also alludes to "eleven daughters of the morne (1. 67)—as opposed to the usual twelve noble dancers—who have been "as you see . . . condemned to prison." Matters seem somewhat confused to the casual glance because twelve "she-fools" and twelve "Muses' Priests" dance and sing respectively before the eleven "daughters" come down to dance Part 1 (1. 336).

20. See *SPV*, 12:101. As she watched *Oberon*, Anna remarked that she expected to give her own masque on the following Sunday, a Twelfth Night date around which three of her previous masques are clustered (*SPV*, 12:106).

21. See *SPV*, 12:101. Henry's masquing attitudes may be suggested by his own proposal. On 5 December Correr wrote that Henry would have to return from Royston where he was hunting with the king "to arrange a masque for Christmas." Correr added: "He would have liked to present this masque on horseback could he have obtained the King's consent" (*SPV*, 12:79).

22. The comments of William Trumbull the Elder, who describes this situation, reveal only the earl of Southampton (besides Prince Henry) as a dancer in the masque, but the group, according to Stow, contained one other earl (probably Essex), three barons, five knights, and two esquires (all not named) to make up the now usual number of twelve. See Jonson, *Works*, 10:518, 522–23.

23. See Jonson, *Works*, 10:522–23. The branle (also "brawl" and often called a *brando* in Jacobean accounts—but this last was a somewhat different dance) was a French chain dance adopted by European aristocracy especially in England as well as France. It was named for its characteristic side-to-side movement and executed by walking, running, gliding, or skipping steps in a chain of couples intertwining arms or hands. Aristocrats frequently performed pantomime branles, one such being the *branle de Poitou*, which some think was meant to pantomime courting. For discussion of this point, see *The New Grove Dictionary of Music and Musicians*, ed. Stanley Sadie (London: Macmillan, 1980), 3:198–201. Skiles Howard, *The Politics of Courtly Dancing in Early Modern England* (Amherst: University of Massachusetts Press, 1998), 72–74, notes several close descriptions of the brawl in Shakespeare and in Marston.

24. The moment, I think, accords with Orgel's sense that "empowering

women was not a Jonsonian ideal, and the Queen was not the patron he sought": see "Marginal Jonson," in *The Politics of the Stuart Court*, ed. David Bevington and Peter Holbrook (Cambridge: University Press, 1998), 174.

25. For an allusion to the queen's practicing for this masque, see Thomas Birch, *The Court and Times of James I*, 2 vols. (London, 1849), 1:148.

26. In the previous year, when Henri IV of France had been assassinated, all the men as well as the women in the English court had donned black mourning garments. See Barroll, *Politics, Plague*, 184.

27. See *Malone Society Collections* (Oxford: Malone Society, 1986), 13:49. Although the prince presented a masque this season, most signs indicate, I think, that it was not *Love Restored*, as often argued. Nothing in the text confirms a date of 1611–12, which has been assumed because of an allusion in *Restored* to a pickpocket operating in London and apprehended at the end of December 1611 (Chambers, *The Elizabethan Stage*, 3:387). But Jonson's *Bartholomew Fair* (presented at court 2 November 1614) also alludes to this cutpurse: see 3.5.120–128.

28. See Nichols, *Progresses*, 2:161; Chamberlain, *Letters*, 1:249.

29. See *SPV*, 12:142. Significantly, Dunbar had helped Somerset become a Groom of the Bed Chamber, an appointment which seems in line with James's policy of advancing the younger sons of the lairds whom he elevated into the Scottish nobility. The future Somerset was Robert Ker, fifth son of the laird Sir Thomas Ker of Ferniehirst to be created Lord Jedburgh. See Maureen M. Meikle, "The Invisible Divide: The Greater Lairds and the Nobility of Jacobean Scotland," *Scottish Historical Review* 71 (1992): 70–87.

30. At this time James seems to have been applying himself to Cecil's duties. In June the channel for all packets was through the Lord Chamberlain (the earl of Suffolk) directly to James. During the same interval, the last of the original English group around James, the earl of Northampton, was performing Cecil's old duties of Lord Treasurer when James was away, the place not yet having officially been filled. See *SPV*, 12:376, 387, 438; Chamberlain, *Letters*, 1:359.

31. See Chamberlain, *Letters*, 1:346, and compare this to remarks about Anna and Maitland in Scotland (chapter 2 above).

32. Chamberlain, *Letters*, 1:331.

33. See Arthur Wilson, *The History of Great Britain* (London, 1653), sigs. H4, K^v, L3^v, who also regards the death of Cecil as the removal of an obstacle to the advancement of factions. Wilson was seventeen in 1612 and a gentleman-in-waiting to the young earl of Essex in 1614, and he is thus, unlike Weldon, a relevant source. For an account of his life (1595–1652), see *Dictionary of National Biography*, ed. Leslie Stephen and Sidney Lee, 66 vols (London: Smith, Elder, 1885–1901), 21:552–53.

34. See *The Manuscripts of the Earl of Mar and Kellie . . . Supplementary Report*, ed. Henry Paton (London: HMSO, 1930), 41. That Anna and Henry were a faction at this time is further suggested by a competition for another of Cecil's old offices, the secretariat of state. Sir Ralph Winwood, vying for the position, had returned to London in July from The Hague where he was ambassador. He apparently thought it necessary to visit both Anna and Henry, for he was described as having spent Tuesday "with the Queen who used him extraordinarily well, and had long talk with him and commanded him to come to her again before his departure" and

"yesterday he took his leave of the Prince and had the same usage" (Chamberlain, *Letters*, 1:368; cf. 369).

35. See Chamberlain, *Letters*, 1:359–60. Of these two office seekers, the first, Winwood, had not been appointed by the time Henry died in November 1612. Winwood's subsequent behavior is indicative of how this death cleared the way for Carr. Winwood was reduced to giving Carr elaborate wedding presents (Chamberlain, *Letters*, 1:496, 499) and depending wholly upon him, according to John Chamberlain, before Winwood was finally appointed principal secretary 29 March 1614 (Chamberlain, *Letters*, 1:521).

36. Chamberlain, *Letters*, 2:32.

37. From the political viewpoint, the end came for Prince Henry's followers on 31 December 1612 (Chamberlain, *Letters*, 1:399) when his household was discharged and all the young nobles, including John Harington and the young earl of Essex, found themselves in need of a new power base.

38. *Mar and Kellie Supp.*, 52.

39. See Stow, sig. 4G6^v (p. 913). As William Camden reported about Anna: "As she had her favorites in one place, the King had his in another. She lov'd the elder brother, the Earl of Pembroke; he the younger whom he made Earl of Montgomery." See William Camden, *Annals*, in W. Kennet, *A Complete History of England*, 2 vols. (London, 1706), 2:685.

40. Chamberlain, *Letters*, 1:314.

41. See Godfrey Goodman, *The Court of King James the First*, ed. John S. Brewer (London, 1839), 2:143–44. For the general Overbury situation, see Beatrice White, *Cast of Ravens* (London: John Murray, 1965), 22–23.

42. See *L'Isle MSS*, 5:65 (9 November 1612). Although several Commonwealth and Restoration histories tell of a spoken insult by Overbury to her that Anna overheard in her garden, Wotton's account (above) is the only contemporary comment I have found on the subject: see Logan Piersall Smith, *The Life and Letters of Sir Henry Wotton* (Oxford: Clarendon Press, 1907), 2:19. For the commitment to the Tower, see Chamberlain, *Letters*, 1:443.

43. For extended discussion of the "nullity," see David Lindley, *The Trials of Frances Howard* (London: Routledge, 1993), ch. 3.

44. Wilson, *History of Great Britain*, sig. K4, observed that Essex even had to endure the further indignity of repaying Frances her marriage portion and selling one of his holdings, Bennington in Hertfordshire, to do it.

45. *Mar and Kellie Supp.*, 51.

46. For Overbury's separation from Rochester, 29 April 1613, see Chambers, *The Elizabethan Stage*, 1:444; for Frances Essex and her dealings concerning her divorce with the wise woman 6 May 1613, see Chambers, 1:49.

47. See Linda Levy Peck, *Northampton: Patronage and Policy at the Court of James I* (London: Allen and Unwin, 1982), 38–40. For other discussions of this marriage, see Lindley, ch. 4. Indicative of the queen's probable viewpoint is a later communication from Northampton to Somerset concerning his troubles, the former remarking on Somerset's fear that "the Queen inflamed with passion and rage should out of her hatred to me disorder the main state of the proceedings": see Lindley, *The Trials of Frances Howard*, 84.

48. See *Manuscripts of the Earl of Mar and Kellie*, 58–59.

49. For these matters see Chamberlain, *Letters*, 1:485–89.

50. See Chambers, *The Elizabethan Stage*, 3:246.

51. See Chamberlain, *Letters*, 1:487. When Lady Drummond had a daughter several years later, Anna and the countess of Bedford were the two godmothers at the christening at Greenwich Palace (Chamberlain, *Letters*, 1:626). Lady Drummond had sufficient standing with Anna in 1602 that she was in attendance on Prince Charles, perhaps as his first governess. See Walter W. Seton, "The Early Years of Henry Frederick, Prince of Wales, and Charles, Duke of Albany, 1593–1605," *Scottish Historical Review* 13 (1916): 366–79.

52. See Samuel Daniel, *Hymen's Triumph*, ed. John Pitcher (Oxford: Malone Society, 1994), v–ix. Pitcher presents a near-diplomatic transcript of the manuscript of the pastoral now in the Edinburgh University Library. The pastoral was also published in octavo in 1615 and then in Daniel's posthumous collected edition of 1623.

53. Pitcher, 11.

54. See John Orrell, "The London Court Stage in the Savoy Correspondence, 1613–1675," *Theatre Research International*, n.s. 4 (1979): 82–83. See also *Hymen's Triumph*, xiii–xiv.

55. See Chamberlain, *Letters*, 1:514. "Servants" in this context were nobles who were honored by being appointed to such duties as pouring the sovereign's wine, carving the meat, and the like. See note 8 above.

56. It is interesting to note that both James and Anna discouraged the plans that a group of countesses had made for a Twelfth Night, 1618, "Masque of Amazons" involving nine ladies. "Whatsoever the cause was," wrote John Chamberlain (Letters, 2:125–26) on 3 January, "neither the Queen nor King did like or allow of it and so all is dashed."

57. I am preparing a detailed discussion of James's independent use of and variation from Anna's model for the court masque: "King James I of England and His Masques of Men."

58. See Birch, *Court and Times of James I*, 1:339–40 and, for Northampton's death, Chamberlain, *Letters*, 1: 541.

59. *Mar and Kellie Supp.*, 56.

60. Chamberlain, *Letters*, 1:553.

61. Chamberlain, *Letters*, 1:541–42.

62. Chamberlain, *Letters*, 1:545.

63. See Wilson, *History of Great Britain*, sigs. L3ᵛ–L4, and for his possible reliability, see note 35 above.

64. See William Sanderson, *Aulicus Coquinariae* (London, 1650), sigs. M3ᵛ–M4. He also wrote *A Complete History* of Mary Queen of Scots and of James that attacks errors not only in Weldon's *Court and Character of King James*, in *The Secret History of the Court of James I*, ed. Sir Walter Scott (Edinburgh, 1811) (and still cited by some as an authority on James's court), but also in Wilson. Sanderson was secretary to Henry Rich, earl of Holland (1590–1649) and is thus a relevant contemporary source.

65. Sir Henry Wotton, *Reliquiae Wottonianae* (London 1651), sig. D3, mentions that Villiers first met James at Apthorp. According to Wotton, Villiers, when

he came to court, had fallen in with Sir John Greeham, one of the gentlemen of the Privy Chamber who advised him and at first served as go-between with James. Roger Coke, grandson of Sir Edward Coke, wrote *A Detection of the Court and State of England* (London, 1697) in which he observed that James first saw Villiers at Cambridge when the king attended the Latin comedy *Ignoramus* (74). The event is specific enough at least to be plausible, but this would postdate the July 1614 meeting of the Pembroke group, because the king saw *Ignoramus* in March 1615.

66. For these matters see *Mar and Kellie*, 56, and Chamberlain, 1:559.

67. *Mar and Kellie Supp.*, 27.

68. See John Rushworth, *Historical Collections* (London, 1721), 1 and cf. Goodman, 1:224. Abbott's own close relationship both to this faction and to Villiers himself may be gathered from his letter to Villiers of 10 December 1615, some months after Villiers had become a Gentleman of the Bed Chamber, and from his general account reprinted in Rushworth.

69. Sir Anthony Weldon, *The Court and Character of King James* (London, 1650), 118–19; see also Goodman, *The Court of King James I*, 1: 224.

70. See S. R. Gardiner, "On Certain Letters of Diego Sarmiento de Acuna, Count of Gondomar, Giving an Account of the Affair of the Earl of Somerset," *Archaeologia* 41 (1867): 168.

71. See *SPV*, 14:45 (6 October 1615 by English dating).

72. For the date of Somerset's committal to the Tower, see John Finett, *Finetti Philoxenis* (London, 1656), 28.

73. See *SPV*, 14:58 (7 November 1615). Wilson, *History of Great Britain*, sig. L4^v, also indicates that Anna was instrumental in blocking this pardon.

74. See *SPV*, 16:393–95.

75. Anna's treatment of Somerset contrasts with that which she accorded his wife. As the Somerset trial approached, Anna was "an earnest suitor" for Frances, who was to be arraigned on 15 April (Chamberlain, *Letters*, 1:619). Mercy was expected from the king, she was treated gently at the trial on 24 May, and she was indeed pardoned by 13 July 1616 (Chamberlain, *Letters*, 2:17), no objection having been entered by the queen. Frances had given birth to a child on 9 December 1615 whom she was forced to leave behind when she was committed to the Tower on 27 March 1616 (Chamberlain 1:619), and Anna's forbearance here leads one to recall her own separation from Henry. Frances' child was interestingly named Anne. It may also be relevant that Frances, when countess of Essex, had been invited to dance in two consecutive masques by the queen, who may thus have had a personal liking for her.

76. In *The Masque of Beauty*, dancing for the first time was Althea Talbot, a daughter of the earl of Shrewsbury and thus the sister-in-law of the earl of Pembroke who had married her sister, Mary, in 1604. Althea herself had married in 1606 Thomas, the son of Philip Howard, first earl of Arundel, who had been imprisoned and attainted during Elizabeth's reign, dying in the Tower in 1595. Thomas (thus Northampton's great-nephew) was, in 1604, at the age of nineteen, restored in blood by King James and re-created earl of Surrey and earl of Arundel. Althea (at least from the evidence of masquing) seems to have become part of Anna's inner circle, appearing in all of the queen's masques subsequent to *Beauty*. (She would

also ride in the procession of Anna's funeral as Chief Mourner.) The wealthy Nort-hampton, who died in 1614, had made Arundel his sole heir, and Lady Arundel, like her husband, was a well-known collector and patron of art. Both she and her husband seem to have become members of the Pembroke-Southampton faction to which the queen and the countess of Bedford were inclined.

77. Chamberlain, *Letters*, 2:18.

78. Chamberlain, *Letters*, 2:18–22. See also the group of letters written by Anna's lord chamberlain, Robert Sidney, to his wife, *L'Isle MSS*, 5:408.

79. In "Restoring Astraea: Jonson's Masque for the Fall of Somerset," *ELH* 61 (1994): 807–27, Martin Butler and David Lindley associate Villiers's triumphant moment with this masque, and I differ from them merely in my addition of Anna to the political ambience that they delineate. The events of Christmas 1615–16 have long been obscured because Jonson, *Works* (ed. Herford and the Simpsons), erro-neously revised the dates of two masques, *Mercury Vindicated* and *The Golden Age Restored*. But John Orrell, working with Florentine and Savoyard embassy docu-ments, has shown that *The Golden Age Restored* was the masque for the Christmas of 1615–16 ("The London Stage in the Florentine Correspondence"). Thus, as Butler and Lindley remind us, the commentary in Jonson, *Works*, 10:546–48 and 552–58 should be reversed: the circumstances associated with *Mercury* applying to *Golden Age* and vice versa.

80. Robert White, *Cupid's Banishment*, ed. C. E. McGee in *Renaissance Drama*, n.s. 19 (1988): 226–64.

81. Anna had been associated with martial strength, wisdom, and also jus-tice in *Tethys' Festival*. She had Zephirus, played by Prince Charles, deliver to his brother a gift from his mother: the sword of Astraea, of Justice.

82. Long after the deaths of both Anna and James, Jonson's Second Folio (1640), *reversed* the ending of the masque by giving Astraea the final speech, But Pallas is the final speaker in the 1616 (F1) text of *The Golden Age Restored* published during Anna's lifetime. Indeed, that F1 is the preferred reading is borne out by the fact that if we adopt the order posited by F2, the masque curiously ends with the "*Galliards and Coranto's*" of F2 rather than with the *sorti* of F1 — the exit that Pallas's last speech calls for.

83. See *The Diary of Anne Clifford: 1616–1619*, ed. Katherine O. Acheson (New York: Garland, 1995), 64–65. I have adhered to the editor's punctuation but have otherwise modernized her text.

84. Clifford writes again of these lawsuits "in which business King James began to show himself extremely against my mother and me. In which course he still pursued, though his wife Queen Anne was ever inclining to our part and very gracious and favorable unto us; for in my youth I was much in the court with her, and in masques attended her, though I never served her." See *Lives of Lady Anne Clifford . . . and of Her Parents Summarized by Herself*, ed. J. P. Gilson (London: Rox-burgh Club, 1916), 38. For the limits of Clifford's masquing, however, see Chapter 4, note 34.

85. The king "compounded the controversy twixt the earls of Cumberland and Dorset in this manner that Cumberland should enjoy the lands in suit, paying 20,000 pounds to Dorset in two years, and if the Countess of Dorset should outlive

her husband and molest her kinsman, then Dorset hath bound sufficient lands for the repayment": Chamberlain, *Letters*, 2:63. After the death of her first husband, Clifford married the widowed earl of Montgomery, Pembroke's brother and husband of the late dedicatee of Lady Mary Wroth's *Urania*, an action that suggests in what circle Clifford felt safe reposing her trust.

86. Chamberlain, *Letters*, 2:47.

87. Chamberlain, *Letters*, 2:104.

88. This adventure is famously described by G. P. V. Akrigg, *Jacobean Pageant* ch. 1, who cites the account of Robert Carey carried by Nichols, *Progresses*, 1:34–35.

89. When Charles was, at age five, created duke of York on 6 January 1605, we recall, he had to be carried by four nobles throughout the ceremony. The queen at that time was said to wish to be appointed Charles's governor.

90. Robert Carey, *Memoirs*, ed. F. H. Mares (Oxford: Clarendon Press, 1972), 73–76.

91. See Chamberlain, *Letters*, 2:45, 102: "The lady of Roxborough is gone from court and the Lady Grey of Ruthen, though with much opposition, succeeds her in her place."

92. See David Mathew, *James I* (London: Eyre and Spottiswoode Mathew, 1967), 91–92.

93. He became Viscount Fenton in March 1606 (see *Peerage*, 5:294) and a Privy Councillor 31 January 1611: see John Stow, *Annals* sig.4G6 (p. 910).

94. Chamberlain, *Letters*, 2:58. The "Jacobus" was a sovereign (worth 20s).

95. *Salisbury MSS*, 22:44. Some indication of Anna's relationship to Buckingham at this time may be glimpsed from short notes she sent to him, in one of which she writes "your letter hath been acceptable to me. I rest always assured of your carefulness" (100). In both letters saluting him as "my kind dog" she writes in a second note that she wants Buckingham to "continue a watchful dog to him [James] and be always true to him." See *Original Letters*, 1st series, ed. Henry Ellis (London, 1824), 3:100–101.

96. Henry Rich (the future earl of Holland) was the son of Penelope Rich, a woman for whose child Anna might have felt some loyalty.

97. See *Salisbury MSS*, 22:45–56.

APPENDIX. ANNA OF DENMARK
AND CATHOLICISM

1. A. W. Ward (1885), in *Dictionary of National Biography*, ed. Leslie Stephen and Sidney Lee, 66 vols. (London: Smith, Elder, 1885–1901), s.v. "Anne of Denmark."

2. Wilhelm Plenkers, *Er Frederick II's Datter Anna, Dronning of Storbritanien, gaaet over til Katholicism?* [Was Frederick II's daughter Anna, queen of Great Britain, as convert to Catholicism?] (Kjøbenhavn: B. Lunos bogtrykkeri, 1888).

3. See Ward's review of Plenkers in *English Historical Review* 3 (1888), 795–98.

4. E. H. Dunkley, *The Reformation in Denmark* (London: SPCK, 1948).

5. N. K. Andersen, "The Reformation in Scandinavia and the Baltic," in

The New Cambridge Modern History, ed. G. R. Elton (Cambridge: University Press, 1990), 2:149.

6. See Paul Douglas Lockhart, *Denmark in the Thirty Years' War, 1618–1648* (Selinsgrove, Pa.: Susquehanna University Press, 1996), 67 and 284n. 17.

7. Lockhart, *Denmark*, 75, 288n. 34.

8. See Chapter 2, n. 40 above.

9. Walter W. Seton, "The Early Years of Henry Frederick, Prince of Wales, and Charles, Duke of Albany, 1593–1605," *Scottish Historical Review* 13 (1916): 366–79, at 372.

10. Seton, "Early Years," 376.

11. Seton, "Early Years," 370 n. 7.

12. Magdalena S. Sánchez, *The Empress, the Queen, and the Nun* (Baltimore: Johns Hopkins University Press, 1998), 105–6, 124–25.

13. David Mathew, *James I* (London: Eyre and Spottiswoode, 1967), ch. 24.

14. *Calendar of State Papers . . . of Venice*, ed. Horatio F. Brown (London: Historical Manuscripts Commission, 1900), 10:40.

15. Maximilian de Bethune, duke of Sully, *Memoirs* (Edinburgh, 1805), 200.

16. Chamberlain, *Letters*, 1:245.

17. *SPD*, 9:299.

INDEX

Abbott, George, archbishop of Canterbury, 146–47, 153, 172, 210n68
Abercromby, Fr. Robert, 163–64
Acting companies, 53, 56, 64, 67–68, 83, 197n21
Akrigg, G. P. V., 173n2
Althorp: reception at, 62–65, 192n101
Ambassadors-extraordinary, 79–80
Anna of Denmark, queen of England: administration of material assets, 40; archbishop of Canterbury and, 172; artists favored by, 57–58, 66–71; Lady Bedford and, 66, 67, 68, 69–70, 71, 194n126; Catholicism and, 162–64, 166–72; ceremonies of childbirth and christening, 104–7; childbirth expenses, 201n59; children of, 20, 25, 26, 27, 105, 107, 176n7, 178n29, 202n66; Anne Clifford and, 152–53, 198–99n34, 211n84; Council, 82, 177–78n19; critical perceptions of, 2, 7–8; death of advisers to King James and, 131; first name of, 173n1; Gowrie problem and, 25–26, 27; *Hymen's Triumph* and, 140–42; identity as queen and royal consort, 4–6, 73, 74–75, 97–98, 103–4, 113–14, 115, 123–26; illness of, 151–52, 153, 158; last description of, 158–59; Sir John Maitland and, 17–20, 22, 23, 25, 177n12, 178n22; marital matches considered for children, 168, 170–72; marriage to James, 17, 176n6; as member of ruling council, 153; miscarriage, 29; music and, 58, 190n84; opposition to Robert Carr, 12, 133–34, 135, 140, 142, 143–48, 208n46; Thomas Overbury and, 136–37, 208n42; parents of, 15–16; personified as wisdom, 150–51, 199n35; political activities, 9, 11–12, 15, 17–35, 152–58, 179n34; Prince Charles and, 154, 155–56, 212n75; Princess Elizabeth's guardianship and, 45–46; relationship

with James, 23–24, 25–26, 177n15; residences of, 38–39; servants of, 53; siblings of, 16, 175n3; transition from Scotland to England, 34–35, 36–37; George Villiers and, 143, 146, 147, 148, 212n95
— and Prince Henry: guardianship conflict over, 20–21, 22–25, 28–34, 36–37, 120; Henry honors in *Oberon*, 129, 130; Henry's death, 11, 134–35; relationship with, 72, 73, 114, 115, 117–18, 119–20, 121–22, 126, 131, 207–8n34
— English court of: Althorp reception and, 62–66; artistic appointments of Jonson and Daniel, 66–71; arts patronage and, 9–10, 15, 37, 47, 57–58, 66–71, 115–16; ceremonials, purpose of, 114–15; compared to James' court, 71; cultural environment of, 8–9, 47, 54–58, 61–62, 72–73, 115–16, 160–61; Essex circle and, 71, 72; household officers, 182n4; Howard/Essex duality in, 72; Lord Chamberlain of, 59–61; noblewomen in, 49–56; origins of, 39, 40–48, 62–66; peers associated with, 56–57; Queen's Council members, 177–78n19
— masques of, 4; Anna's control over, 110–11; Anna's queenship signified with, 73, 74–75, 97–98, 103–4, 113–14, 123–26; cessation of, 142–43; chronological order of, 200n48; court status and, 101–2; dual masques presented with Prince Henry, 130; effect and purpose of, 10–11, 58–59, 73, 74–75, 97–98, 103–4; King James and, 99–100, 143; later masquing, 117; *Love Freed from Ignorance and Folly*, 126–29; *The Masque of Beauty*, 59, 108–12, 204n79, 210n76; *The Masque of Blackness*, 48, 50, 67, 69, 93, 99–104; *The Masque of Queens*, 112–14, 127; noblewomen in, 59, 90–93, 101–2, 111–12, 126; number of, 99; performed for Prince Henry, 77, 204n3;

Queen Anna's New World of Words (Florio), 150
Queen consort: Anna as, 4–6, 115; Anna's masquing and, 73, 74–75, 97–98, 103–4, 113–14, 123–26; in European monarchies, 4–6
Queen's Arcadia, The (Daniel), 70

Radcliffe, Elizabeth. *See* Ramsay, Elizabeth
Ralegh, Sir Walter, 181n62
Ramsay, Elizabeth, Viscountess Haddington, 206n18
Ramsay, Sir John, Viscount Haddington, 206n18
Regency: European monarchies and, 21–22
Religion, Anna and, 162–64, 166–72
Rich, Sir Henry, 158
Rich, Penelope: arts patronage and, 51; Lucy Bedford and, 43; disgrace of, 191n87; in the first Christmas masque, 86; life and politics of, 42; marriage to Devonshire, 69; in Anna's court, 10, 42, 51, 62, 185n33; in Anna's masques, 59, 91, 92, 94, 101, 102; Robert Sidney and, 61
Robert, Prince (son of James and Anna), 27
Rochester, Lord. *See* Carr, Robert
Romeo and Juliet (Shakespeare), 76
Roper, Sir John, 133
Roscommon, earl of. *See* Stuart, James
Rosso, Andrea, 48–49
Roxburgh, countess of. *See* Drummond, Lady Jean
Roxburgh, earl of. *See* Kerr, Robert
Russell, Anne, 76–77
Russell, Francis, earl of Bedford, 43, 44, 95
Russell, Lucy, countess of Bedford: arts patronage and, 10, 44, 54–56, 58; *Cupid's Banishment* and, 198n33; Samuel Daniel and, 66, 67; Lady Drummond and, 187n48, 209n51; Essex uprising and, 43; first associations with Anna, 43, 44, 45; in the first Christmas masque, 86; guardianship of Princess Elizabeth and, 118–19; John Harington (brother) and, 118; Ben Jonson and, 66; opposition to Robert Carr, 145; pregnancies of, 191n86; in Anna's court, 10, 49, 62, 66, 67, 68, 69–70, 71, 72, 186n37, 194n126; in Anna's masques, 59, 91, 92, 94, 101, 102, 112; Shakespeare and, 55–56, 160; Robert Sidney and, 61; George Villiers and, 149

Russell, Margaret, countess of Cumberland, 66, 77
Ruthven, Barbara, 25, 27, 166
Ruthven, Beatrix, 25, 27, 166
Ruthven, William, earl of Gowrie, 176n11
Rutland, countess of. *See* Manners, Elizabeth
Rutland, earl of. *See* Manners, Francis; Manners, Roger

Sackville, Anne (née Spencer), countess of Dorset, 63
Sackville, Richard, third earl of Dorset, 63, 139, 152–53
Sackville, Robert, second earl of Dorset, 63
Salisbury, earl of. *See* Cecil, Robert; Cecil, William
Sanderson, William, 145, 209n64
Savoy, Emmanuel-Philibert, duke of, 21
Scaramelli, Giovanni Carlo, 81, 166, 169, 170
Scrope, Lord Emmanuel, 139, 183n13
Scrope of Bolton, Thomas, Lord, 183n13
Scrope of Bolton, Lady. *See* Carey, Philadelphia
Second Book of Airs (Dowland), 55, 58
Servi, Constantino de,' 58
Seton, Alexander, Lord Fyvie, 31, 166–67, 170, 179n39
Seymour, Edward, earl of Hertford, 40, 50, 96, 145, 186n40
Seymour, Edward, Lord Beauchamp, 50
Seymour, Frances (née Howard), countess of Hertford, 40, 49–51, 86, 91, 92, 94, 136, 186n42, 187n47
Shakespeare, William, 3–4; acting company of, 64; earl of Rutland and, 139; First Folio, 57, 115–16; Hampton Court and, 38; Lord Strange's Servants and, 64; *Love's Labor's Lost*, 56; *A Midsummer Night's Dream*, 83; patrons of, 55–56, 160; receives acting company patent, 67; *Romeo and Juliet*, 76; Stuart cultural environment and, 1, 47; *The Tempest*, 130–31; *Titus Andronicus*, 56, 160
Sidney, Barbara Gamage, viscountess L'Isle, 43, 192n96
Sidney, Elizabeth. *See* Manners, Elizabeth
Sidney, Sir Philip, 51, 160
Sidney, Sir Robert, Viscount L'Isle, 24, 53, 137, 145, 160, 182n4; arts patronage and, 10; court factionalism and, 135, 144;

ACKNOWLEDGMENTS

This book, like all others, could not have moved from first idea to final material object without much help from many persons whom I am delighted and honored to be able to thank. Susan Cerasano of Colgate University, Lena Cowen Orlin of the University of Maryland (Baltimore County), Linda Levy Peck of George Washington University, Peter Stallybrass of the University of Pennsylvania, and Susan Zimmerman of Queen College CUNY read and often reread portions of the work. I had helpful and stimulating conversations with Rebecca Weld Bushnell of the University of Pennsylvania, Philippa Berry of King's College, Cambridge, John Pitcher of St. John's College, Oxford, Raphael Falco of the University of Maryland (Baltimore County), and Gustav Ungerer of the University of Bern. Laetitia Yeandle, curator of manuscripts at the Folger Shakespeare Library, and Georgianna Ziegler, reference librarian, have been unstinting in their generous advice and help. I am also extremely grateful to Catherine Belsey, Director of the Centre for Critical and Cultural Theory at the University of Wales, Cardiff, who read the manuscript for the press and from whose judicious advice I have greatly benefited, as always. My access to the extensive knowledge and experience embodied in this group of scholars is my good fortune.

The constantly wise guidance of Dr. Jerome E. Singerman of the University of Pennsylvania Press, who received my submission of this manuscript and advised me in many particulars, has my special thanks as does Noreen O'Connor, my editor.

The Folger Shakespeare Library, where most of this work was pursued, has been most hospitable and the staff there unfailingly supportive. The Reading Room staff under the guidance of Elizabeth Walsh has been patient and always helpful: Harold Batie, LuEllen DeHaven, Rosalind Larry, and Camille Seeratten are always kindness and consideration themselves.

Lightning Source UK Ltd.
Milton Keynes UK
UKOW02n0926270116

267212UK00006B/127/P